LOVING THE ENEMY

Building bridges in a time of war

Andrew March

Halwill Publishing

First published in Great Britain in 2021 by Halwill Publishing, 99 Buckingham Rise, Coventry CV5 9HF

ISBN 978-1-7398051-0-4

A CIP catalogue record for this book is available from the British Library.

Cover design: Nikki Bovis-Coulter

Cover image: 'Dresden. Blick von der Neustadt', SLUB Dresden / Deutsche Fotothek / Wilhelm Stein

For Alicia, Isabelle, and Ben.
May you build bridges and dare to love.

Contents

Part Three –
RIKE: THE REALITY OF DEATH 1939-1946

Part Four –
FRED AND RIKE: JOY FROM ASHES 1946-1948

Foreword

Since the dark days of the Second World War, the city of Dresden has been close to the hearts of the people of Coventry. We not only share common ground in some of the horrors of our past, we have built our future upon it, sowing the seeds of reconciliation and nurturing a spirit of mutual trust and peace.

The young Fred Clayton, a recent graduate in Classics from Cambridge, got there first, building bridges between England and Germany in the mid 1930s – not a minute too soon, we can say with the benefit of hindsight. By the time bridge building was on our minds, untold damage had already been done: countless lives lost, cities destroyed, Dresden's Frauenkirche and Coventry's Cathedral both reduced to rubble.

In this story of friendship, cultural exchange, and love, Andy March has allowed us to hear Fred Clayton's prophetic and visionary voice in the midst of a Europe which, clearly in our eyes now – and no less clearly in his eyes then – was sleepwalking into war. In 1936, Fred sets out to Dresden 'with vague ideas of bridge building.' By 1939, with the outbreak of war, he contemplates whether 'the bridges he'd built would surely be destroyed.'

Ultimately, Fred's bridges would withstand the traumas of war and hatred in ways which he, and we as readers, might never have imagined. Through his wrestling with the outrage of conflict and destruction, he captures the sense in which love and hatred are sentiments of a totally and categorically different order. They are not conventionally competing with each other in the way two opponents do battle, one force trying to overcome the other in displays of confrontational power. And so, where human bonds of love and friendship are involved – where, in Fred's own words, one becomes 'emotionally involved' with the people one is being conditioned to hate – the utter madness of war, hatred and evil becomes apparent. It is senseless and corrupt. It provides no lasting solutions to the needs of humanity. In the end, love wins out for Fred. The point is, though, that love was never engaged in battle in the first place. Love overcomes precisely by resisting the effects of hate. This is something of what it means to say, 'love your enemies'.

I have been privileged to visit Dresden many times. Regularly taking part in the annual Commemoration of the Destruction of Dresden, and doing so in the presence of survivors of the dreadful night of 13 February 1945, count among the most moving moments of my life. Andy March, one of Coventry's parish priests, joined me in 2015 for the 70th Anniversary Commemorations of the bombing. I was deeply touched by witnessing Andy retracing the steps taken by his grandfather, and by following him as he accessed the story of his grandfather's remarkable life and the love that grew between Fred and Rike, Andy's grandmother, whose home city was Dresden.

I am delighted that Andy has now published the results of his very personal research into his family's past. He has captured Fred's frame of mind, his sincerity, and the richness of his thoughts as they reacted to the powerful and horrific forces which swamped Europe in the 1930s and 40s. At the heart of the story, however, is not ideology or politics, but people, places, meaningful encounter and the careful nurturing of relationships. It is a journey which demands tremendous courage of Fred in his open tackling of the dangerous ideologies emerging in 1930s Germany, in his attempts to provide refuge to children from the continent, and in coming to terms with the fact that, following the bombing of Dresden, 'barbarism on our side as well as theirs has beaten tolerance.' To quote the prayer that lies at the heart of Coventry Cathedral's ministry of peace and reconciliation, *all* must say, 'Father, forgive'. And to borrow from Bonhoeffer, Fred's peace is one which 'must be dared.'

Cultivating these meaningful relationships, acknowledging these wounds and, in the fullness of time by God's grace, healing them, is at the centre of Coventry's mission. We live in a very different world, of course, and readers will be struck by advancements in technologies of travel and communication. But just as Fred built bridges which weathered the severe storms of his time, so his story will stand the test of time itself. It is my hope that, thanks to Andy's efforts, the story will inspire you as much as it has inspired me, and that it will find its place as a signpost, even a landmark, along the path of reconciliation, trust and love which links Coventry and Dresden; Britain and Germany.

Rt Reverend Dr Christopher Cocksworth,
Bishop of Coventry

PART ONE

Fred: The Disquiet of Peace
1931-1939

CHAPTER ONE
1931-1936: A journey of discovery in Cambridge and Vienna

It was May 1934. Frederick William Clayton, small, slight with sharp blue eyes emphasised by a splash of jet-black hair, was twenty, a year younger than the rest of his cohort, when he completed his final paper for his undergraduate degree in Classics. He already knew what his next challenge would be whilst waiting for his Masters to begin in the autumn; he skirted round the freshly mown lawn, flicking through the pages of the German textbook, delicately balanced on a dictionary he was cradling in his arms. Here was an opportunity to get to grips with another language and culture, to discover new worlds, to read the works of Goethe, Hegel, Schleiermacher, and other Romantics in their native tongue. Here was an opportunity too to gain an understanding of this new movement, this revolution, spreading like a disease across Germany. Little did he know this decision would shape the course of his life.

Fred had begun life at King's College, Cambridge in 1931 and his time there had coincided with an increase in political tension all around a world still reeling from the impact of the Great War and from the Great Depression. In Germany the wounds and recriminations still festered, leading to the rise to power of Adolf Hitler, who promised to restore Germany's national dignity. Meanwhile, in the East, a Red Beast rose up, with Soviet Russia claiming that it was the only country that had rid itself of the warmongering clique that had been responsible for the Great War in the first place. There was no escape from these issues, not in the debating chambers of Oxford or Cambridge, whether in the dining

hall, in fellows' rooms over lunch or tea, or on the lawns, where
the rise of National Socialism and Communism and their various
merits were topics of hot debate. Indeed, while the Oxford Union
voted in February 1933 to 'never again fight for King and Country'
causing uproar in the national newspapers, with the Daily
Telegraph   announcing,   'DISLOYALTY   AT   OXFORD:
GESTURE TOWARDS THE REDS', a substantial number in
Cambridge turned to Communism as the only safeguard of peace.

In contrast to his peers at King's and the other colleges in
Cambridge, who hailed from Eton and other public schools, Fred
had been brought up in a semi-detached house in Mossley Hill, on
the outskirts of Liverpool and educated in a state grammar school,
the Liverpool Collegiate School. Whilst his peers' relatives were
overwhelmingly wealthy, his father, William, was a headmaster of a
small village school near Liverpool, his mother, Mary, was a
housewife and among his relatives were post-office workers and
shopkeepers. Fred's older brother, Don had been prevented from
pursuing his own dreams of university because his parents were
unable to afford the costs involved, instead working for the
Pioneer Assurance Company in the city. Fred could hide all this,
pretend he wasn't so different, until he opened his mouth. His
Scouse accent gave the game away. At King's he was a fish out of
water, a novelty and, he suspected, a figure of fun. He hadn't been
entirely happy at first, being made aware of his Lancashire accent
and his being 'different', even by people meaning to be kind.
Someone even suggested he change his name – people called Fred
didn't go to King's – Francis or Hilary (weren't those girls'
names?) were proposed as acceptable substitutes.

It had been a heady time, socially as well as academically.
Despite his initial feelings about not fitting in, thanks to his
precocious academic brilliance, the red carpet was laid out for him
and he was welcomed into the cabals of the intellectual elite. Here
he made good friends, people to whom he was passionately
attached. He dined in refined company such as the world-
renowned economist, Maynard Keynes, and literary giants, E M
Forster and T S Eliot. Keynes had invited him to dinner once and
lunch twice in his rooms in Webb's Court, which had oak panelled

Left – Fred as a young man, before his King's College days. Right – Detail from Fred's matriculation photograph at King's College – Fred is in the front row, 2ⁿᵈ from the left. Alan Turing, who would become Fred's friend at King's, is in the top right of this photograph.

Fred's full year group at King's College, autumn 1931.

walls dominated by eight extraordinary murals by painters Duncan Grant and Vanessa Bell depicting the muses of arts and sciences.

Fred wasn't much of an arts aficionado himself, but he knew that Keynes was and had the good sense to ask about the work that Keynes himself had commissioned. At the second lunch, Keynes had invited Fred along with Basil Willey, an English Literature fellow of Pembroke College and T S Eliot. Though he had been greatly anticipating socialising with someone so renowned, Fred was disappointed; Eliot hardly said a word, which Fred had thought strange, only to learn later that this was not uncommon. This particular lunch was turning out to be an excruciatingly awkward social occasion and Willey managed to escape early. In desperation, Keynes turned to the topic of Fred's dissertation, and much to everyone's relief, Fred entertained the remaining guests as he shared his passion for his subject.

'Did I conquer King's by being so novel—so naive but potentially promising?' he was later to wonder. He never attempted to deny his origins, developing a good-humoured critical awareness of English class snobbery, chuckling at the naivety of the elite classes as much as his own. He enjoyed telling how, at a dinner party given by Keynes, he was faced with a plate of oysters for the first time in his life. Fred was visibly embarrassed, not sure what to do with this disgusting looking delicacy especially when his host asked 'Well, Clayton, which are you, a swallower or a chewer?' The uproarious laughter of his fellow diners made him suspect there was more than a hint of innuendo in Keynes' question. Ignoring this, he tried to focus on the task in hand, deciding to go for swallowing, as it would surely go down quicker, trying not to think of all those faces looking at him. Later on, he would be able to see the funny side of this incident, even if he didn't at the time.

Though he eventually got used to the teasing, Fred was irked more by the way that his background made him a target for those who wanted to enlist him in their political cause. He experienced this one evening in November 1933 when he was having drinks with his new friend and fellow Kingsman, Alan Turing in the Junior

Common Room of Trinity College. Fred had first got acquainted with Turing through rowing. Though he wasn't sporty, his slight size did give him certain advantages and he became cox for Turing's boat. They quickly became friends, discovering a mutual recognition and understanding of their intellect and their shared experience of being outsiders – Fred, because of his diminutive size and working-class background, and Alan, his sexuality. Fred was very interested in exchanging views and emotional experiences, and was drawn to Turing, who was always very frank and open with Fred about his homosexuality, sharing stories about his experiences at public school. Fred was in awe of Alan's confidence in this area, as he himself felt more than confused – he'd been told by a Fellow he seemed 'a pretty normal bisexual male', but this was completely out of his experience. He didn't know what he was and besides, even if he felt drawn to his own gender, he knew he would never be able to explore this; not only did it seem culturally impossible for a man of his background, but it was also illegal. To make matters worse, Fred had almost no access to or experience of any woman other than his mother. He felt he'd never had the opportunity to be attracted to women – any he'd come across seemed either formidable and frightening, or seemed to barely acknowledge his existence, probably because he was too small, a boy in their eyes.

Fred was an avid reader, devouring Havelock Ellis's *Psychology of Sex* and Freud, and also made discoveries in the classics which he would convey to Turing who was a mathematician and knew little of Latin and Greek. Fred was in the middle of sharing his latest discovery with Turing in the Common Room bar when they were approached by a man with movie star good looks wearing a striped suit jacket, spotted tie, and cream trousers – ostentatious, even for Cambridge. He nodded to Alan, and focused his attention on Fred. 'Hello, I don't believe we've met. Can I get you a drink? I'm having a Gin Fizz – would you like the same?'

'Oh, thank you – no, half a mild, thank you.'

'Right you are.' The man sauntered towards the bar.

'You've caught someone's eye,' Alan muttered. 'Believe me, I can tell.'

'What do you mean?' Fred protested. 'Oh stop it, Alan.'

Turing raised his eyebrow, but before the conversation could continue, the man returned to the table. 'Mind if I join you?' and sat down without waiting for an answer. 'So, you're clearly not from around here.'

'No, I'm from Liverpool.'

'Liverpool? How interesting! I've heard things are terrible up there. Thousands of people unemployed. It just goes to show that the capitalist system is utterly bankrupt. I'm sick of it and so are a lot of us, I suppose that's what took me into the Party. They're a great bunch. There's a demonstration happening at the weekend for the Armistice Day celebrations by the War Memorial. Why don't you join us? I've heard you'll be there, Turing, won't you?'

Turing nodded.

'Well, I, err, I'm not sure what my plans are yet,' Fred replied.

'Oh, right,' the man responded, seemingly affronted, 'Anyway, I must be going.' He proffered his hand, 'Nice to meet you – '

'Fred Clayton.'

'I'm Burgess. Guy Burgess. I'm sure we'll meet again.'

Fred felt perplexed by this encounter. At first, he was flattered by the interest shown in him, but he wasn't sure what it was about him that had piqued Burgess' interest. Over time, though, he came to realise that because of his modest origins, it was assumed that he would be naturally sympathetic to the burgeoning Communist movement, but it wasn't quite that simple for Fred – things never were. He found it galling that upper-class public schoolboys, Old Etonians, like Burgess, were trading on their style and charm and sounding off about the working class, whilst knowing very little. They pressed Fred very hard in their attempts to convert him. But he distrusted their dogmatism, the extension of Marxism to all the spheres of life, and sometimes their remarks seemed plain daft. He couldn't get over his suspicion that he was a target so that he could become the token working class member of the Communist party and he also didn't like their tactics. He didn't like being encircled.

Another day, Fred was sitting with Turing on the Bodley's Court lawn (it was a favourite spot that year as Turing's room was on the 3rd floor of Bodley's building; they would often make their way over there after dinner). They were sitting on the impeccably cut lawn, enjoying the evening sunshine, looking out to the trees by the river, when they heard the familiar clipped voice. 'Turing. Clayton. Together again. Thought I'd find you here.' Without waiting for an invitation, Burgess sat down and continued, 'You know, Clayton, of all the people here you really should join the British Communist Party – we understand the sufferings the oppressed working classes, I'm surprised at you, really, coming from where you do...'

Fred and Turing exchanged exasperated looks; Fred had lost count of the number of times Burgess, Blunt and their associates had attempted to recruit him. Until this point, he had joined in their discussions, good-humouredly batted their attempts away, but after Burgess ignored his polite refusals a second time, something snapped.

Fred stood up. 'Look, Burgess. I know you'd like me to be your poster boy and you go on as though you really know what it's like for us poor backward people in the depressed North. You pontificate about the working classes and lecture me on their sufferings, but you don't have a bloody clue what you're talking about. I doubt you even know anyone in the working class – and no, I don't really count, do I? You think that Communism is the sole safeguard of peace on earth, but refuse to look at the atrocities that are being done to opponents of Stalin and his cronies in Russia – the only peace for those who don't toe the line there is in the grave. Quite frankly, I've had it up to here. I won't be joining you, now, or ever.'

Fred glanced over at Turing who could barely suppress the grin on his face. 'I'll see you later, Alan, I'm going back to my room.' He swept off, leaving Burgess with a stupefied expression on his face, for once, speechless.

Despite this resistance Fred was a political animal. He was a convinced pacifist, but he wouldn't pin his beliefs to one particular political mast; he refused to be boxed in. He distrusted the national stereotyping that was painting all Germans as villains, and he never lacked the courage to weigh into the political debate and air his own political opinions, however controversial. Thus, when he was appointed editor of the important *Cambridge Review* – the youngest ever, at only 20, as well as the first to come from a non-Public School, he was determined to shake up what he saw as a rather grey, dull, publication. He excelled at the job, but it made him sick with worry. He never re-read what he wrote, hoped it was good, and was always rushing on to next week, all the while trying to write his fellowship dissertation, which, after all, was what he'd got the grant for.

As well as the staple of reviews of theatrical performances and new books, Fred saw his tenure as editor of the *Cambridge Review* as an opportunity to raise awareness of the political debates that he found himself embroiled in, publishing articles first criticising then defending Marxism. Then, inspired by his own experience, in February 1935 he penned a satirical article entitled, 'Conversations with Communists'. This alluded to the way that Communists would manage to relate every topic and conversation to the class struggle. The article envisages a new parlour game:

> The object of the game might be described as not so much to keep the ball rolling, as is done in orthodox conversation, as to roll it on to the class-struggle. It is assumed by your opponent, for the purposes of the game, that a point is scored whenever the class-struggle emerges naked and unashamed on to the carpet. I say 'for the purposes of the game,' because it is doubtful whether any further end is served.

The article then continues to give advice about how one might play the game successfully and concludes:

> How cynical you are allowed to be is a difficult question. I think it should be considered a foul to say 'Blast the masses!' On the other hand, some players consider that all's fair in this game. My own opinion's that, if used at all, this species of body-line should be reserved for when your opponent threatens to produce 'the facts'. But, even then, may I say, here and now, that I consider it in the worst of taste?

Fred knew he was stirring a hornet's nest and he continued to do so a fortnight later by publishing letters on the subject as well as an article that defended Communism and criticised him:

> Only a self-conscious and intelligent writer like F. C. must realise just how much he is rejecting. He is saying, in effect: the suffering and oppression of the majority of men does not interest me; I refuse to allow it to interest me; I shall laugh at the idea that it interests anybody; and it certainly has no relevance whatever to anything that I may think or do.

In the same issue of the *Cambridge Review*, he published an article about the forthcoming visit to Cambridge of Sir Oswald Mosley who would be attending a dinner of the University Branch of the British Union of Fascists. Warning of the dangers posed by Fascism in Britain, contributor Colin Clout argued,

> It is hardly necessary to point out the disaster that would overtake English culture if Fascism should gain the ascendency in England. The Fascist state has no use for advanced culture. It cannot utilise the inventions of scientific workers. It does not want highly trained critical brains, but dull-witted brawns that will serve its interests and fight its wars without criticism or question.
>
> As yet Fascism in England is only a small cloud on the horizon, no bigger than a man's hand. But in times of storm and crisis such a cloud may swell until it darkens the air. Let this be a warning to all those who have the interests of culture at heart, who are concerned for the future of Cambridge and all it stands for.

These articles in the *Cambridge Review* were provocative both to Communist and Fascist students and staff and also those dons who didn't seem aware of the strong wave of somewhat startling, very radical opinion that was sweeping the university. At first it was fun, as he enjoyed imagining the raised eyebrows in Senior Common Rooms across the city; however, it became less so as he realised he had pushed it too far, ending his tenure as editor having offended both sides of the argument and a threatened libel on his hands.

Fred and his King's College year group at graduation in 1934. Below, Fred is in the 2nd row, 2nd from the left. Alan Turing is on the front row, 2nd from the right.

He also caused a stir at home when, half-sick with fear, he announced to his father, William – who, like many, had fought in the Great War – that he was a pacifist. His daring declaration, 'You're talking nonsense about the Germans. Your war was pointless,' was instantly rebuffed by his father:

'Mark my words son, you'll get to know what the Huns are really like.'

Typically for Fred, his father's admonition gave Fred even greater motivation to learn German. He would indeed get to know the Huns, and show his father what they were really like. So, in summer 1935 he planned to visit the country, improve his German and find out the truth for himself in the long vacation. After all, the books he'd been reading could only take him so far; he needed to immerse himself in the language and culture. A friend of his had a contact in Vienna willing to put him up for a night or two while he tried to find somewhere longer term to stay. This seemed perfect – Vienna was a place brimming with culture and renowned for its beauty.

When he arrived in Vienna, Fred's priority was to find somewhere more permanent to stay. Thankfully, after a rather uncomfortable night sharing the cramped apartment of his friend's contact, Fred was informed that a lady round the corner might have a spare room. She was a young Jewish widow, Helene Schneider, he was told, who lived alone with her two half-Jewish sons, Robert and Karl, and could probably do with the money.

The next day was May Day, 1935. Long red and blue pennants in the colours of Austria hung from the buildings all over the capital, a city and nation clinging onto its sovereignty, though still feeling the aftershocks of the previous year's chaos, orchestrated by the Nazis, in which in an attempted coup, Chancellor Dollfuß was assassinated. Though the Army had intervened to back up the government, the atmosphere was still tense. The shadow of Hitler loomed large over the nation. Fred wondered whether the fluttering flags would prove to be enough to keep Herr Hitler at bay. People thronged the streets for the May Day celebrations, reminding Fred of a street soccer scene. He made his way through the crowd to the Weihburggasse near the city centre where he'd been told the lady lived. Before he knew it he had been welcomed into their home; perhaps it was the novelty of offering hospitality to a foreigner that made the family so willing to give him a room.

Over the next few weeks Fred spent increasing amounts of time with them, and it was not long before he felt part of the family. When he learned that their father had committed suicide, this brought him even closer for reasons he did not fully understand.

Helene and the boys gave no hint as to when this tragedy had hit this family, how long, how much they grieved. But clearly the paternal absence had created a father-shaped hole in their lives – one that Fred, to his surprise and satisfaction, found himself filling.

He discovered that they too, filled a hole in his life. He was yearning for tenderness and affection, tired of the make-believe and need to put on airs and graces that made up much of Cambridge social life. As one who had always been the youngest and always the smallest in his class at school, at King's – he was also desperate to be looked up to, to be needed. Even his younger brother, George, nine years his junior, was socially confident and had never needed looking after by his older brother. Helene's son Karl, aged ten, small and slight with thick black hair, on the other hand, looked up to Fred as a father figure. Fred felt needed and admired for the first time in his life, and it was gratifying. He grew fond of this boy, a fondness that became love.

Karl took Fred to his first ever football match – despite it being in June, and, as Fred murmured, hardly soccer weather. Despite being no football fan, Fred found himself drawn by the rhythm of the Austrian roars, and in spite of himself, felt his own blood rise until he roared along with them. It was his first experience of the power of mass-hysteria.

Before Fred knew it, it was time to return home to Cambridge. Although his stay in Vienna had only been brief, Helene and her boys had captured his heart. No sooner had he returned to England, than he began to arrange another, shorter visit to Vienna, for the spring of 1936. His excuse was that he wanted to improve his language, although his real reason was that he wanted to see the family once more and Karl in particular. He did not fully understand and in any case could not stop the feelings that grew in him uninvited, unbidden, within him. He couldn't help but get involved. Towards the end of this second stay, the three went together on an evening walk. Karl was kicking a pebble along the street, bored by the adult conversation going over his head. After a while, he exclaimed, 'This is *zwecklos*' – aimless, he said.

'Ach, Karl,' his mother replied with her tired smile, 'all life is aimless, and yet we all like living.' Fred reflected how, unexpectedly, his life had been turned from being *zwecklos* by this family who'd shown him the joy of living.

After his return from Vienna, Fred continued to write to Karl and sent him a birthday present. He had brought one photograph of young Karl back with him to Cambridge, which took pride of place on his desk. A friend walked in, saw the picture, and remarked, 'Good-looking boy, but aren't you baby-snatching? Ten? Nearly eleven? All right for your classical Greeks but it's not quite the thing these days old boy?'

'Don't be disgusting,' Fred snapped, 'The boy likes getting letters, and it gives me the chance to practise my German. There's no harm in it, don't paint me with your public-school vices!' His friend looked sceptical. Fred, though, could feel no harm, no wrong in his feelings for this boy. Though he was confused, one thing he was certain of on his return – his visit to Vienna made Fred feel more consciously than ever how much he wanted to be a father, and what a fine father he'd make, given the chance.

Then, in July 1936, just as Civil War broke out in Spain, Fred received a letter from Helene. She and her sister ran a hat-shop in Vienna and were contemplating emigrating to London or Liverpool or Dublin. Business in Vienna was bad, and she was writing to ask for advice about the possibility of such a move. Fred replied, writing an ultimately discouraging letter. He knew something of the difficulties of immigrants, refugees from Germany, as regards jobs, work permits, adapting to life in England. The uprooted boys would find it very difficult to adjust, and he knew German Jews who were not very happy in their adopted country, as a result of the antisemitic sentiment they had encountered. Besides, he argued, they would have plenty of time to get out should it be necessary. Though he had seen plenty of signs of antisemitism in Austria, which Helene had lived with and was used to, Fred felt optimistic about the prospects of peace enduring in that country. No, he concluded, Helene and the family were better off staying in Vienna.

Shortly afterwards, the correspondence with Karl and Helene ceased, but his experience in Vienna had awakened a hunger, another obsession, a growing and deepening hatred of Hitler. Fred read *Mein Kampf* while in Vienna – which was more than most Nazis did, despite it being their bible. He found it pretty unreadable. In his opinion, *Mein Kampf* was from start to finish, rubbish. At the age of 21, with perhaps youthful rashness, he decided that Hitler was 'a moron', a maniac, and a murderous would-be Napoleon.

The question that kept niggling at Fred was, could the German population really believe this Nazi doctrine preached by Hitler and his cronies with such violence? There was only one way to find out; by experiencing it first-hand. He wanted to go to Germany to find out what was happening, what the Nazi system was really like. As well as the search for truth, he was also attracted by the idea of making human contact in spite of everything, to somehow build bridges. Perhaps it was the optimism and idealism of youth, but he thought he could make a difference.

And so, having come to the end of his undergraduate studies and secured a fellowship at King's for three years, he decided to delay taking this up in order to carry on his German studies. Fred made enquiries with the *Deutsch-Englisches Akademisches Austauschbüro* (Anglo-German Academic Bureau), which organised the exchange of students and teachers between Germany and the United Kingdom (they probably hope to make a good Nazi out of me, he mused), and he received an offer from Dr. phil. Max Johannes Carl Bogumil Helck, the Principal of the Gymnasium zum Heiligen Kreuz (School of the Holy Cross; hereafter known as Kreuzschule) in Dresden inviting him to teach English for the year 1936-7. Dresden had earned a reputation as one of Germany's pre-eminent cities, renowned for its beautiful architecture, education, and culture. It had even had a large English-speaking population before the first World War. The school itself, he learned, was the oldest school in Dresden, renowned for educating the world-famous choristers of the Kreuzkirche (Church of the Holy Cross) since the thirteenth century. All in all, Fred felt like it would be the perfect place to spend the year.

Fred would be entering an environment that would engender a maelstrom of emotions and conflicts: the heady hysteria and cruelty of Naziism, the confusing emotions of being at the centre of young men, boys who would offer him the respect and admiration and even affection he craved. Fred had the intelligence to recognise the white-hot crucible he was entering, but the single-mindedness of youth, the stubbornness of his personality and the unstoppable curiosity of his intellect drove him through these concerns.

So, Fred travelled to Dresden in the late summer of 1936, a fresh-faced twenty-two-year-old, flush from a highly successful academic career. The prospect of spending time in an illustrious institution with history going back over 700 years such as the Kreuzschule, which numbered the likes of Richard Wagner among its alumni, caused Fred to reflect on his own academic career during the long journey across Europe.

It was nearly two days' travel on the train from Cambridge to Kings Cross, across London to Victoria, from Victoria to Dover, across the channel on the ferry to Ostend, back on the train to Dresden, changing once more at Berlin. He had plenty of time to reminisce. Looking out of the window, he recalled the feeling of excitement a few years previously when he learned he'd won a scholarship to study at King's College, Cambridge. (This was one of one of only four open scholarships which were not reserved for Etonians.)

Fred had been only 16 when he sat the entrance exam for King's, and on his 17th birthday, on 13 December 1930 he had the best birthday present he'd ever had. He was in his room, immersed in one of his books, a gift for his birthday, when he heard his mother calling up to him, 'Fred – a telegram boy is at the door – I think it's for you!' His mother stepped aside as he rushed down the entrance hall towards the front door. A boy was standing there, dressed very smartly with a round pill-box hat, highly polished leather pouch fixed onto a belt with shiny brass buckles, his uniform was immaculate, and his bicycle was spotless. 'Telegram for Master Clayton?' he said.

'That's me.' Fred wondered if this was a birthday message or something. The boy handed over the sealed envelope and Fred tore it open, reading with increasing disbelief, 'Mother, it's from King's College, Cambridge. They've offered me a place. I start in October!'

Fred (left) with his parents, William and Mary, and his brother, George.

Fred was still 17 when he began his life at King's in the autumn of 1931. He flourished academically, sweeping up prizes as he went. A Latin essay prize in 1932 followed by the Porson Prize in 1933 for translating a passage from Shakespeare's Henry VIII into Greek, and he won the Chancellor's Medal for English Verse the following year for his poem, 'The English Countryside, Lines written in the Suburb of an Industrial city'. This was a lament to the lost landscape caused over the years by the urbanisation whose beauty you only learn to appreciate once it's gone. In it he asks,

Oh, if I love that blue, why hate
Blue smoke drifting on blue slate,
Steel-blue swords of light that quiver
On the gasworks, by the river,
Where slag makes hills and where oil makes
Many-coloured water-snakes?
Why should I loathe those rainbows there,
And love a rainbow in the air? ...
But, whatever comes, I'm cheated,
I'll not see my foes defeated:
I'll not see the meadowsweet,
Back from exile, in this street.
I'll not have the earth to tread,
When the fools fly overhead.
But certain is it that I hate
This red of brick and blue of slate,
This England that I know so well,
This *other* Eden, demi-hell.

More awards followed, culminating in a prize fellowship, which he'd been awarded as a result of his dissertation on Edward Gibbon. While he had always loved Shakespeare, his studies in Greek and Latin had opened whole worlds to him in which he could immerse himself. He had always seen beauty in languages, the power of words to move and create new worlds, new possibilities as well as educate. And when he wrote, he discovered he could use that power himself.

He loved the academic life and the protection afforded him by King's, but just a few hundred miles over the sea, people were being radicalised by this extraordinary and frightening revolution called National Socialism. Curiosity and acute political consciousness made him to want to see first-hand what was happening in Germany under the rule of these so-called 'Nazis'.

CHAPTER TWO
Autumn 1936: Dresden – An introduction to the Büttner-Wobst family

At last, the train was nearing Dresden, his destination, and the place that he would call home for the next year. He craned his neck to catch his first glimpse of the silhouettes of the Old Town on the southern bank of the Elbe River – on the left, the dome of the Frauenkirche (Church of Our Lady) shaped like a stone bell and topped off with a golden cross that glittered in the sunshine, and the baroque opulence of the spires of the Hofkirche (the Catholic former church of the Saxon court) and the Royal Palace in the centre, competed to dominate the view.

Fred's first view of the famed Dresden skyline would have been like this. Here, the Frauenkirche is on the left and the Royal Palace on the right.

Other spires and church domes punctuated the skyline and Fred gasped at the beauty that had earned Dresden the title of 'the Florence of the Elbe.' He had spent happy hours poring over photographs of the old city in the library in Cambridge but the reality before him, even glimpsed from the train was better than he had imagined. He could not see the baroque quarter from the train but he knew it was in there somewhere and he was excited to explore it properly.

Once the train had crossed the Elbe, it was another ten minutes until he arrived at the main station, and he watched, mesmerised, as the train took him past one remarkable building after another, including an exotic structure with a dome that could have been at home in the Orient. Later he would be bemused to learn this oriental palace was no more than a cigarette factory. But even a cigarette factory in this beautiful city was a sight to behold.

Fred stepped down from the train, his luggage beside him on the platform, and he paused to look around. The station was similar in size to King's Cross station, through which he'd travelled; it seemed like an age ago. The Dresden station was impressive with its huge curved, glass roof spanning the platforms, with daylight streaming through. After he loaded his suitcases onto a trolley, he made his way towards the main station building, whose vast vaults lent the station a cathedral-like quality; a temple to the German gods of industry and engineering.

Dresden Altstadt's Hauptbahnhof, where Fred arrived in Dresden.

His attention was arrested by a vast poster, depicting the German eagle, perched on a rock in the foreground, with palm trees and a snow-capped mountain in the background and the Nazi flag flying across the sky. Across the bottom of the poster, the Gothic text proclaimed, '*Deutschland, Deine Kolonien!*' – 'Germany – your colonies.' Fred understood it was a demand for the return of the German colonies in Africa that had been stripped from the nation after the end of the first world war. There was no escaping the times he was living in. He wondered if the return of the colonies would satisfy Hitler's appetite for *Lebensraum*.

Fred had been told someone from the Kreuzschule would be there to meet him at the station and show him to his lodgings, so he stood in the middle of the entrance hall, wondering how long he would have to wait. When a few minutes had passed he began to fear he had been forgotten, or that someone had been told the wrong time.

He was relieved when he was approached by a young man, who introduced himself as Friedrich Jehn, a mathematics teacher. He picked up a couple of Fred's suitcases. 'Herr Clayton, you are most welcome in Dresden. I hope you don't mind, but we'll take the tram to your lodgings – they're not far from here.'

'No, not at all,' Fred replied, 'and, please, call me Fred.'

Jehn had soft, worried brown eyes, black hair, soft hands. He clearly had a nervous disposition; he looked around constantly, perhaps fearful of being watched, even followed. Is this what life in Dresden is like? Fred wondered. Must one always watch one's back?

Sure enough, it wasn't far from the main station to Fred's digs at 20 Lüttichaustraße, which would be his home for the next year. The street was a wide avenue comprised of multi-storey buildings with hotels, guesthouses, and shops. There was a graceful uniformity to the buildings with their large windows and stone frontages. Conveniently, the tramline went just past Fred's lodgings. Jehn told him that this was at the heart of what had become known as the English colony. At its peak at the turn of the century up to a thousand Britons had lived in Dresden, congregating mainly in this small area of the city. 'Those days seem a distant memory now,' Jehn commented sadly. 'The Great War put paid to all that. Very few British people make this great city their home now.'

'Well,' Fred smiled, 'I hope to, at least for this year.'

They alighted from the tram and walked a short distance along the road to the accommodation. Fred thanked Jehn for showing him the way.

'That's no problem,' Jehn replied. 'I look forward to seeing you at school.'

'How far away from the school are we?'

'Not far; it's just round the corner from here.'

Fred was relieved; at least one thing seemed to have gone smoothly so far, and in Jehn he might have found a friend. He wondered if any of his other colleagues at the Kreuzschule would be as friendly.

Fred was greeted by his landlords, Mrs and Professor Günther, who showed him to his room, on the second floor of the apartment building. Though only sparsely furnished, with a desk, bed, chair and wardrobe, it was comfortable enough and the large windows meant that the room had a light and airy feel. He appreciated the desk being placed in front of the window, looking out onto the street below and, as he sat down, he smiled as he thought about the hours he could spend daydreaming while watching the life of the city go by beneath him.

Fred had a couple of days to acclimatise before the new school year began, so he made the most of it by getting to know the area. He'd been given a map by his landlady and he first found his way to the school where he'd spend most of his time. The neo-Gothic building of the Kreuzschule, with its square pillars and cloistered arches, was imposing and impressive, and reminded Fred of his own school.

He headed across the city and found the Prager Straße. This was Dresden's equivalent of Oxford Street, a wide avenue of grand

buildings that conveyed luxury, the epitome of 20th century
bourgeois life and style. People, Fred was told by his landlady,
travelled from all around to go there and shop, although he
himself couldn't see why anyone would travel any distance for
shopping – a necessary evil, rather than a pleasure.

*The imposing neogothic Kreuzschule building, built in 1866. Like many others, it would
not survive the air raid in February 1945.*

Thoughts of his first day at the Kreuzschule filled him with a
mixture of exhilaration and trepidation. His first day at the
Liverpool Collegiate School was seared into his memory for life.
Recognised as intellectually gifted, he'd begun grammar school a
year early. His French teacher and Form Master, Gussie Terton
had ignored Fred's increasingly frantic signals to be allowed to the
lavatory and he had burst into tears and wet himself. It was an
ignominious beginning to a school career for Fred who was not
only the youngest and smallest in the class but hopeless at games
and apt to burst into tears when the going got tough. Fred had
been, one might think, born to be teased and bullied, especially
when he repeated the weeping part of the performance on several
occasions. But in the following seven years, joshing became no
more than teasing and Fred, eagerly affectionate himself, enjoyed
protective friendliness from the others. He hoped to be able to
treat the young boys in his class in the Kreuzschule the same way
he had been treated himself.

That first morning was bright and sunny. On his short walk to the school, he was grateful for the late summer sunshine and gentle breeze that helped calm his nerves. Fred felt very self-conscious about walking onto the school grounds for the first time, weaving through the crowds, aware that he was a stranger. He felt that everyone was looking at him, whether they were or not. He wondered if he looked convincing in his trilby, white shirt, formal tie, knee-length overcoat and black leather briefcase, or could people see through him to the boy he was?

Fred on the Lüttichaustraße, dressed for school.

He'd been told that his first class would be teaching the fifteen and sixteen-year-old boys with a Herr Klinge, who would meet him at the main entrance to the building. Was Klinge, Fred wondered as he sprinted up the stone steps to the entrance hall, an ardent Nazi? Were his colleagues? Although Fred had steered clear of politics in his conversations with Jehn, he doubted that Jehn was a devotee of Hitler.

Klinge was waiting for him already. He greeted him stiffly, 'Heil Hitler!' and Fred raised his arm in response; he didn't know what else to do, he was loath to get off on the wrong foot with his colleague. Klinge, however, seemed unimpressed, as if he detected the lack of conviction in Fred's action. 'Herr Clayton, I believe you are with me this morning,' he said abruptly. 'Follow me.' Klinge then promptly clicked his heels and turned around, Fred following him a couple of feet behind, feeling like Klinge's pet or servant.

Fred made an inauspicious start in the classroom when he stumbled over a boy's satchel, whereupon he reacted in English with an automatic, 'I'm awfully sorry!' Sixteen pupils looked at him in amazement. He'd given the game away immediately. The next awkward moment came immediately with the Hitler salute.

'Heil Hitler!' barked Klinge.

The class chorused, 'Heil Hitler!' in unison and Fred knew he was being watched. How would this foreigner react to the greeting?

To his later shame he found himself mumbling, 'Heil Hitler', albeit with scant enthusiasm. He reflected later on what his King's friends would have thought had they seen him – but what other choice did he have?

'You'll notice we have a guest among us. This is Herr Clayton from England. He has come to teach with us this year.' Fred's face flushed as he felt the eyes of sixteen pupils bore into him; some were welcoming, others challenging and most, simply uninterested.

Fred managed to get off on the wrong foot with Herr Klinge from the very beginning. A boy, Wilhelm Schmidt, was asked to read an English essay out loud, which he did in an unintelligible accent. He also kept repeating the phrase, 'That will say.' Fred felt he had to step in and offer some criticism.

'Wilhelm, I think you need to work on your English accent and if you don't mind me saying, we don't use, 'That will say' in English – this is a French idiom – it isn't used in English.'

Suddenly, all eyes turned on Herr Klinge. He had obviously taught them this. 'Ahh yes, thank you, Herr Clayton, for your interesting criticism. It is so valuable having a *natural* English speaker with us, isn't it?' The class responded with a typically unenthusiastic grunt of assent. Klinge then made sure he had the final word: 'Boys, you should notice that Herr Clayton's English accent is not pure. It is marked with a lesser regional accent. One shouldn't copy him – that isn't, how do you say, how the King speaks.' Fred smiled, wincing inwardly. Lessons with Klinge would no doubt be challenging.

Indeed, in their next lesson, Klinge deliberately took Fred by surprise by delivering the whole class over to the Englishman. 'Talk to them in English. Talk to them about English public schools. They will understand.' Fred was rather taken aback by this. Klinge clearly believed in the success of his own teaching. Fred was more than a little embarrassed. He could feel he was blushing, but there was nothing he could do. Soon he was stumbling, mumbling, hesitating, speaking almost apologetically, as he tried to say something coherent and useful to the class while wondering how much they really understood.

He could see by the blank faces that the majority understood very little, but he noticed a particular boy whose blue eyes were accentuated by the sky-blue pullover he was wearing. He wore black corduroy shorts and no tie – there was nothing very uniform about the lads' attire in the school. He was regarding Fred with an amused smile. They exchanged glances conveying their shared appreciation of the absurdity of the situation. 'We both know,' the glance said, 'that you probably don't understand what I'm saying. But it's OK, I wouldn't worry about it – it's the most awful rubbish anyway. It's absurd, isn't it?' The joke was on Klinge, who clearly wasn't as good at teaching English as he thought he was.

Soon after this lesson, Fred bumped into the boy just in front of the Kreuzschule's stone steps. They only exchanged a brief greeting. The boy spoke first. 'Heil Hitler!' he said, with perfect gravity.

Fred paused for a moment, and responded, with equal gravity, 'Heil Hitler!' and that was it, that was all he could manage. Afterwards he wondered if, again, there was a shared understanding, a shared joke, even, in their exchange of the German greeting. Fred knew it meant nothing to him, and

wondered what the boy himself meant by it. Exchanging the
greeting in front of a class or group of people was one thing, but it
was something completely different to exchange the greeting when
there were just two of them. Was he joking, or was he issuing the
Englishman a challenge – would Fred rebel, be openly defiant?
Only time would tell.

They bumped into each other again; this time, Fred was
determined to make more of the opportunity to build some sort of
relationship with someone outside the confines of the school
community. He asked his name. 'Götz Büttner-Wobst.'

'And how do you find school, Götz?'

Götz shrugged, 'I don't really like it.' Then he blurted out, 'I
know I'm a disappointment at home. Mother always tells me I
should work harder. But it's boring.'

'Well, perhaps I can help you with your studies? Do you think
your parents would like it?'

He hoped that he sounded more composed and professional
than he felt; longing for connection, for friendship, for
understanding. Perhaps this young man would be a route to
friends, to his family. He was already imagining the conversation
Götz would have at home. He would say, as if not much
concerned, that, by the way, there was this Englishman at school
who had wondered if he might help him with his schoolwork.
Would his parents welcome the idea, would they be interested in a
young foreigner, a visitor from the wider world?

Not long afterwards, Fred was delighted to be contacted by the
boy's parents, asking if he would be a tutor to Götz and his
younger brother, Wolf. Fred wondered whether they would
welcome a teacher or simply another adult who would have a real
interest in them as individuals, who thought them worth talking to,
who would take them seriously. He asked Klinge for more
information about them. 'Young Götz Büttner-Wobst is not up to
standard. He is undersized, unathletic, no great scholar. Not
surprising really; he's the class weakling. Wolf isn't too blessed
with brains either.'

Fred learned that the boys travelled from Langebrück, outside the city, by train and walked from the Hauptbahnhof to the school, which took only ten minutes. They were a wealthy family. His father was a doctor – a specialist in tuberculosis – whose practice on the first floor at number 1 Mosczinskystraße wasn't too far from the school, on the edge of the Altstadt. This was round the corner from Fred's digs.

The next day, there was a knock at the door of the staff room. Götz appeared and delivered a very polite invitation to tea on behalf of his parents. 'Mother seems very pleased that you've agreed to teach us,' he said, 'and she said that perhaps it would do me good if we could speak a little English together.' Fred was relieved that, a month after his arrival, the monotony of Sunday afternoons spent playing patience with his landlady would be broken for this weekend.

That Sunday, Götz met Fred at Langebrück Station. Langebrück was a small town ten miles from the city centre. Fred found Götz polite, not unfriendly, but perhaps a little wary. Conversation seemed stilted. They crossed the little square in front of the station in silence. Finally, Fred broke the silence. 'Why do you live out here, so far out from the city?' he asked.

'Oh, I don't know. My father thinks it's healthier. He says that lots of people suffer from lung and breathing problems in the city.'

'Your father's a doctor,' said Fred – making a statement, rather than asking a question.

'Yes, how did you know that?' asked Götz, surprised.

'Klinge told me. I asked him about your family.'

The awkward silence fell upon them again. Fred racked his brain for something to say. 'We have something in common.'

Götz smiled politely, vaguely interested. 'Yes sir, what's that?'

'We're both class babies. I was the smallest and the youngest in my class,' Fred explained, and continued to give Götz a potted biography of his school life. He knew he babbled, but he couldn't help it. Either way, it seemed to work – Götz relaxed as Fred chatted away.

When they neared the house, Götz suggested they take a more scenic route through the Dresdner Heide, the huge forest that overlooked the Büttner-Wobst family house. As they walked, Fred looked around at what struck him as a quintessentially German landscape. 'It reminds me of *Grimms' Fairy Tales.*'

'Maybe,' Götz replied, 'but to me it's just home.'

'Well, I'm used to getting up on a hill like this one at home in Liverpool and seeing the sea. But I can't even sense it here behind the hills. The woods are so dark. It must be an easy country to feel lost in.'

There was a short silence. 'Our house is just at the bottom here. We've come right round. Now we can go straight down although it's quite steep.'

'Homesickness is a funny thing,' Fred mused.

Götz looked at him sympathetically. 'I suppose you can't go home yet?'

'No, not for a long time. And I don't want to. Only half of me is homesick, the other half is almost afraid of going home.' Fred wasn't sure he was making much sense, but he continued anyway, 'One feels it's terrifying to have left the land, but now – one must go on to the other shore.'

Götz looked a little baffled, so Fred stopped trying to explain. Instead he asked, 'Have you ever thought of visiting England?'

'No, but I've often thought I'd like to visit Italy.'

'"*Kennst du das Land, wo die Zitronen blühn?*"' quoted Fred, unable to resist the urge to show off a little.

'Do you know a lot of German poems?' asked Götz.

'Hardly any actually. I learn quickly and forget quickly.'

'So do I.'

'"*Du liebes Kind*" – "Sweet lovely child,"' Fred began, in a strange mocking tone. He saw that Götz started at these words for a moment – wondering if Fred were addressing him, and then an expression of realisation crossed his face – it was another quotation – '"– *komm', geh mit mir!*" – "Come, go with me!"' continued Fred.

'I know that,' said Götz, smiling.

Fred began at the beginning of Goethe's 'Der Erlkönig' – 'The Elf King', melodramatically:

'"Who's riding so late where winds blow wild?"'

They were coming down the hill quickly now. After the first verse they found themselves taking parts in the poem. Götz was the boy, squeaking with terror. Fred was the ridiculously gruff father and a really sinister Elf King. The darkness and the bushes played their parts too, even if the wind had to be imagined. Down they came, laughing, caught up in the fun of it all, taking a half-line of the poem at a time.

"'The father shudders, –'"

"'–his ride is wild,'"

"'–In his arms he's holding – '"

"'–the groaning child, – '"

"'–Reaches the court – '"

"'–with toil and dread.– '"

Götz rang the doorbell, and they recited the last line together mournfully:

'The child he held in his arms was dead.'[†]

4 Blumenstraße, home of the Büttner-Wobst family

The house on the Blumenstraße, like many others in Langebrück, was very large. Langebrück was clearly the place where wealthy citizens of Dresden moved when they wanted to escape from the city. The family seemed particularly affluent; Fred noticed that they

---

[†] Johann Wolfgang von Goethe, Erlkönig, 1782 (translated into English 'The Elf King' by Edwin Zeydel, 1955)

owned a car and garage, one of the few he'd seen in Langebrück. He wasn't thinking of this, however, but rather of the family he was about to meet. He had a dim idea that there were sisters as well as the two brothers.

A maid answered the door, and Fred and Götz were ushered into the drawing room. The first member of the family Fred met was Wolf, whose class in school he had not yet encountered. Wolf had crisp blonde curls, and his blue eyes seemed strangely mobile, glittering with interest and mischief, whereas his brother's were still, quiet, almost brooding. Wolf had a more positive attitude. Foreign might mean fun, made of or with the foreigner. Their mother and two sisters joined them for tea. He felt very anxious: he was desperate to make connections; and while he met boys every day, with girls he didn't even know where to start.

Here the situation was no different. Traudi, who was seventeen, had a young man in her life already. Anyway, she seemed a bit silly and not in the least interested in Fred. This was typical; he had been abashed and irritated since adolescence by this feeling that girls could so readily dismiss him with such easy superiority. Mädi, aged twenty, the elder sister and firstborn, was intellectual enough but Fred's desire, at odds with his size, was to play the manly, protective part to someone younger and weaker who might need him. Mädi certainly didn't need Fred, or, she communicated, any man at the moment. She would take her time about that. Anyway, with women – with the girls, and with the mother as well, Fred found this baffling barrier, not felt with men or boys. He felt uncouth; he didn't react with instinctive attention to women, still less pay compliments. He didn't quite see why one had to play this uncomfortable game, start talking in a different style and find the wavelength of their interests. Why was there the need for all this artifice and work when he was trying to relate to those of the opposite sex when relationships with men and boys seemed so natural in comparison?

Later, on his way home, reflecting on this first encounter, Fred would muse on whether he should have bowed, and certainly been better dressed, more attentive to creases and clashing colours, if he were to make the right impression and he wondered whether relationships that relied on making that much effort would be really worthwhile at any rate. Surely any relationship worth its salt would enable him to be himself?

The conversation over tea with the boys' mother was polite enough. 'How do you like Germany?' she asked.

'I....'

'He thinks it's too big,' said Götz, 'because you can't see the sea.'

Everyone laughed. Fred found himself having to explain their conversation in the Heide. Out of desperation for something to talk about more than anything, Fred brought up the subject of opera as he'd heard of Dresden's reputation in this field, cemented of course by the world-famous Semper Opera House. Fred remarked on the high standard of musical education in Germany. 'I'm as unmusical as they come,' he explained, 'so I envy anyone who is musical.'

'Unfortunately, Götz doesn't have a real talent for music either,' replied his mother. Götz rolled his eyes and Fred felt for him, as she continued, 'He's bottom of his class.'

And she turned to her son, 'Well, did you talk a lot of English with Herr Clayton?'

'He said something in English once when he slipped,' said Götz wickedly.

His mother laughed a little uncomfortably, and, turned to Fred. 'What would *you* do with a boy like this?'

Fred felt himself being pulled to the grown-ups, and made an appealing, apologetic glance at Götz as he mumbled 'Yes. I suppose it's a problem...'

'Quite seriously, it is... Of course, he's young for that class. Sometimes I think the work is really a little difficult for him... He isn't stupid, but he is so sensitive. I wish he would work harder and pay more attention. He could do so much better if he applied himself more, instead of staring out of the window.'

Fred felt mortified for poor Götz. He longed to help and knew that the immediate way of doing so would be to change the subject. And soon enough he managed to steer the conversation away from the disappointing older son towards something else, talking in sweeping terms about how the Kreuzschule compared with his school back in Liverpool.

Fred could tell both boys – Wolf and Götz – were relieved when tea finished and they could take Fred upstairs to show him their room. They exhibited something of their present hobbies and past playthings. They seemed to get on well enough together. Fred could imagine Wolf being the provoker of quarrels rather than Götz.

Fred had felt slightly ill at ease with the boys' mother; he wasn't sure where he stood and believed he needed to be very careful with her. Fred had no problem with making the right impression on the doctor, who arrived midway through Fred's time at the Büttner-Wobst family home. They heard his voice downstairs and went to greet him. Fred was immediately struck by how haggard the man looked – he was clearly ill, and illness had aged him beyond his years. He learned that the doctor's job as a lung specialist meant he was not often at home – on weekdays his surgery and visiting times were in the afternoon and evening. He would only see the children on Sundays, if the Hitler Youth did not otherwise decree.

The doctor told Fred of his visit to England before the War; how he had even had a brief romance with an English girl, and his later experience as a prisoner of war. He recounted a story of an unpleasant Frenchman and a nice Scotsman who had apologised for the behaviour of the 'Fucking Frogs' – Fred and the doctor both laughed immoderately at this story and the boys joined in, perhaps because they found it so funny to see the men both laughing. It struck Fred as remarkable that the doctor's experience as a prisoner of war hadn't stopped him from warmly welcoming him into their home. Fred asked him about the unusual family name of Büttner-Wobst, and the boys groaned, as it set the doctor off on one of what was clearly his favourite topics, the history of the family. They were a long-established family in Dresden, with connections to Saxon royalty.

Soon they all went into the study, the walls of which were covered with portraits of the Büttners, the Wobsts, and other ancestors, all rather small and badly painted. The doctor went through each one, explaining who they were, and then concluded by putting his hand on Wolf's shoulder and playing with his ear affectionately. 'And this is the last picture.'

'I congratulate the artist,' Fred said.

'Well, practice makes perfect,' said the doctor. 'He is the fourth child.' He looked paternally at Wolf, who blushed, clearly embarrassed but also pleased at the compliment.

Fred looked at the clock on the doctor's desk, 'Well, thank you for your hospitality today, but I must be getting back home.'

'Let me see you to the front door.' The doctor rose from his seat and Fred followed. At the front doorstep, the doctor asked, 'And you have seen the motto above our door?'

'Yes, I did notice it earlier, – "*Thue recht - scheue niemand*" – "Act justly – fear no one",' Fred read.

'That's right. This has been our family motto for generations. I had those words chiselled into the stone when we moved into Blumenstraße in 1920.' The doctor lowered his voice conspiratorially, as if afraid of being overhead, 'I don't want to speak too politically today – '

'Good!' exclaimed Wolf. 'That's a relief!'

'As I was saying,' the doctor said, looking pointedly at his son, who grinned mischievously, 'we won't talk politics today, but if ever there was a time for us to live by this motto, it's now.'

In a louder voice, the doctor continued, 'Goodbye, Herr Clayton, thank you for your kind visit. We look forward to seeing you again soon.'

Fred left the Büttner-Wobst family that afternoon with a peculiar mixture of perplexity and excitement. He certainly wanted to see the family again, to continue to build the bridge that he had begun and he wondered whether the feeling was mutual. He reflected on the family motto and the doctor's determination and defiance; how costly would it be to adhere to these values?

* * *

As the weeks in Dresden passed, Fred found himself getting into a fairly well-established routine, aided of course, by the regular rhythm of the school week. He was determined to immerse himself in the German culture and language and looked for opportunities to read as much literature as he could and converse with as many people as possible, although his contacts and conversations were predominately with those connected with the small community that revolved around the Kreuzschule. This gave him the opportunity to get to know and observe the Büttner-Wobst boys well over time, and he found himself discussing them with more than one colleague. One of them, Zetsche, who'd got to know the wider family, commented, 'That is an absurd family. The girls are terrifically clever, but not exactly beauties. The boys are beautiful' – he used the term *bildschön* – 'but not exactly scholars.'

'Wolf's no fool,' Fred argued.

'But he can't concentrate on anything,' Zetsche maintained. 'Every fly on the wall has his attention wandering.'

Fred had to concede that Wolf certainly didn't waste much of his cleverness in class at the time. Even with Fred, he was no model pupil. But Fred was grateful to him when he gave some of his scarce concentration to a piece he read in English which came to a comic climax. Wolf grinned encouragingly with his glittering, mischievous blue eyes at just the right moment. Fred had beaten that fly on the wall!

Indeed, although it was Götz who had initially caught Fred's attention, Fred found a bond developing with Wolf, and they spent time together outside class. This had been encouraged by the boys' parents. Their father, Werner, often invited Fred to Langebrück, with whom he enjoyed discussing politics. Fred wondered how openly this subject was broached when there wasn't a foreign visitor for the Doctor to impress – how much influence did their father have on his children?

He soon got his answer one afternoon after school, when Wolf and Fred were walking together in the Großer Garten, Dresden's biggest park. Fred felt he could breathe easily in the wide-open spaces of the lawns and tree-lined avenues that dissected the park. After a companionable silence, Wolf asked, rather abruptly, 'What do you think of the political situation in Germany?'

'Are you interested in politics?' Fred answered, taken aback by Wolf's sudden question.

'Very.'

'I see – what do you expect me to say? It's a big subject.'

'Well,' Wolf paused, 'anything you like– it interests me. I'm uninterested in English and – and French and stuff, just mechanical learning. I like history and things with ideas.' Wolf spoke earnestly, hoping no doubt to persuade Fred that he was a boy who deserved to be taken seriously, 'I mean, certain things must strike you about life here.'

'Yes … in fact, it's so different that one doesn't know where to begin. It's much harder than I had imagined possible. It's like two worlds. Words don't mean the same in them.'

Fred was aware that he was being abstract and unconvincing. He found speaking in German incredibly restrictive. His limited grip on the language meant that he was unable to convey his thoughts and ideas as effectively as he wished. His intelligence – so vaunted in England – was infuriatingly fettered in the German language. He had to simplify, crudely and unsubtly. So, he slowed himself down, and persevered. 'Just before I came here, I met at a friend's house a lady from Germany who was in England for a short visit. She wanted to read the papers mostly. She said it was the dreadful way – the way the young were poisoned with propaganda – she said they knew nothing of the world outside and what really was going on. …'

'That's nonsense,' Wolf countered. 'One can read foreign newspapers and listen to foreign stations! In fact, although Father doesn't think I know, he listens in secret to the BBC. But I bet he's not alone. Why, I don't suppose more than half the chaps in our form are really Nazis.'

Fred couldn't hide his sense of surprise at this statement. Wolf continued, 'Well, I mean, you know Heinz Sandmann, Traudi's male friend, well, he's flying planes in Spain – we all know he is, and yet no one's supposed to be in Spain. So, you see, we do know what's going on. And personally, I have my doubts about the whole business. I don't trust Italy.' And he continued giving his reasons – or were they, Fred wondered, his father's reasons that Wolf was now repeating? Fred felt Wolf was trying to prove himself to him. His ears particularly pricked up when Wolf mentioned, 'National Murder Week.'

'What's that?' asked Fred, intrigued. He'd not heard that turn of phrase before.

'Oh, – you know. As if everyone hadn't known about the *Schweinerei* for months!'

Fred couldn't help but be impressed by this precocious fourteen-year-old and his knowledge of Hitler's *Night of the Long Knives* in which he had slaughtered 150-200 of his supposed allies within Germany two years previously. 'You certainly know more than I give you credit for,' he commented, wincing inwardly at the dry schoolmasterly note that had crept into his voice. He certainly didn't mean to talk down to Wolf. Perhaps it was safe to touch on the Reichstag, which Fred was convinced had been torched by the Nazis. 'Do you know the joke about the Reichstag?'

'Yes, but go on …' Wolf replied.

'Chap comes to Herman, tells him the Reichstag's on fire. He says, '*Mein Gott*, already?''

They both laughed. As it happened, Wolf knew all the jokes about the Reichstag, and he told them all. Fred realised that here in his young companion, was a kindred spirit – Wolf was mischievous, wiser beyond his fourteen years and, indeed, although Fred was meant to be his teacher in Dresden, it would often be the other way round. Wolf was a holy terror, an intellectual vandal who flicked every pebble of a joke he could pick up in that appalling glasshouse of the German regime.

Soon afterwards Fred made his next visit to the Büttner-Wobst house. He hadn't been invited, but he was lonely and homesick, and the Büttner-Wobsts were the closest to family that he had in Dresden. He trudged the whole way from Dresden-Altstadt, through the Heide, to Langebrück, only to discover that the

Doctor was at home, in bed. The maid denied Fred entrance and so he had to trudge all the way back home again. It had been for nothing.

Fred wasn't completely deterred by this negative experience, however, and appeared, uninvited, another time. This time, only Wolf seemed to be about. 'Hello Mr Clayton,' he said, 'it's nice of you to visit. I'm sorry, but I've got to go out soon – it's Hitler Youth and I need to get changed into my uniform. You're welcome to stay; my parents will be back soon.'

'Thank you. So you're going to go and be a Wölfling,' remarked Fred, unable to resist making a silly pun on Wolf's name. Wolf rolled his eyes – a dead loss, then, and then headed back inside to finish getting ready. But then a little girl appeared with solemn blue almond eyes and pigtails, obviously drawn by curiosity from the veranda outside. She had a book called, *Viel schöne Sachen zum Lesen und Lachen – Many Nice Things for Reading and Laughing* – and Fred asked her, 'Are the *"Sachen"* really *"schön"*?'

She shrugged and said, 'I've read them all before.'

'So now they're a bit boring?'

'Yes, a bit,' she admitted. Fred noticed this girl – whose existence he hadn't even been aware of before – had an odd guttural voice – it wasn't a matter of language, but as if she had a heavy cold or something else wrong with her throat.

She withdrew as Wolf appeared in his uniform, a novel sight to Fred. 'I'm sorry you're unable to stay,' he said.

'It's OK,' replied Wolf, settling himself down on the settee, 'I'm not really in a hurry.'

'Oh, OK. I didn't know you had another sister,' Fred gestured towards the veranda where the girl with the pigtails had disappeared once more.

'Ach, Rike,' said Wolf dismissively, 'she's ten – the baby of the family.' Wolf didn't expand any more on Rike, and soon enough their conversation moved on.

Fred wondered why Wolf hadn't left to go out to the Hitler Youth. Perhaps he was going to give it a miss after all. Perhaps the unexpected arrival of the English guest whom he was left to entertain since everyone else – except his younger sister, was out –

gave him an excuse to miss a session. Wolf said none of this in so many words, but simply showed an air of indifference to the passage of time, as if punctuality were not all that important in the Hitler Youth.

At last, a key was heard to turn in the front door, and Dora Büttner-Wobst came in. She was visibly taken aback at seeing Fred, but said, 'Good afternoon, Herr Clayton, what a lovely surprise!' She smiled politely, although Fred wasn't convinced that she was really pleased to see him, 'Would you like some tea?'

'Yes please, Frau Büttner-Wobst.'

She then turned her attention to her youngest son, 'Wolf, I thought you were going to Hitler Youth this afternoon?'

'I was, but Herr Clayton came. I felt it was rude to turn him away.'

Dora grunted as she headed to the kitchen. Fred felt that she was embarrassed and did not really regard it as proper for him to pay unannounced visits and give Wolf an excuse for skiving, which might get him into trouble. Fred didn't realise it at the time, but this family, which was known by the Nazi regime for its non-conformity, couldn't really afford any more black marks with the Party. An English guest did not appear to Dora to be such an ideal excuse to skip Hitler Youth.

Fred found he made more headway and reached more of an understanding with the boys' father. He took advantage of the close proximity of Werner's medical practice on the Mosczinskystraße to his own digs, to make frequent visits to the surgery. Werner was a Stahlhelm man – as Conservative as they came. He made no secret of this – the steel helmet symbol of the Stahlhelm was featured above the main entrance to the family home which marked him as a supporter of the exiled monarchy – he longed for a Hohenzollern restoration by the army. In short, he wanted the pre-1914 world back again. He had a straightforward approach to the Nazis. They were just 'Canaille' – a pack of dogs, and Hitler was a lunatic.

In his surgery he had the obligatory picture of the Führer, and had chosen one of Hitler in top hat and tails, bowing to Hindenburg. Seeing this, Fred murmured, 'Moss Bros,' to himself, for this awkward, humble, thrilled little plebeian had obviously borrowed his unaccustomed attire for the great occasion. To the doctor Fred just said, 'The Bohemian Corporal', and, from the way Dr Büttner-Wobst's eyes lit up, saw he had scored a bull's-eye.

'I heard that you came round to our home the other week when I was alone, unwell, in bed. Our maid turned you away. I'm sorry about that. I should have been told. I would have welcomed your company for an hour or so.

'You see,' continued the doctor, 'I have a lung disease. It will kill me eventually. Most of the time I can live with it and carry out my work, but there are times when all I can do is stay in bed.' Fred felt flattered at the doctor's willingness to share his own vulnerability with his young English guest.

Later on, Fred mentioned that he'd discussed 'National Murder Week' with Wolf. The doctor shook his head. '*Pack schlägt sich, Pack verträgt sich,*' he remarked, delivering his verdict on the butchery of Röhm and his cronies in 1934. Fred made a note of these words and did his best to translate it into English – 'Dog greets dog, dog eats dog' – 'Shits salute, shits shoot' – No, he couldn't quite translate it.

In 1934 Martin Niemöller, along with other Protestant Germans, had risked the ire of the Nazis by forming the Confessional Church. It opposed the so-called German Christians and the changes that were being forced upon the traditional Protestant churches in Germany, and now in 1936 he was one of the Pastors who signed a petition against the 'Aryan paragraph' – which excluded Jewish people from membership of the church – denouncing it as being incompatible with Christian beliefs. The doctor was clearly worried about Niemöller's safety. 'Niemöller is a brave man,' the doctor said, 'but I worry for him. He has made himself a target, someone to be shot at.'

'But he's a respected pastor, they wouldn't dare,' Fred argued.

'Look at what they did to Röhm and he was Hitler's friend. I don't think there's anything they wouldn't dare to do – no one's safe – not even pastors.' Werner paused and smiled, 'You know Wolf has got it into his head that he wants to be a pastor at the moment. I think it's just because they're standing up against the Nazis. He's a *Trotzkopf* – a natural born opposer – like his father.' When Fred looked it up later his dictionary defined a *Trotzkopf* as 'a wayward, stubborn person,' but that missed the element of defiance, the impish devil of opposition in Wolf.

While Fred found himself forming a bond with Wolf and indeed the boys' father, the relationship with Götz was more difficult. In Götz, Fred saw a young man, who was struggling –struggling with the burden of parental expectation under which he laboured; struggling with the tumult of the world around him – the politics at home and at school and in the streets. While his younger brother, Wolf, went along with the doctor's dismissal and scorn of the Nazi regime, for Götz it wasn't that simple. He rebelled against that purely negative, almost lazy, shallow dismissal of Nazism. For him it was too easy to reject National Socialism wholesale; Götz was drawn to the deep water, wrestling with the times he was in, reading the works of Oswald Spengler, whose *The Decline of the West* predicted that western civilization was in terminal decline, that the Prussian people would be those who were appointed to defend and preserve the remnants of its culture.

Götz was clearly out of his depth here, but Fred couldn't help but admire the way he was trying to brave the gathering storm. He was nearing the end of his school life, and soon would be thrown into the Reichsarbeitsdienst – the National Labour Service, where he, like every young man between 18 and 25, would serve for at least six months. It was all right for his father, much of whose life was behind him, but it was different for Götz and his contemporaries; they had no real power over their future. All power, it seemed, was in the hands of the state. Could Götz really afford to rebel, even if he intended to?

When Fred looked at Götz he looked at a boy who was lost, whose blue eyes that had so captivated Fred were those of a boy more puzzled and struggling than brilliant. Fred felt that he himself had been given a superfluity of brain that wasn't really being put to good use, and he wanted to reach out, to help him, in whatever way he could, to reach out to him while he was still within hailing, warning distance. Fred, unlike Götz, had been clever, to whom studying, particularly Latin and Greek, came naturally and easily – perhaps he, Fred could help Götz navigate those particular choppy waters, but how could he convey this to the boy around whom Fred found himself particularly tongue-tied?

One day after school, they walked together down the Prager Straße to the Hauptbahnhof and stood together on the platform as Götz waited for his train home. Götz seemed preoccupied and quiet. Fred wondered whether his presence exacerbated Götz's confusion about his future and where his loyalties lay. After all, the boys a year senior to Götz had suddenly had their Abitur brought forward, their time at school reduced, in order to speed up their entry into the National Labour Service and the Armed Forces. Was he afraid? Fred didn't know what to say; he was just trying to show him sincere sympathy. As they stood side by side looking down the track from where the train would come, Fred said, '*Sie tun mir leid.*' – 'I'm sorry for you' – knowing how clumsy his words would sound. Fred never felt secure enough in their relationship to use the informal 'du' with Götz, only Wolf. With Götz there was always that level of formality, that distance between them. And it widened in that moment.

'*Ich brauche niemandem leid zu tun.*' – 'I don't need anyone to feel sorry for me,' Götz replied brusquely. Fred had hit upon decidedly the wrong note. An unhappy silence fell as they waited for the train.

In November Fred spent a fortnight in Rankenheim, a small village outside Berlin. He was invited there to teach on a residential course where German schoolmasters and mistresses had been summoned to learn English. Under the National Socialists, English, rather than French, had been made the main foreign language to be taught in all German schools, so teachers who could speak the language well were at a premium.

He was glad for the invitation as he had time on his hands. And, he reflected, it would give him something other than Götz's struggles to think about.

When Fred arrived, he found he was among around eighty other attendees. He'd hoped that others who were attending would be the same age as him and that this fortnight would offer him the opportunity for further connections and new relationships. He was disappointed. The vast majority were middle aged or older. Moreover, all were in uniform – the ladies in white blouses and blue skirts, the men in grey.

The certificate Fred received for attending the course in Rankenheim. It reads: 'Mr Frederick Clayton, Liverpool (England) has taken part as a lecturer in English in the English course at Rankenheim/Mark organised by the Deutsche Zentralinstitut für Erziehung und Unterricht [German Central Institute for Education and Teaching] at its Centre there. In addition to taking groups for English practice he has given lectures. Mr. Clayton's cooperation has been very valuable, a fact recognised on all sides.'

There was uniformity too in the way that people were to address each other – as '*Kamerad*' and not '*Herr*' or '*Doktor*'. The idea was that all would be seen as equals, although Fred felt that people were actually being denied their individuality. They were part of the mass. The mass was what mattered.

In an article, "How to learn English – A Nazi plan", published in an English newspaper, Fred described a typical day:

> Those innocents who had assumed that they were assembled for a fortnight solely to devote themselves to the brushing up of rusty English were early disillusioned. As early as 7 am the dormitories were called to life and hurried to parade for a quarter of an hour's physical jerks. An hour later (no excuse for untidiness, you see) the camp leader, appointed from headquarters, inspected all dormitories while the occupants stood to. A simple breakfast followed as a reward; nothing warm – one did not quite deserve that – except coffee of doubtful origin and unsweetened, but still a meal of sorts. Each table waited on itself, and fatigue parties were detailed for washing up, which they often did to a burst of sentimental song. After breakfast the German – or should one say the Nazi? – flag was hoisted. The comrades then divided up for an hour's labour service – chopping wood, preparing ground, general cleaning of common-rooms and stairs. The purpose of these activities was "ideological" rather than practical; the virtue in manual labour was to be brought home to the academic mind.
>
> Not until 10 o'clock did the camp cease for an hour to be an organisation for the good of men's souls; the teachers, on an average at least half as young as their pupils, took their classes for English conversation. Afterwards came a lecture in German, lunch, rest hour, route march, an English period for reading and discussion (using Priestley's *English Journey* or Inge's *England*), coffee, a lecture or two again, supper at seven, flag parade, and at eight the evening gathering, which expressed itself in many ways from the general airing of grievances about East Prussia and the Polish corridor to the full-throated if somewhat unmelodious singing of the more popular English songs. At ten o'clock came "lights out".

On the Sunday, instead of a Christian act of worship, there was music for violin and piano and a reading telling the story of a cavalry captain who lost his life in a battle against the Russians. New heroes, new mythologies, were taking their place at the heart of National Socialism, elbowing out the old, Christian God and making a new God in its own image. So much for the Nazi government's professed desire not to interfere with the church, Fred thought grimly.

National Socialist ideology permeated the lectures too – war poetry by Rupert Brooke and Siegfried Sassoon were held up for comparison: Brooke's, "If I should die", was presented as a great piece of work, patriotic, idealistic, all a war poem should be, but Sassoon's, "The Dreamers", showed the typical Jewish negative attitude, and could not, indeed have been written by anyone but a Jew. Shakespeare, too, was brought into the debate. Clean-living, and, therefore, considered more than halfway to being a good Nazi, he was compared favourably to his contemporary, Christopher Marlow, a rake. It would have been funny, Fred reflected, were the whole situation that this country found itself in, not deadly serious.

By the time Fred returned from Rankenheim, it was nearly the end of the first term. Fred was presented with a gift from some of the senior boys who were leaving, to thank him for the extra help he had given them. He felt, 'These boys are in a way, older than I am, sadder and wiser. They are aware of the acceleration of events. While there is yet time, these decent, well-bred lads wish to indicate they, at least, are innocent of national prejudice, and not all the Nazi propaganda will make them hate a nice individual young Englishman who has no hatred in his heart for them.'

Many of these boys as individuals seemed to go out of their way to say no hard feelings, even if they did clown with him in class as mercilessly as with any other weak master. He suspected they were better than many of their elders, men nearer Fred's own age, who believed they must build a new world at any cost and, as for the younger generation, they would have to be brave as well.

On the last day, as Fred was leaving the school principal, Helck's study he met Götz outside, about to give a letter to the principal. Helck took it from Götz and returned into his study.

'Going home?' Fred asked. 'Do you mind if I walk with you?'

'Not at all.'

'I've been in a camp for teachers,' Fred told Götz cheerfully as they left the school together, 'for teachers of English. Chaps like Klinge in convict uniforms. I can't still make out whether I was supposed to teach English or be taught politics. There was a chap who gave a long lecture, taking us "behind the scenes" of English policy, making us responsible for Spain and China and God knows what. It was fantastical. Then there were minorities, every evening a new one; Schleswig, Tyrol, Silesia, Memel … I've got to go to another camp in January. Then I come back here, and then I go skiing with you – with your class, I mean.'

'With us? I didn't know we were going this year?' Götz queried.

'Yes, you're going with Reinhardt, and a couple of other classes.'

'I see.'

'I'm going away for Christmas,' Fred continued. 'We must have another walk before then. Perhaps you would have tea with me?'

'I can't,' Götz replied hurriedly. 'My mother says I've got to do more work.' Then, more abruptly he asked, 'Why don't you ask Herr Reinhardt to tea?'

'Oh, it's no use asking any of the Herrn Kollegen to tea. They never have time.'

'We're very busy in Germany.'

'I know,' Fred replied. 'No time to think. Kept moving all the time. "Remember the movement".'

As they were talking on the street corner, a group of boys from the school passed them. Two were from Götz's class. 'Heil Hitler!' they cried, with a mixture of friendliness and mockery; more friendliness, perhaps, in each, more mockery in the mass. Fred flushed, frowned, smiled, gave a perfunctory greeting in reply.

'You don't like doing that,' said Götz sharply.

'What?'

'The German greeting.'

'In Rome one does as Rome does.'

'But it goes against the grain.'

'It becomes a habit.'

'But you don't like it,' Götz persisted.

Fred frowned. 'Why do you want me to admit that?'

'Oh I don't know,' began Götz, but then it all came pouring out. 'You can't be expected to understand it all. … You think of the poor Jews and the poor Communists and the terrible camps. Don't look at me like that – I hear what my parents say – I know about Dachau, it's near where my grandparents live. That's where the political prisoners get sent. I'm not as ignorant as I look, you know. Why did you come here, if you're so anti-German?'

'I'm not,' Fred protested. 'I may be anti-Hitler –'

'Ach, it's the same thing, and you know it. What do you want? Why don't you leave me alone? Why can't you go and find some other victim of your propaganda campaign?'

'What's the matter?' Fred asked, taken aback. 'Has something happened?'

'No,' Götz shook his head. 'It's no good. Look, I've got to go now.' He turned and almost ran away. Fred felt numb, hoping their relationship hadn't completely disintegrated. They would not meet again until after the Christmas holidays, and it was galling to end the term on such a sour note. So much for building bridges!

After Christmas there was a strain in Fred's relationship with Götz who, he sensed, was keeping him at arm's length. Fred felt constrained in their lessons; the need to conform to the regime, and Fred's desire to question, challenge and sow seeds of doubt in him was too much for Götz to handle. Fred reflected on that conversation before Christmas and wondered if he had pushed the young man too far. Not only was Götz, at sixteen, going through the maelstrom of impending adulthood, he was also having to handle the burdens of parental expectation; a dying father at home whose illness cast a shadow over the family; as well as the constant barrage of propaganda to which he was exposed through school and the Hitler Youth. Perhaps, Fred realised, Götz needed to conform simply in order to survive. It was best to leave him alone.

Fred would make one more uninvited visit to the Büttner-Wobst home. He met the boys' mother just outside the house. This time, she made no attempt to mask her unease at the Englishman's presence. 'Good afternoon, Herr Clayton. It is good of you to come, but I'm afraid you cannot keep coming like this outside the lessons. You're disturbing, upsetting the boys. We're not sure if your coming round in this way is helpful for them.'

Fred's mouth went dry, his breath caught in his mouth and his stomach churned. The message was clear. He was effectively banned from making social visits to their home. He felt inclined to be indignant, to challenge the ban, to demand open explanations from her. To be turned back from the very door like this was so humiliating. He did not deserve it.

But what choice had he but to endure? He merely bowed his head, meekly apologised to the Frau Doctor for disturbing her, and wished her good day before trudging back to the station, still numbed by the rejection he had experienced, wondering why he'd been turned away.

Fred found out later that Dora's sister-in-law had warned her off him as a dangerous propagandist for the anti-Nazi cause. The doctor's sister had married one of the masters at the school. He had never been very friendly to Fred, having been a prisoner of war in England in the first war and attributed to the bad treatment and bad food he had experienced there a curious persistent complaint. Hearing this, Fred had vaguely apologised on behalf of his country.

He fretted about what was being said about him to the boys. Would they hear things said or hinted against him, unheard, undefended? That thought was unbearable, and in his heart, he appealed to God, whose existence he doubted, against the keen injustice he felt. To have to face them in school, Götz, Wolf, not knowing what exactly they knew or believed! He had no choice. There was nothing he could do, except try his best to demonstrate who he was, to at least retain his innocence in the boys' eyes. He hoped that they wouldn't be swayed or persuaded by the propaganda that whirled against him.

CHAPTER THREE
1936-1937: Politics in the Kreuzschule

Throughout his time in Dresden Fred moved in middle-class circles, trying to measure, fathom, take soundings. What made men accept or reject the regime? He wasn't afraid to challenge and criticise the Nazis – he made open propaganda against them. It may have been unwise, but he couldn't help himself. He was born free and garrulous. He protested instinctively at the absurd, the unreasonable, the unjust, the glib generalisation, as he had done at school, as he had done all his life. He protested against the way that being anti-Nazi was being equated in many quarters with being anti-German, but that was definitely not the same thing at all, and he strove to make this point to anyone who would listen. Many did – he was a friendly breath of fresh air to many of his pupils, but he made less impact on the masters, many of whom were Nazis. He used a discussion he had with Reinhardt during a mid-morning break to press this point:

'Maynard Keynes, you've heard of him?'

'Yes, the famous economist. What of him?'

'Well, he was against reparations. He was never anti-German.'

'No?'

'No. But he thinks this regime are a bunch of gangsters. So do I.' Reinhardt flared with anger, made as if to reply, but kept silent. Fred hoped that by his example, his open-heartedness, he had demonstrated palpably that he was not anti-German at all even if he remained firmly against Hitler and the Nazi regime. Some might have called him foolish, but he carried on his one-man propaganda campaign, and was gratified when he scored the odd point.

In the Kreuzschule every Monday, and on political anniversaries, there was a sermon, religious or secular, after prayers. This took place in the Kreuzschule's grand auditorium, spanning two floors at the front of the building. To get there you walked up the wide wooden staircase and through the entrance door, into the vast room, which had two galleries at the front and was decorated with rich paintings and carvings. Above the entrance door there was a painting framed by carved turrets, which depicted the instruction of students by wisdom. To the right and left of the door were life-size paintings showing examples of the love of God (Abraham's sacrifice) – Fred wondered how long this Jewish scene would last intact in the febrile antisemitic atmosphere – love of truth (Socrates emptying the cup of poison), love of country (Marcus Curtius sacrificing himself for his country in Rome), and intellectual courage (Luther before the Diet of Worms). In this extraordinary location, teachers gave discourses from a podium, often delivered with great fervour, on a range of subjects, which, although lacking somewhat in form, were well directed at all the fine and generous impulses of youth and its discontent. They preached virtues of loyalty – to school, friend, fatherland, whatever faults may be found in them; of industry – the using of every moment of one's life so that it had purpose and bore fruit. Fred thought this was all very well, but questioned the value of unthinking loyalty. 'Criticism has its place, surely?' he wondered. In the staff room he argued this point with Rudert, a teacher of English with hard features and harsh voice, of humble origin, but distinct and strong personality, discussing with him the merits and demerits of democracy.

Rudert had irritated Fred by saying, 'All I want is a clear command – *Ich will nur einen klaren Befehl haben.*' Fred wondered at this. Rudert made passivity and fatalism sound somehow heroic.

Rudert seemed instinctively hostile to the doctor's family, seeing them as pampered upper-class types who had had it all too easy. He, more than any others that Fred came across, gave the socialist half of the 'National-Socialist' label some meaning. He was certainly anti-capitalist, and was dismissive of the doctor's family, who had been friendly with some rich Jewish bankers. When Fred mentioned that the Doctor had a very modern radio which he had shown Fred with some pride, Rudert said sourly, 'They would have.'

With Fred, with England, he seemed to have a curious love-hate relationship. They argued long and bitterly about politics, yet an odd kind of reluctant respect, almost friendship, persisted. Walking down the Prager Straße one lunchtime Fred was arguing that Hitler was a war monger. 'I've been reading Bertrand Russell's *Power*. Listen to what he says here – "Hitler and Mussolini, since they teach that war is the noblest of human activities, could not be happy if they had conquered the world and had no enemies left to fight." – I'm not the only one who thinks as I do.'

'That's rubbish! Anti-German propaganda as usual,' exclaimed Rudert. 'Same as all the others.'

'Actually, that's not true,' replied Fred. 'Russell was a pacifist in the Great War. He spoke out publicly against our country going to war against yours and suffered for this – he lost his job as a lecturer, even spent six months in prison. He's more entitled to criticise Hitler than rabid anti-Germans. You can't tar us all with the same brush.'

'The bombs,' said Rudert harshly, 'will not discriminate.'

Fred thought this was a damn silly pseudo-fatalistic argument, and he retorted, 'Bombs are boneheads. Men discriminate, or forfeit their claim to be men.'

One day grudgingly, Rudert gave a little ground. He admitted that he had to agree with many criticisms of the less satisfactory features of the Nazi regime. Then suddenly he exclaimed, *'Und doch sagen wir ja'* - 'And yet we say yes.' It may have been fanciful, but with instant instinctive perception Fred said to himself, 'This man had held a plebiscite in his heart and come out with a 51% vote in favour of the regime. So the regime is his government and can do what it will with him.' Later he mused that Rudert might as well have no opposition at all to the Nazis since he had given himself wholeheartedly to serving the regime; his pride could come to no other conclusion. Fred wondered whether people like Rudert had doubts about the regime to which they could no longer admit. It was pride that made men pretend to themselves that they accepted all this, that they were free agents, not slaves, that they were acting according to their mature judgment. They would then adapt actions, and even thoughts, to their enslaved state. Yes, he concluded, it was Pride that made that awful, stupid Hitler a great man. No one was going to admit that some strange caprice of chance or choice had made them bow down before a moron.

Fortunately, amongst the staff not everyone shared the strident views of Rudert, the 'and-yet-yes man.' Friedrich Jehn, for example was someone Fred liked much more than any of his other colleagues. He was a great lover of Austria – the non-Nazi Austria. He was quite a good teacher with small, eager pre-teenagers, but teenagers were harder to control, though Jehn with endless patience and good humour did his best. Jehn had no proper pride, no heroic stance of the 'and-yet-yes man', no pretence of liking that monstrous regiment of war men. His instinctive distaste for aggressiveness, his distress at hatred was as great as Fred's, and in this way, he was a man after Fred's own heart. Though he was the antithesis of the Aryan strongman so lauded by most of their colleagues and was often teased by the others for being soft and flabby, Fred saw his deeper qualities; his honesty, integrity, and deep discomfort with living in this regime, and discerned that Jehn was not simply happy to swim with the tide.

And – he had to talk, he was hopelessly indiscreet and worried after the event. He told Fred a story about the early days of the regime. One worried, rebellious boy felt he could not accept the compulsory 'German greeting', the new salute, and consulted Jehn on this problem. 'I told him,' said Jehn, 'that one did after all conform in certain formal forms to one's company. One did as Rome did. For instance, in a synagogue, one would keep one's hat on.' It dawned on him, the moment the boy had gone, the comparison of the Reich with the synagogue was not exactly a happy one. He hoped the boy would have the sense not to quote this interesting parallel.

Jehn was always liable to remind Fred not to repeat things, but his own transparency, arguably a sort of courage of the harmless and helpless, made him the greatest risk to himself. In a lecture to his colleagues on a trip he had taken through Austria and Italy, he came to the South Tyrolese people and their groanings under the Italian yoke – 'which, of course, we do not mention, now that we are one heart, one soul – *ein Herz und eine Seele* - with our Italian friends and allies.' He beamed at the whole group as he said this. Fred started – the implied criticism over the way the Nazis and their allies rode roughshod over minorities would have been obvious to anyone who was listening. This was so out of character for Jehn that Fred wondered if Jehn was being deliberately brave or whether this was a lapse in character. Fred wondered whether Jehn slept easy in his bed that night, or whether he turned over what he had dared to say. Any of his colleagues more loyal to the regime could use his words to get him into trouble.

One evening Fred said to Jehn, over a drink of Moselle in his small flat, 'I'll outlive the lot – Hitler, Mussolini, Stalin – the whole damn lot.'

'You're young,' Jehn replied sadly. 'You may have that luck. But those dark weeds go very deep; no one's going to uproot them any time soon.'

'We will outlast them,' Fred insisted. 'Both of us. We have to. We are worth more to the world than they are. It is the meek who shall inherit the earth. Here's to the meek! Prost!' Fred was a bit drunk, of course, but under this meekness was steely resolve. He meant every word. He was determined to survive, determined somehow that good would win out.

In the new year, Fred was surprised when he observed a very thorough rehearsal of air raid precautions. All the windows were blacked out, all the streetlights were switched off. It was, Fred thought, very well done, with characteristic German efficiency. Although the people didn't take it entirely seriously, jostling each other in the blacked-out Prager Straße rather as if it were all a joke, Fred wondered about the implications of this exercise. Was the regime preparing for war? He didn't suppose any such exercises had been done in England. The English were many steps behind and Fred thought this could turn out to be incredibly costly.

At the end of January came the long-anticipated skiing trip in the mountain resort of Oberwiesenthal in the Erzgebirge, on the border with Czechoslovakia. Fred was accompanying School Director, Reinhardt, and three classes from the Kreuzschule for the week. He, of course, had to borrow skis, having never been skiing before, and he knew he would make a fool of himself. He could imagine his father raising his eyebrows at the idea of his middle son hurtling down the mountains with two planks of wood attached to his feet. As he did so often, he tried to mask his self-consciousness with humour, greeting the assembled group as they met together on the platform of the Hauptbahnhof, with an amused, '*Grüß Gott!*' He also felt self-conscious, because he had never spent such a concentrated time with the boys, and Götz was part of the group. The memory of their last conversation before Christmas cast a shadow.

As the little train climbed slowly up into the mountains, and the snow lay ever thicker on the ground (it hadn't been snowing at all in Dresden), Fred felt increasingly as if he was entering another world. This sense grew as the party from the school trudged the two miles from the train station through an unfamiliar snowy landscape, past vanished fields to their hostel, remote and set apart from the wintry, silent village. Fred found himself caught up in the group – everyone wanted to join in with the clowning around, the joking, the singing. He was, indeed, at the centre of it, as the great novelty, and he couldn't resist playing up to that, telling stories mainly to get a reaction, to make people laugh. It helped that on the first evening he was invited to give a brief talk in German on the English school system, which meant that even those pupils who hadn't had the chance to get to know Fred before could become more aware of who he was. Afterwards he was congratulated on his excellent talk and German accent, and was delighted to have made such a good impression.

In Oberwiestenthal, here with the schoolmasters supervising the trip.

Of course, he was hopeless at skiing, as predicted, but he enjoyed being part of the party – it was probably the time when he'd felt most accepted in his whole time in Germany; he came to be treated as a person, not as an *Englander*. After a time, he even enjoyed skiing, sticking to the easy slopes near the hostel. He lost himself in the activity and rhythm of the sport and was grateful for the opportunity during the day to give his mind a break from its constant ruminations. He could lose himself also in the mass gathering in the long evenings which began at about four. It was too cold to stay in the bedroom so he'd be drawn back into the warmth of the two big rooms downstairs. In Fred's group, with Götz and the headteacher, there were twenty, and there were forty in the other. Guitars and accordions were played during these evenings, hearty songs sung and cards played. There were jokes and scuffles too. After supper, the Course Director, Reinhardt, read, well and passionately, out of a prescribed novel – *The Village on the Frontier* – all about the Sudeten struggle. Fred felt that over time Reinhardt had grown increasingly frustrated with him, due at least to his tendency to treat even the weightiest subjects irreverently. This wasn't always deliberate for, on difficult subjects, Fred found his German was more clearly patchy and imitative and self-conscious, like the language of a child. Reinhardt was jealous of Fred's popularity with the boys: his slight size made him look more like one of the lads than one of the teachers. You couldn't say the same for Reinhardt, who was tall, stocky, and bald – it was a long time since he'd been one of the lads. Fred wondered if the obvious tension between the two of them would ignite by their sharing the space and competing for the boys' attention over such an intensive time.

And still, although they had little time alone to converse – limited to a strained silence and the muttered 'Good morning' on the stairs, there was Götz, to whom Fred wanted to reach out but had no idea how.

On 30 January, the party was subjected to listening, under compulsion, to a speech given by the almighty Führer on the fourth anniversary of the Nazis coming to power. The Führer was lauded by so many for his great oratory, but Fred saw his speech as the ravings of a lunatic.

'Surely nobody will doubt the fact that during the last four years a revolution of the most momentous character has passed like a storm over Germany. Who could compare this new Germany with that which existed on 30 January four years ago, when I took my oath of loyalty before the venerable President of the Reich?'

'No,' Fred thought, 'there is probably no comparison between the Germany of four years previously, and it's certainly a whole lot worse than it has been. The black clouds of the storm still persist and I suspect that they'll only become darker and more threatening.'

'... The National Socialist Revolution was almost entirely a bloodless proceeding ... This was the first revolution in which not even a window pane was broken. ...'

Bloodless proceeding? Try telling that to Röhm and 150 or 200 others who had foolishly allied themselves to him or dared to stand in the way of Hitler. The voice went on and on, extolling the virtues of the most extraordinary revolution in human history and Fred looked around to see how Hitler's words were being received. They were away from the meeting, not infected by the mass hysteria common to football matches (he remembered being caught up in the excitement of that match in Vienna) or political rallies. They were listening to this man shouting down the wireless. And the boys were bored as hell. They dozed off, woke up with a guilty start, dozed again. He had begun to get to know some of those boys well, and it was evident, some of them loathed the regime. Many were sadly fatalistic about it all. But many too no doubt might have been infected by mass hysteria, had they but been there. More reasonable, reasoned, calmer oratory was surely more effective than that ranting rubbish, Fred thought. That was just as well, because he was alarmed about the content of the message – the talk about racial purity, the desire to prevent the Jews from disrupting and thus gaining power over the nations. Fred also shivered at the promoting of the mass over the individual. Individual lives were to be sacrificed for the sake of the party. He was talking about these boys, Fred worried. They would be sacrificed for the sake of the Greater Germany, for the German Volk. Hitler would have no problem in ordering them to lay down their lives.

Fred's ears pricked up when Hitler went on to discuss foreign secretary Eden and the British government …

' … I have already tried to contribute towards bringing about a good understanding in Europe and I have often given, especially to the British people and their Government, assurance of how ardently we wish for a sincere and cordial cooperation with them … '

Of course, Hitler spoke about his desire for peace and good relations with other nations, but Fred simply did not believe him. His words about the 'most malignant poison' and 'world peril' of Bolshevism against which Germany was arming itself, for its own protection against the threat that would apparently come from Russia – were alarmist and the talk of a war-monger, not a man of peace.

'What did you think of our Führer's speech?' asked Reinhardt in front of the whole group – it was clearly a barbed question. Fred paused. He didn't know of any good way to answer, but answer he must, somehow. Before he had time to reply, Reinhardt continued harshly,

'What are you?'

'What am I?'

'Yes, politically, I mean.'

'I'm not a politician. But, I suppose I should call myself a Liberal, I espouse the liberal attitude of mind – '

'That's no more than the luxury of not having an attitude, of not making up one's mind. That's the Liberal all over. Like Hamlet, you demand hundred-percent certainties before you act. Life doesn't provide them.

'I agree,' said Fred, 'I agree. But my scepticism – '

' – is an excuse for not acting.'

'Your conviction is an excuse for not thinking.'

'It is more important to act than to think,' said Reinhardt. 'Life is not thought, but action. It is not our duty to understand but to act. We are not here to find answers. We are here to create forces, to bring about decisions. Academic, intellectual scepticism – liberalism – denies life. The National Socialist revolution is a conservative revolution, a revolution of unqualified, unconditional Life against the thousand and one conditions and qualifications of the liberal mind.'

'I'm not sure I know what that means,' began Fred, speaking slowly now, trying to find the right words in this foreign tongue. 'It sounds as if your acceptance of Life could also be an excuse to the leader for failing to abolish misery and an excuse to the follower for accepting without question all that the leader does as part of life. It's an excuse, in fact, for making him God.'

Reinhardt ignored Fred's point and countered, 'You can't abolish misery! That is a liberalistic dream. Medicine won't abolish death, or governments get rid of poverty, or the League of Nations exterminate war.'

'Death is outside our scope, war and poverty are not.'

'You choose to think so.'

'You do not even want to think so.'

There was a pause in the discussion for a moment; Fred was fighting to make himself understood – by Reinhardt, by the group at large, by Götz above all, for whose soul he felt he was fighting. Götz, he knew, had been watching the conversation keenly.

'Bolshevism,' Reinhardt continued, pushing out his chin, 'Is the logical conclusion of Liberalism, with its false, materialistic conceptions of freedom and happiness, and its equally false egalitarianism. The liberalistic idea of freedom is escape from obligations and responsibilities, and happiness is satisfying the greatest numbers offering a suburban villa of the same size for everyone, leading humanity to the Moscow cul-de-sac. No, I don't believe in your happiness. Happiness is not the goal of life.'

'And National Socialism?' asked Fred, genuinely interested to know what Reinhardt thought.

'National Socialism is a break with the whole materialistic falsity of the nineteenth century, the age of the machine, of the mass, of the economic man. Modern society has dethroned the Great Incomprehensible that men call Fate or God, and set up idols of its own, Intellect, Matter, Self. It forgot the great truth that he who saves his life shall lose it, that there is a greater deeper life than that limited to a man's few decades on earth, that he is part of something bigger than himself.'

'The Reich?' asked Fred.

'Exactly! Death is the climax, the highest expression of life, and there is no greater death, no greater love than when you lay down your life for your friend.'

'Or your State,' Fred interjected. 'You say that happiness is not the aim of life. What is then?'

'Life itself – life more abundantly, as Christ puts it. Life in all its intensity, realisation of all the heights and depths, the abysses and dangers, the tragedy and greatness. Hitler said once that only the shallowness of the bourgeois mind could ever have called the middle way, the way to heaven. Hunger and hate have produced greater things than comfort and satisfaction.'

Fred was appalled – Christ and Hitler in the same mouthful, the one being used to support the other. This was a step too far.

The discussion moved on and on, over and over. Reinhardt talked about the waning importance of truth. 'We are in love with Reality. We accept and affirm Life, which follows its own laws without demanding a Truth. We are sceptical about truths that do not prove to be forces, realities, powers.'

'Forces! Realities!! Powers!!! Was this crescendo music or philosophy or politics? It's all the same here,' thought Fred, 'all opera. What a beautiful language, and how dangerous!'

'Surely,' he said slowly, 'that destroys any basis for argument or understanding. Only intellectual processes are intelligible, only their results – truths, not realities – are communicable.'

'Well? That also is something I accept.'

'Do you? Do you? … You can't.' argued Fred. 'You can't create a myth of the twentieth century and then believe in it. You can't, as an intellectual, go back to instinct, any more than you can become a child. Your conservative revolution means tearing down the Big City stone by stone, in order to return to grass and forests. In practice, there is a massive contradiction at the heart of this society. You want war almost as badly as you want peace, and you know it. You sing, "We will march on, though worlds in ruin fall: Today this land is ours, tomorrow all!" – and, as you sing, you mean every word of it, especially worlds falling in ruin. You want to die and not to die, to destroy and not to destroy.'

'That's all you see at the moment, I grant you that. Believe me, there are forces underneath in Germany, strong forces – of destruction if you like, but also of new birth, not only for us, but for all Europe. Hitler may only be the beginning. And for all of us to return to instinct may be impossible, as you say, but a new generation will arise – '

'It is a dream, or a nightmare.'

'It can be dreamed true!'

Fred looked at Reinhardt, who stood there, flushed with the heat of the room and with his own defiance, grotesque and tragic, and wondered whether it was a German characteristic to want to dream nightmares true and be proved right by ruin? How many others believed in this coming apocalypse which would herald supposed new birth for all of Europe? Fred shivered and decided he'd had enough of the debate.

'Talking of dreams,' he said aloud, 'I think it's time to go to bed.' The party dispersed and they retired for the evening.

The rest of the week passed uneventfully, although Fred could not forget that conversation with Reinhardt, particularly when the issue of the Sudetenland raised its head. The apparent mistreatment of the Sudeten-Germans at the hands of the Czechs was a constant refrain over the week – Zetsche, one of the teachers, was very contemptuous of the Czechs, and exasperated, Fred asked, 'What do you actually want?'

'The dissolution of this hyphenated hybrid state,' Zetsche said, with his hammering histrionic gestures. That statement, this almost hysterical denunciation of the Czechs, more than anything else Fred heard, really worried him. Zetsche was not a Nazi, and this made it so much worse. He taught English, he had been quite friendly to Fred, he was perfectly sane, and yet he seemed to want his neighbouring country – only twenty-five miles away from Dresden – wiped off the map. The Führer was still talking peace – at least that's what everyone said to Fred. But peace at what cost?

On his return from the mountains Fred's obsession with Hitler grew. He studied every word from every speech. He took note of all the propaganda that was posted around the city: the anti-Czech exhibition in the town hall to which schoolboys from the Kreuzchule had been taken; the exhibition that demanded the return of Tanganyika and other former German colonies; the demands for more *Lebensraum* for the German people; the anti-British rhetoric in the newspapers; it all added up to a conviction that Hitler was dangerous and would not settle for the current status quo. Fred believed that troops would be on the march – but where? His visits over the past year to Austria meant that he knew there were so many Nazis in Austria that the branch of the German family tree was ripe for stripping at any moment – it was only a matter of time – it was a matter of *when*, not *if* German desires for expansion would be realised. His thoughts naturally went to the Schneider family in Vienna. He hoped they would have time to run before the storm came that would sweep all away.

Fred felt he had to do something. He couldn't just stand idly by. So, rashly, he knew, he decided the Czechs would be first in the line of fire and wrote a letter to the Foreign Office suggesting the British should call Hitler's moral blackmail bluff and offer him a colony or two, which was, Fred reckoned, no use to either the British or the Germans. He knew the letter was mad and would make no difference, yet he desperately waited for a reply, clinging to hope that this insanity could surely be stopped, that someone in power would take decisive action in favour of diplomacy and justice and reveal Hitler for the madman he was. It came not as a surprise but just a disappointment when the response he received from the Foreign Office treated him as a jittery young fool, rushing in where official angels feared to tread.

While Fred knew he was powerless to stop Hitler and his cronies, he did still hope to be able to win the hearts of the boys in his care and his colleagues. He hoped to alert people to the dangers of the Nazi creed, and to demonstrate that the boys shouldn't simply heed, unquestioningly, every word of Hitler's speeches and everything produced by Goebbels' propaganda machine. More than that, Fred hoped to show the boys that he loved and felt for them, and that his nationality was no bar to him doing so.

* * *

The English became the source of staff room gossip in February when Joachim von Ribbentrop, appointed German Ambassador to the United Kingdom since the previous October, gave the Nazi salute to King George VI. The gesture nearly knocked over the king, who was walking forward to shake Ribbentrop's hand at the time. Fred couldn't help boiling over at the embarrassing ambassador. (He had already felt uncomfortable at the attention paid to the abdication crisis a few months earlier.) He remarked to one of the masters, Herr Schmidt, 'Ribbentrop was tactless.'

Schmidt stiffly retorted, 'This is now the German national greeting, and it must be accepted.'

'In Rome,' Fred countered, 'do as Rome does. In London ditto. Look at me. You must have seen me day after day doing as one does in Dresden, and that has political implications, whereas Ribbentrop could observe the normal forms without committing himself in any way to royalism.' Herr Schmidt looked outraged and stormed out of the staff room.

Fred later recounted the episode to Wolf. 'He hasn't spoken to me since, you know.'

'That's no loss,' remarked Wolf wryly, 'I wish he wouldn't speak to me either but I have to listen to him.'

Soon afterwards, at the end of February, Fred realised he was more than halfway through his time in Dresden, and thought he'd try to reflect on his experiences and finally get round to doing the writing he'd been intending to do all along. He would at least clear his head and give himself something to read back over at a later date, despite the lack of clarity that characterised this surreal experience. What were his conclusions so far, and what would they sound like in a year or two's time, he wondered. Maybe just the muddled and naive anxieties and dreams of youth, he sighed, as he put pen to paper.....

When I came here, I suppose I regarded myself as a sort of amateur journalist. I was going to find out all about the Third Reich and what people think and say and eat in it. And I was going to convert them, too. And I was going to get a lot of work done – new ideas in Classicism and Romanticism. But I find out nothing: I write nothing. I have desultory arguments, contacts which I don't follow up. I suppose in any case it was a mistake to think that there were a lot of facts one would neatly tabulate, or a lot of conclusive arguments – truth to buy and truth to sell. There probably isn't for me. And then these wretched boys disorganise my life. I can't stop thinking, agonising over them.

I am afraid I have pushed Götz away. He feels too much the pressure to conform. The boys' mother too seems to have been warned off me. She worries about the boys, she sees Wolf as rash and impressionable and has tried to come between us. I know she's simply trying to protect him, to keep him safe as any mother would, although her rejection of me does hurt. Still Wolf and the boys' father are open. They see me as a friend. They don't believe what others may whisper against me. I hope in time Götz will also see that above all, although I know I am clumsy and push him sometimes too hard with what I feel is the truth – as far as we enlightened English see it – it's genuinely well meant. I mean no harm. I sincerely love and pity him and Wolf – as well as other German boys.

So the job of learning the truth about Germany and telling the truth to Germany does not progress. I feel anyway, that I am not made for this sort of journalism. If I get anything positive out of this at all, it will be only truth about and the truth to a number of individuals, because my curious passion will have given me in those cases the will to know and the will to convert. For there is this intellectual side to it – an intense curiosity about their minds and an intense desire to conquer them. One might wonder what I want to convert them to – after all, I get less sure what I believe in every day, in this confusing atmosphere where facts hardly exist. But I do believe in facts. I believe in logic – so that monstrous distortions of truth or reasoning make me wild. And I believe in toleration and justice and things like that. I conceive that something in Germany is being done to people's minds against which everything in me cries out.

* * *

The months rolled on, and Fred began to prepare for his return to England, and to say farewell. He knew it was difficult, particularly bidding farewell to the Büttner-Wobst family he had grown to love. While he knew he would stay in touch with Wolf and Werner, with whom his friendship had blossomed over the year, with Götz the relationship had remained strained, and he didn't expect to be receiving many letters from him. He only hoped to part on good terms.

'I wanted to say goodbye properly – I don't want to feel like we've left with a misunderstanding between us. I'd like to get it straight.'

'I think it's better to leave it,' Götz replied.

'But I feel like I've made such a mess of it. I don't know whether it's the language thing, but I don't think the words I say come out the way I want to say them,' Fred faltered, knowing how clumsy his words sounded. 'I know things aren't easy for you. I wouldn't want to be in your shoes at all. You cope incredibly well, and I admire you for that.' He paused. 'You're very brave, Götz. I only wish you didn't have to be so. Anyway, I wanted to say good-bye and make sure there were no hard feelings.'

Götz shook his head and smiled. 'No hard feelings. Goodbye, and thank you for trying to understand.'

They shook hands.

This felt more of a definitive departure; Fred doubted that he'd hear from Götz again and, if he was honest, he feared for the young man over whom the shadow of the Nazi regime loomed large.

Fred packed up his bags, and took one last walk through the Altstadt, meandering through its beautiful streets – through this city that he'd grown to love above even his own– and he sought to drink it all in, recalling conversations, laughter, moments he'd shared. As well as a profound sense of sadness, Fred felt fear. He feared for the future of this city and for its people.

And what had he learned in Dresden? He'd learned that no one virtue of head or heart, would suffice to combat the Nazi virus. Many of those with whom he'd argued and debated had endless love-hate arguments with England and with Fred. They saw the points he made but, he thought sadly, refused to be pierced by them. They made concessions and yielded not an inch. They were full of proud self-sacrifice, the sacrifice of their own freedom to think. Men like that had too much pride to admit they acted and spoke other than they thought, that they were slaves out of fear. To Fred it seemed they feared fear itself. They derived their identity from the regime and ignored the murderous prejudice that came with it. They wanted clear commands. These, Fred felt sure, would come.

Above all, Fred found he had got emotionally involved with the people he'd met in Dresden. It was made worse – almost like a fever at times – by the feeling that the pupils in the Kreuzschule were trapped by a regime which they had been too young to choose. He feared that war between their two nations was inevitable. This generation of innocent young men would be amongst the many victims of such a conflict. His attention and sympathy had been first drawn to Götz and Wolf and their whole family, but extended to other pupils too, for whom Fred could not help feeling moments of pity and affection mixed with foreboding. He'd come to Dresden with vague ideas of bridge building, but now felt that any anti-Hitler talk of his might merely have tormented rather than helped them. Perhaps some bridges had been built; whether they would stand the test of time was another question.

CHAPTER FOUR
1937-1939: The return to England

Fred found it hard to adjust to life after Dresden. He enjoyed being back in the comfortable surroundings of King's, where he began his three-year Prize Fellowship, earned for his essay on Edward Gibbon. His time was taken up between the library and lecture halls as he mixed academic research with the odd bit of teaching of Latin and Greek, and amongst friends.

Meanwhile, he followed international developments with great interest and sought to combat his growing sense of impotence by founding the New Peace Movement with a friend, also from Liverpool, Tom Lyon, which explored every aspect of war and its prevention. There were a number of speakers, from economists, MPs both Labour and Conservative, historians, and psychologists.

Fred also set about forming a group to study the Sudeten problem, trying to get hold of propaganda from both the German and Czech perspectives. Of course, it was futile, but Fred couldn't just sit there and do nothing. None of these initiatives lasted long, but at least he had tried to do something.

Dresden and his new friends, particularly those boys and their families, were never far from his thoughts. He wrote to Wolf and others too, all the time, continuing to argue the case against Hitler – so much so that he was accused by Wolf of only really being interested in political developments. Wolf kept him updated on the family, and it was through his letters that Fred learned that Götz had passed his Abitur and was beginning life in the Labour Service. He smiled when Wolf sent him photos from the school skiing trip. Wolf himself got on with school, where teachers complained about his handwriting – they had to use a microscope to decipher his German script - and he planned for his future, wondering about becoming a missionary or a doctor. Fred meanwhile continued to fret and tried to cover his anxiety through action, throwing himself into his studies.

When Hitler annexed Austria in March 1938, Fred's anxiety grew, and he wondered about the plight of Helene and her sons in Vienna. They had lost touch since the letter he wrote encouraging them not to attempt to begin a new life in England and he regretted the advice he had given them. He hoped that others in Austria had given her the same counsel; he couldn't bear the thought of being solely responsible for Helene still being in Austria. Again, Fred felt an overwhelming sense of powerlessness and threw himself into his work even more.

However, there was a ray of light when, in July 1938, he was joined by Wolf and another boy from the Kreuzschule, Heinrich Vollmann, who was one year older than Wolf, for his family's summer holiday at Port Erin on the Isle of Man.

Fred met the two boys in London and they spent some days there seeing sites including the Law Courts and House of Commons. They had just visited the National Galleries and were on their way back to their hostel when they passed a modernist stone monument with a statue of a lady wearing a nurse's uniform on a plinth. 'What's that?' Wolf asked, and he stood in front of the monument reading aloud, '"Edith Cavell ... Brussels ... Dawn ... October 12th 1915". Who was she? What does that mean?'

'Edith Cavell?' Fred replied. 'She was a British nurse during the War. She had treated soldiers from both sides without discrimination, but then she was arrested for treason by the Germans for helping two hundred Allied soldiers escape from German-occupied Belgium. The court martial found her guilty and sentenced her to death. Well, you can imagine the outcry this caused – governments from all over appealed for mercy. It made no difference. She was shot by a firing squad. The Germans were condemned universally for that act of brutality.'

Wolf winced at this reminder of his nation's atrocities and shook his head. 'I'm not surprised. You know, I've never heard that story before. Well, I wouldn't have, would I?' He contemplated the statue for a moment and then saw the inscription at the base of the plinth and read it out, '"Patriotism is not enough. I must have no hatred or bitterness for anyone."'

'She said those words to her chaplain the night before she was executed,' Fred commented. 'A good lesson we all need to learn today.' Wolf nodded, bright-eyed at his friend.

Fred found Vollmann infuriating. He was a young Nazi, prone to find everything in England inferior to that of Germany. He made constant generalisations about the English, which Fred and Wolf both resisted. Wolf reflected on the experience of being a German boy in a foreign land, 'Sometimes, I want to forget about me and Vollmann being German and you being English – I want to forget about those so-called national differences. Why can't we simply be people? Other times, though, it's like we can't escape from our nationalities, no matter how much we try. I'm trapped being German and you're stuck being English and there's nothing we can do about that.'

For Vollmann, however, it was, apparently, much simpler. Anything inferior was blamed on it being English. When a sash-window in their cottage on the Isle of Man suddenly gave way and drew blood from Fred's mother's finger, Vollmann commented on the stupidity of English windows while Wolf rushed quickly and efficiently for his little first aid kit.

Wolf was charmed by Fred's mother, and it was mutual. Here was a mother who cooked with the aid of one of Fred's cousins – and did everything, without domestics, chauffeur and cook as at home. Here was a close-knit family, and he savoured the whole unfamiliar atmosphere as much as the foreignness, including food. Fred couldn't help laughing when Wolf tried Marmite and referred to it as '*Affenschiss*'– monkey shit – but he ate it, nevertheless. Fred had wondered how his own father, so staunchly anti-German, would react to Wolf – but even he was taken with him. 'The little beggar!' he said gruffly. 'There's some kids you can't help liking.'

There was a film called *Lancer Spy* on at the local cinema about World War I. Fred carefully enquired whether it would be likely to hurt or offend two young Germans. He was assured that it was a very good film and could give offence to no one. So one evening he took the boys to the Strand Cinema, recently opened and still looking fresh and new. They seemed impressed – perhaps this was up to the standard of what they had in Germany. The film was far less impressive. It paraded and parodied German officers with monocles and mocked the German national anthem. Even Wolf was indignant, not least because it proved to the biased Vollmann that the Nazi newspapers were justified in claiming that the anti-German, not just anti-Nazi, propaganda machine was in full swing in England.

Fred found himself having to argue with both of them, defending his fellow countrymen and the spirit of certain remarks in the film: '*Du hast ein ganze Menge missverstanden,*' – 'You've completely misunderstood!' he almost shouted at Wolf. This shook Wolf's confidence in his own first impressions, but Fred was lying. He felt so angry and ashamed, which his family didn't seem understand, looking blankly at him when he expressed this. Fred remembered a similar experience of how embarrassed young Karl had been at a war film in Vienna where *die Engländer* were the enemy and not always very nice. That sensitivity of a mere child for his English friend's feelings shamed the so-often insensitive adults.

Afterwards, Fred had reassured Karl that he didn't mind; to him it was just funny. But now, reflecting on these incidents, Fred felt like he, Aryan Wolf and half-Jewish Karl were doing their desperate little bit for the brotherhood of man simply by loving each other while filmmakers on both sides were doing their damnedest to keep the war fires of hate alive.

Overall, though, the time at Port Erin was blissful. Swimming at the sheltered bay bordered by the tall cliffs of Bradda Head, playing tennis and games in the evenings – Fred relished every moment – it seemed like an island of peace in the choppy seas of international turmoil. Not that they could ever escape it completely as politics was never far from their lips. Once, at the end of one of their arguments, Wolf exclaimed, 'What's the use? We know nothing. We're not allowed to know anything.' Fred was shaken by this exclamation and it dawned on him that while he could play politics as if it were a game, it would be a matter of life or death for Wolf.

After leaving Port Erin they stayed for a couple of days in Liverpool, and Wolf noticed that Fred had a whole bookcase of German books in his room. He was particularly attracted by the various anti-Nazi books published in Switzerland, Austria or Holland which were, of course, banned in Germany. He motioned to Konrad Heiden's *Das Leben eines Diktators*. 'I'd like to read that. I feel so ignorant and want to do something about it.'

'Shouldn't you be reading some English books if you want to read?' Fred queried. 'You can read German books at home, can't you?'

'Not like this.'

'It would be better for you to read some English while you have the chance. After all, we want to be able to tell your parents how much English you've learned.' Wolf reluctantly agreed and they read an English book together.

Next morning, Fred walked into Wolf's room to wake him up and noticed the Heiden book on the bedside table. 'My God,' he said, picking up the book and looking to see how much Wolf had read, 'you stayed up late to read this – wow, you're halfway through – you've stayed up very late. No wonder you're so sleepy. Anyway, you can't read it tonight. You've got to go tomorrow, and you need your sleep.'

'Well, let me finish it,' countered Wolf. 'It's very interesting. It's important to know the truth.'

Yes, thought Fred, although he wasn't entirely sure how helpful the truth was. Aloud he said, 'We have a busy day ahead of us today. I really don't think we'll have the time.'

That evening, the final one of the holiday, they listened together in silence to Schubert's Unfinished Symphony played on Fred's portable wind-up gramophone, which perfectly encapsulated the swathe of emotions that Fred felt – melancholic, portentous, the sense of waking up from a dream.

Soon, the dream was over. Wolf bade goodbye to Fred's family. 'Tell your mother,' said Mrs Clayton, 'that you've been a very good ambassador – even if you've not learnt much English.'

'*Auf Wiedersehen,*' said Fred, utterly miserable as he waved off his friend at the station.

Next day Fred felt bereft. He sat with his mother on a bench by the boating lake in Sefton Park. He remembered being a small boy sobbing passionately at the inexcusable passage of time, at the sudden realisation that something was 'all over', such as his days in the village school. She put her arm around him as she had done all those years ago. Perhaps she didn't fully understand his feelings, but Fred was comforted by the fact she did at least sympathise with his sorrow.

* * *

In September came the Munich crisis. The wireless was full of reports of Hitler's threats to invade Czechoslovakia unless his demands to incorporate the Sudetenland into the Greater German Reich were met. Fred listened to these events unfold and, convinced that conflict was imminent, felt physically sick. Food stuck in his throat, and he took an hour to chew two pieces of toast. When the Munich Agreement was reached on 30 September, with Chamberlain proclaiming he'd won 'peace for our time,' Fred was relieved that the immediate danger of conflict had been averted, but he couldn't share the joy of the crowds who were celebrating across the country, including in front of Buckingham Palace where Chamberlain greeted them from the balcony with King George VI and Queen Elizabeth. In this agreement, Hitler had seemingly got what he wanted; the Sudetenland, about which Fred had heard so much while in Dresden, had been 'restored' to Germany.

The relief didn't last long. Fred heard Hitler's speech in Saarbrücken – on 9 October, where he lashed out against the

Conservative anti-appeasers Winston Churchill, Alfred Duff Cooper, and Anthony Eden, whom he described as a warmongering anti-German faction. Hitler's speech made Fred's heart sink with sick foreboding.

'Did you hear Hitler yesterday?' he asked his friends as they were eating in the King's College dining hall. 'Hitler isn't satisfied. He's not content at all. He thanks Chamberlain half-heartedly and pours out the vials of his vitriolic wrath on Churchill, Eden and Duff Cooper. It's clear he resents Chamberlain's interference. He wanted to march into the Sudetenland alone, to prove that no one could stop him, that he was Napoleon or God knows who. He wants to dominate.'

Fred could feel his anxiety rising as he spoke. He continued, 'Haven't you read the papers? They're saying the same thing, sounding alarms about Hitler's petulance.'

Gerald Shore, who was a thoroughly nice socialist and pacifist leant back on his chair, 'You and the papers are such doom-mongers. They're overreacting and you're making far too much fuss. Why shouldn't Hitler criticise English politicians who did not spare him?' Fred shook his head in disbelief. He was amazed at how Gerald could be so deaf to the menacing undertones of that speech.

What made it even worse was that later Fred found out through a letter from Wolf, that Götz, only 17, had been on parade, in the ranks of the Führer's soldiers that day. He was a pawn in the Great Leader's chess game, his life at the mercy of this megalomaniac's unquenchable quest for power.

Soon after Munich Fred received a postcard from his colleague in Dresden, Jehn. They had kept in regular touch since Fred's return a year before. Most of his letters were filled with news of pupils and students at the Kreuzschule – he steered clear of political discussion. But after the Munich crisis, he wrote:

We were all pretty well informed about the course of events via foreign radio stations. So for example we heard Chamberlain speak in person. We are of the opinion that, if there is peace, we must above all thank Chamberlain as well. Once the tension had faded we all felt a great joy. At least we're glad that we can now <u>hopefully</u> live long in peace.

Reading this, Fred could not help smiling at the statement, 'if there is peace, we must above all thank Chamberlain as well.' It was a sudden sign of caution – 'as well'. As well as whom? Fred wondered, Mussolini? It was so typical of Jehn – the rash slight indiscretion, the immediate fear that he had revealed too much of his real feelings. Fred was grateful that he could be somewhat freer to express his own feelings.

Despite his nervousness at the end of 1938, as 1939 dawned with no sign of further hostilities Fred began to allow himself to hope that Chamberlain had done it after all. But then the Ides of March came, when the Germans invaded the rest of Czechoslovakia. He feared the torrent that would overwhelm them and leave their love and their hopes, in the words of Byron, 'in one red burial blent'.

The events in Czechoslovakia left Fred in a dilemma. He had been invited to return to Dresden for a holiday with the Büttner-Wobst family in July, and even set out half-heartedly, getting as far as London, where he stayed with a friend who had married a Jewish refugee. While he was there, he saw much of her relatives, including her self-assured Marxist brother, Josef, who seeing Fred's unease, asked him over dinner, 'Why are you dithering so much? What are you worried about?'

'Because I think the atmosphere in Germany's going to be unpleasant at best, but above all, I'm afraid of war suddenly breaking out, leaving me trapped,' replied Fred.

Josef smiled pityingly at Fred's apparent 'innocent naivete', 'There'll be no war between Chamberlain and Hitler,' he asserted. 'Dog won't eat dog.'

'Dog might,' retorted Fred.

No, Fred couldn't banish his sense of unease, and so decided reluctantly to stay at home, writing from London to Dr Büttner-Wobst to apologise for not making the journey and expressing his concerns. Werner's response was typically gracious. He agreed that a trip to Germany at this time with the atmosphere that existed in the country wouldn't be entirely pleasant. Fred knew Wolf particularly would be disappointed. They had, after all, had such an enjoyable holiday on the Isle of Man just the previous year.

Fred remembered on the return journey how Wolf remarked, 'Goodbye, Isle of Man, I think, forever.' When Fred's brother, George had asked him why he'd said this, he answered that he didn't know exactly, but he just wasn't sure he'd see those shores again.

Maybe he'd been right. Would he survive these tumultuous times, with war seemingly inevitable? Would Götz? Would Fred? He recalled how just a year previously he and Wolf had stood together as friends beside the Edith Cavell memorial. He had felt that they'd shared a deep understanding that their friendship would somehow withstand national boundaries and made a silent concord that, even if they would have to shoot each other, in that moment, they would opt out of the hollow hate-mongering slogans of nationalistic propaganda.

Now, this would be put to the test more than ever. His friends, he felt, would soon be his enemies. They had written many long letters since Port Erin. Fred wondered when – if ever – he'd next hear from Wolf.

PART TWO

Fred: The Futility of War
1939-1946

CHAPTER FIVE
1939-1941: The Outbreak of War

'This morning the British Ambassador in Berlin handed the German Government a final Note stating that, unless we heard from them by 11 o'clock that they were prepared at once to withdraw their troops from Poland, a state of war would exist between us.

I have to tell you now that no such undertaking has been received, and that consequently this country is at war with Germany.'

Fred felt very calm when he heard Prime Minister Chamberlain's announcement to the country. He was back in his room in Bodley's building at King's as he listened to the announcement on the wireless. He wasn't surprised – he'd felt the writing had been on the wall for years, that this was simply confirmation of the inevitable. Britain was at war with Germany. The bridges he'd sought to build would surely be destroyed. He looked at Karl, the poor boy who was a refugee, separated from his mother, who was still in Austria, and felt an overwhelming surge of pity. Karl himself looked terribly frightened. He was only a child, not yet thirteen, and already he had been through so much.

Fred had assumed that Karl was out of his life forever – he'd almost forgotten about the young boy and his family. Everything changed after Kristallnacht in November 1938, when a pogrom against Jews was carried out throughout Nazi Germany. Jewish homes, hospitals and schools were ransacked, synagogues burned and thousands of businesses destroyed or damaged. Fred read about these events with a horror that was increased when he received an unexpected letter from Vienna.

Dear Mr Clayton,

I hope you are well. I am sorry to write so suddenly after what must seem like a terribly long time, but we need to ask a great favour of you.

You have heard no doubt of the recent events that have taken place here and all over Germany and Austria. My shop was smashed up in the violence that occurred. I have come to the conclusion that it is no longer safe for us to live here. I fear greatly for my children's future. I hope that Robert will be able to go to an uncle in Switzerland and find a job there, but Karl is still too young to work – he's only a boy. I know that the two of you were very fond of each other – Karl spoke of you often and looked up to you very much. Is there any way you would be able to foster him?

I know I ask a great deal of you, but the situation is so desperate. You are our only hope.

Please help us and save one who is dear to both of us.

With kind greetings

Helene Schneider

This letter shook Fred into action. Having heard that the Government had eased immigration restrictions, allowing unaccompanied children under the age of 17 to enter Great Britain from Germany and German-annexed territories, including Austria, Fred went straight to the office of University MP Kenneth Pickthorn whom he had previously met through organising the New Peace Movement talks and asked for his help on behalf of both boys. Mr Pickthorn in turn pointed him to the Quakers who were organising transport from Germany and Austria. 'But,' Mr Pickthorn warned, 'we cannot guarantee that your friend's sons will be taken. There are many children in danger – too many to help. The Government needs guarantees that each child will not be a burden on the state. They'll need to find foster families, have their education paid for.' Expressing a conviction that he did not feel, Fred said that this would all be fine. He rushed on to the Quakers.

The lady who was responsible for dealing with this was very calm in the face of Fred's agitation. The story he had poured out was clearly one she'd heard many times before. 'Well, Mr Clayton,' she explained, 'it's an intolerable situation, I know. However, you must understand that there are very high numbers of children affected by this crisis. Much as we'd like to be able to, we cannot guarantee each child's safety.'

'Please,' Fred said, 'I'll do anything I can to get those children on the lists. I'll make sure they're fully paid for, that they find foster parents, that their education is covered. I'm their only hope. I can't let them down.'

Eventually his determination was rewarded and she relented. 'Look,' she said, 'tell your friend to contact the Kultusgemeinde in Vienna.'

When Fred looked blankly at her, she explained, 'This is the representative body of the Jewish community there. They act as a sort of buffer organisation between the Nazis and Vienna's Jewish population. They're planning the transport. We can contact them too, explain that you have pledged that all their costs will be paid. We'll do what we can, but we cannot promise anything.'

'Thank you,' Fred said. 'And, the boys' mother?'

The lady shook her head. 'The children have to travel unaccompanied. They're expected to return to their parents when the crisis passes. I'm sorry. There's nothing we can do to help her.'

Fred wrote to Helene urging her to contact the Kultusgemeinde in Vienna and explained that he would happily act as a guarantor for them. He also reassured her that he would do his best to help her come to England herself. He expressed more confidence in his letter than he felt. He wondered whether his rushing around would do any good at all.

December went by and Fred heard nothing until, on Christmas Eve, he received a card from Dovercourt, a coastal town near Harwich in Essex. The boys had arrived there from Vienna and were now in Dovercourt Bay Holiday Camp. They asked if it would be possible for him to visit. Also, could Fred help their mother?

Fred went as soon as he could to the refugee camp. There he met some young volunteers who told him, 'That lad talks about his English friend the whole time. Both boys will be so glad to see you – so few kids this end have people they can call friends.'

Fred was shocked at how many children were being pushed

around from pillar to post in the frost-bound billets, and he knew he couldn't allow Karl and his brother to be in the camp for long. He made several visits to the camp and asked anyone he knew if they could help by becoming the boys' foster parents. His parents and their friends didn't have room and couldn't afford it.

Then, in the new year, the boys' fortunes changed. A rich Liverpudlian bachelor took Robert in and Karl was fostered by a rich Lancastrian family – Clement Fletcher, a widower with children around Karl's age, and his sister Molly. Rossall School, a public school on the Lancashire coast, agreed to waive its fees for Robert and Karl, and a number of other refugee boys. Fred could at last breathe a sigh of relief, but he could not forget the plight of all those boys at Dovercourt.

He told all his friends and colleagues about his visits. One of these was his friend, Alan Turing. Their friendship had grown over time. They both won post-graduate Fellowships in their fields which enabled them to maintain this relationship. This was interrupted in September 1936 when Fred went to Dresden and Alan to advance his already stellar mathematical career at Princeton University, New Jersey. Alan was still in America when Fred returned from Germany and they only resumed contact in July 1938, spending all of their spare time together when Alan went back to Cambridge. It was Fred's nature to be open about every part of his life with his friend, so Alan was well acquainted with Fred's story. Alan's response was wholehearted; he accompanied Fred to Dovercourt one wet Sunday in February 1939, where Alan agreed to foster another child himself, Bob Augenfield. Bob too was able to attend Rossall School. The Lancastrian family agreed to let Karl come to Fred for part of the holidays, and so Alan and Fred planned a summer holiday sailing together with the boys in Bosham. In the meantime, Fred did what he could to find a job for Helene. He made enquiries at various shops in Liverpool, until he heard the news in August, just before the holiday that, finally, she would be able to join her sons in England in December.

On holiday in Bosham. Fred, at the back with (from front) Alan, Bob and Karl.

The holiday in Bosham was a tense affair, full of a number of undercurrents. There was the obvious political anxiety, beginning as it did with news of the Molotov-Ribbentrop non-aggression pact between Russia and Germany. Fred and Alan couldn't help discussing the implications of these previous sworn enemies committing to peaceful relations with each other and giving Hitler a free hand in Europe. They were sceptical about it lasting long-term and were fearful of the short-term consequences. Did it mean that war was imminent?

They tried to hide their tension from the boys, who already had been through so much. Karl and Bob did feel tense, but that was mainly because they hadn't been sailing before and came to the conclusion that Alan and Fred were incompetent sailors. 'It's the lame leading the blind,' remarked Bob to Karl, who giggled.

One day they took a trip across to Thorney Island, and went ashore to look at the RAF planes lined up on the airfield. The boys were distinctly unimpressed. They were even less so when at the end of the day the tide had gone so far out that the boat was stuck in the mud. Alan and Fred looked helpless, and the boys shook their heads disbelievingly at the incompetence of their adult companions. 'What are we going to do, Alan?' asked Fred.

'There's nothing we can do. We have to leave it and come back tomorrow, when the tide's back out.'

'And how are we going to get back home?' asked Bob.

'Wade to the island and catch the bus,' said Alan, shrugging his shoulders.

'What, through all that mud?' complained Karl.

'Yes, we have no choice, unless you want to stay here all night?'

'Of course we don't,' grumbled Karl. And so they waded through the mud to the shore to catch the bus. Their legs were covered with thick black mud. 'We look like soldiers in long black boots,' observed Karl.

And now, less than a week later, the peacetime was over. Thousands of German soldiers with their long black boots had marched into Poland. Chamberlain's ultimatum had fallen on 'deaf ears'. Britain was at war and any chance of Helene coming to England were surely dashed. Fred feared, once more, for her future. Their sailing holiday in Bosham already seemed a lifetime ago.

That night, a frightened Karl woke Fred. Fred felt an overwhelming sense of love and compassion for the lonely refugee. He was the closest to family Karl had for hundreds of miles – to him Fred was a friend and father, the only person in England, apart from his brother, whom Karl could really love. Fred wished he could protect him forever. He whispered, 'It'll be all right, Karl.' He was lying, he knew, but what else could he say?

Next morning, Karl returned to the new school term at his boarding school in Lancashire. Fred was faced with uncertainty – with the introduction of universal conscription he had to register for service and he didn't know when he would be called up. He couldn't stop thinking about Karl, Wolf, Götz, and the other German boys and of Götz and Wolf's father who had written so warmly to him earlier in the summer.

Fred was determined not to allow himself to hate, and the onset of war brought with it a fresh determination within him. Although he didn't know how long he had, he decided to throw all other work aside and write one book while he still had time – a book which would remind people that Germans were humans, to be loved and pitied, and not guilty because they were German. He resolved it must be done before he and his countrymen began to hate too much, whilst it was still possible to think in terms of individuals. At the same time, he would try to be unsentimentally objective about the possible effects of the system on them. He'd had an emotional experience, and exposure to complex truth, which he had to express somehow, before it was too late.

And so, Fred began to write, and as he did so, memories of his time in Dresden came back. It was slow going – he was grateful for the encouragement of George 'Dadie' Rylands, who had been a mentor for Fred while at King's, who helped him when he got stuck – and at times the whole enterprise seemed futile in the light of the frightening progress of the German army. Staring at a blank page one wet afternoon, Fred felt, 'What am I writing this stupid book for? They're going to beat us, and there'll be little point in my sentimentality then. I'd better start feeling sorry for myself and Karl, because these incredibly swift, sweeping victors don't look as though they need anyone's sympathy or understanding.'

Despite these reservations, he ploughed on. His Fellowship having finished, with funds running low, he returned to the family home in Liverpool and found some tutoring jobs to tide him over while every spare minute was dedicated to getting the message out, to build those bridges. He went doggedly, perhaps naively, on, as he wrote to his brother, George, 'I have to say this, if it's the only worthwhile thing I ever do. It's a bit of truth, a bit that's going to be buried the longer this war goes on. And the war itself loses meaning if we're not fighting for the survival of such things as truth and tolerance.'

By the end of the summer, although the Battle of Britain was raging in the skies above the channel, the war didn't seem to be affecting Fred's life too much. This changed at the end of August when he was woken in the night by the roar of explosions and the whine of aeroplanes.

With a thrill of fear, he hurried out of bed and downstairs. 'What's happening?' he asked his father, who was pacing the living room.

'The Huns are attacking us. A bomb came down nearby. They can't beat us in the air, so they're playing dirty now. Typical.'

Fred said nothing, not wishing to further incense his father. They had to live under the same roof for he didn't know how long.

'Shouldn't we go out into the street shelter?' he asked.

'No, it's more dangerous to go out into the open now. The dining room table will protect us, it's sturdy enough.' He spent the rest of the night huddling with his parents under the table, listening out for any approaching aircraft. Thankfully, the sounds grew more distant.

The next morning, they walked together to discover what damage there had been. Round the corner there was a crowd of people gathered outside the parish church, which had been struck in the raid. All its stained-glass windows had been destroyed. Fred shivered. The church was less than half a mile from home. He counted that as a lucky escape. Houses had been destroyed in the area, but no one had died.

That evening, he took refuge in a nearby Anderson shelter; he didn't want to take any chances. The bombers came again, but there was little impact.

No longer feeling safe in his home city, Fred wanted to escape but recognised the futility of this. He expected to be called up at any moment; nowhere would be safe, especially if the war went on much longer.

Although Fred couldn't escape from reality completely, he did look forward to the brief respite that would come in the form of a holiday with Karl in the Lake District. This was an opportunity to ignore a world at war. August was mellowing to September. Leaves warmed, lakes gleamed in the haze of the sun and they were set for a blissful escape, which they both needed, until they came to the

Hotel in Borrowdale. A posh lady noticed them talking together at the dinner table. 'Excuse me, I hope you don't think me rude. I wouldn't ask normally,' she said to Fred, 'I know you're English, but what is he? French?'

'An Austrian Refugee,' Fred replied. The lady got up hastily from the table and went out of the dining room.

'Is anything wrong?' asked Karl.

'No, everything's fine,' Fred replied, again feeling far from it. A moment later the manageress appeared.

'Good afternoon, Mr Clayton, one of our fellow guests has raised concerns about the young man you're with. It says on his form that he's German? I'm afraid we're going to have to call the police. In other times we wouldn't bother, but you know …' She shrugged, 'To my untutored eyes you certainly don't look like spies, but then again, one's heard of Huns dressing up as nuns elsewhere – I know it sounds silly, but you can never be too careful.' Heads nodded as people eavesdropped.

Fred could not contain his anger. 'This poor boy has suffered more than you can imagine. He's more a victim of the Nazis than any of us. He's a half-Jewish boy who suffered persecution from the Nazis in Vienna and now has had to flee his homeland and he's cut off from his mother – possibly for ever. His elder brother has been interned as an enemy alien.'

'What? Interned? You bet our government's got its reasons,' argued another man, who'd been listening in on the conversation.

'Can I go to bed now?' Karl asked Fred suddenly. He looked so tired and bewildered by the attention of these strangers.

'Of course,' Fred said. Karl went to bed while Fred waited for the police to come.

The manageress seemed a little more sympathetic. Watching Karl go, she murmured, 'That's the way things go. The innocent suffer.'

It was ten o-clock before two policemen came. 'Another spy, eh? What a game!' one said.

'He's no spy,' Fred retorted. 'He's a Jewish kid from Austria. I needn't tell you what the Nazis did to Jews there.'

'No,' he replied in a non-committal tone. 'We're just doing our job, sir. Where is he?'

'Well, I let him go to bed; he looked so tired,' Fred said. 'He'll be awake, but he's in bed.'

Undeterred, they went upstairs. Karl was sitting upright in bed. The sergeant, rosy cheeked with a black moustache, looked at him, saw the fear in Karl's eyes and said, 'You look cosy, Karl, that's the name, I see. You're fourteen, nearly fifteen. I've never been to Vienna, although I've heard that it's a beautiful city.' Karl nodded. 'Well, well, pity men can't be reasonable with one another. I shouldn't worry about your brother – your friend will, no doubt, make sure that he's let out.' He turned to Fred. 'Well, we won't keep your young friend from his beauty sleep. You vouch for him, and I don't think Old Winne's going to lose a wink of his sleep over him. Good night. Don't worry. It'll all come right.' He brushed the tip of Karl's black hair with his clumsy, broad, red hand.

Afterwards, the sergeant asked, 'Do you know the mother? Is she a Jewish type like him? I bet she's a black-eyed beauty?'

'No,' Fred replied bemusedly. 'Red-haired.'

When Fred went back upstairs, he reassured Karl. 'Well, thank God for that! What did you say to impress them?' he asked.

'I? I didn't impress them. No, thankfully they had some sense.'

The rest of the holiday passed without more drama, although Karl was unable to escape notice, for he was obviously so different from everyone else. It wasn't quite the escape that they both had craved.

When they returned from holiday, Fred resumed his book, putting all his energies into it. But then, in November 1940, he was called up to the Royal Signal Corps before he had written half. He was tempted to give up the whole idea, but something kept him going – he felt a peculiar mixture of optimism and despair – but conversely, the call up gave him a fresh determination to resume his Magnum Opus, which would be, in the midst of war and hate, a declaration of pity and love for the trapped youth of Dresden. He jotted down odd notes and memories in a small pocketbook, all mixed up with Morse Code, which he would use for his war work. He decided to disguise the location of the novel, lest the Nazis got hold of the book and believed some characters to be identifiable. He wanted to protect his friends and ex-pupils as much as he could. He already felt guilty about having written letters from the safety of England before the outbreak of war that criticised the Nazi regime. He worried that he had risked exposing some of them too much. Now, any indiscretion could be far costlier.

Fred begins military life, 1940.

He began his army life in Prestatyn in the Royal Signal Corps, and then was transferred to Winchester where he joined British Army Intelligence. In Winchester, his clumsiness and poor co-ordination (only hitherto in evidence on the school sports field) resulted in him nearly killing himself as he tried to master the motorbike. In the end, somehow, he actually made it, to the amazement of one instructor, who swore it was a 'bloody miracle'.

Later on, another instructor who seemed more willing to tolerate Fred, whom he found a 'funny little sod', said genially, 'Clayton, you're not actually really much worse than the others.' This made Fred's day.

Overall, he settled down into military life better than anyone expected, including himself; he adapted instinctively, relapsing into his unlearned Lancs–Scouse accent with the addition of a few choice words, which one didn't use at home and which slightly startled his mother. A friend at King's commented how surprisingly happy he seemed to be with army life. He wasn't – not really – but it was a challenge, and he liked to believe he was meeting it. Anyway, Fred had been used, since early adolescence, to putting on a cheerfulness with others, whatever was happening inside him, which, in the moment, beguiled him as much as it did others.

Soon, Fred was posted to Essex, where he was slightly bemused to be given a sloping sort of display counter in an abandoned butcher shop window to sleep on, which resulted in him rolling to the front and waking up every morning with his nose pressed to the glass. It was here Fred began to write again, getting a friendly hotelkeeper to let him work in an empty bedroom. He wrote on leave or in billets. The best thing about being in Essex was that he was back near Cambridge, which had been his home for much of the past decade. This meant he could bike over to Cambridge. In fact, Fred was positively encouraged to 'fuck off' for a long afternoon's practice on that 'fucking' machine, which he seemed still to control somewhat erratically – but Fred suspected that the real reason was that no one could think up any other job for him. They were always trying to think up jobs.

On one such trip out, Fred went to King's, parked up his bike and walked over the grass. He was stopped by a Canadian officer – 'Sarge,' (for Fred was in uniform, wearing his stripes), 'can't you read?' – and he pointed to the sign. 'You're not allowed to walk on the grass.'

'Fellow of the college,' Fred replied loftily and swept quickly into the King's College Combination room. It was an exaggeration – technically he was only an ex-fellow. At King's he had tea with Dadie, who had read more chapters, commenting that he'd been a bit more daring in his writing, as he had previously encouraged him to be. Dadie himself persuaded an, at first, reluctant E M Forster (another Kingsman) to read it, and he wrote both encouragement and criticism. He said Fred should try to put more of himself in the book. Fred tried his best, but found it difficult to expose himself in that way.

While writing his novel, Fred was anxious about portraying the Germans, in particular, the boys, as creatures to be loved. He worried that this would somehow undermine English morale. He expressed this in a letter to his brother, George, training as an air pilot, 'I worry that there isn't a place for this book at this present time. We can't afford to love at the moment, rather, we need to hate the Germans.'

George's reply was typically thoughtful: 'I don't think hate comes into it. It's kill or be killed. It's all about the animal excitement of the moment. One might need to see the Germans in proportion in due time.'

Perhaps there was room for his novel, perhaps someone would dare to publish it. How would it be received? Was the country, at war with the people he'd depicted as lovable creatures, ready to read such a potentially controversial book that would offend their patriotic values?

Somehow, in barracks, in billets, in hotel bedrooms, on leave – Fred got it done. He sent the manuscript off to publishers, and waited. He entitled the novel, *The Cloven Pine* – the title was a cryptic reference to Ariel in *The Tempest*, who had had been trapped by the witch Sycorax in a 'cloven pine' as a punishment for resisting her commands. The boys were imprisoned in the Nazi system, with Hitler playing the role of the witch. And, like Ariel, these boys were trapped, and they needed rescuing. It was a subtle and intellectually sensitive reference, but, perhaps, too lofty an allusion for most readers.

CHAPTER SIX
1941-1942: Passage to India

In early 1941 Fred was posted from Essex to RAF Cheadle for six months, where he worked as a Computor at Woodhead Hall, a Y Station completely dedicated to intercepting German Luftwaffe radio communications. He felt a thrill of excitement when he signed the Official Secrets Act, the sense of feeling at home when he first saw the grand country house – he was used to such lofty environs having spent so many years in Cambridge – and even the 12 ft high razor wire fence couldn't disguise its grandeur.

Although intercepted messages were initially sent to Bletchley to be decoded, the authorities decided it would be more efficient to house those who intercepted the work and those who could decode the messages together in the same premises, and this was where Fred came in. He was part of a team that sat at a large table in the middle of the air-intercept room, with the wireless operators working around them. He would receive messages from receivers who were ranged around the walls and his work would begin. His task was to decode, translate the messages and then pass them to the Warrant Officer in charge. The Warrant Officer would then decide what to do with the messages, and he passed them to the Commands, as he saw fit.

Fred enjoyed his work at RAF Cheadle. He slipped into the routine well and had success, although he often didn't know the significance of the messages he was decoding. For example, he decoded a message about Scharnhorst and Gneisenau – not realising the import of this message until he read in the newspaper in March 1941 that these were battleships that went on to cause havoc, capturing or sinking six ships in a dispersed convoy.

He also had help with his decoding through enemy errors, such as the slow-witted German at Bordeaux who was such a godsend because he never had the new code and had to ask for a repeat in the old code that the British had long-since broken. There were messages about partisans near Warsaw, an officer who wanted to be met at the Anholterbahnhof; and the operator who fooled about saying his estimated time of arrival was Götz. Fred wouldn't forget that name – after all, he was a real boy in Dresden, the hero of his novel, but Götz to that operator meant only a very rude remark in the eminent German playwright J W Goethe's *Götz von Berlichingen*. The actual quote, *"'Er aber,' sag's ihm, 'er kann mich im Arsche lecken.'"*– meant, He can lick my arse. This was the kind of thing, Fred reflected, that the adolescent boys in the Kreuzschule had found incredibly funny, and it brightened up their literature lessons. When he read and decoded this message, it gave him a familiar twinge and he wondered what had happened to those boys. Were they ok? Were they still alive? Was Götz? Was Wolf? But Fred had to push these feelings down. Such sentimentality wasn't a luxury he could afford. There was a war to be fought, a war to be won.

Fred also enjoyed the autonomy that he was granted at Cheadle. Life there, in the middle of the country, with its familiar routine, was peaceful and the war felt altogether in another world. The only downside was that he received the first of the rejection letters, while he was billeted with a nice homely north-country family. The excitement as he saw that the letter had come from the publisher soon dissipated when he read the words – the publisher said that the great defect of the book was that the boy was the only character. Apparently, they were rejecting him purely on literary grounds, but Fred couldn't help but wonder whether there was any ulterior motive behind the rejection.

It was a wrench when he was posted from Cheadle in summer 1941, and after a month as a civilian, sent to Uxbridge to take up a new post. He didn't really know, or care, for that matter why he was moved again – like everyone, he was a pawn, moved about at will by the Powers. The problem with each new transfer was that he had to go through the same drill training, along with the new recruits. And no matter how hard he tried, no matter how much he practised the square-bashing, he never improved. He could never time an order properly. It had been the same ever since he tried the Officer Training Corps while at school. He'd fully learned his limitations then. Practice most definitely did not make perfect.

Fred in his RAF uniform

Meanwhile, he agonised at the ongoing wait to discover the fate of his novel. Would the months of pouring himself into this project ever bear fruit? Would it ever unite readers in a common understanding of the sad plight of young Germans? Would his concern and compassion ever be recognised and shared by others? Another rejection letter came in Uxbridge. Each rejection stung – it felt personal, like they were rejecting him, and the gloom of depression descended on him. Fred was consoled by a kind letter from Karl, by now a 16-year-old schoolboy, who wondered whether writing really made one happy. 'Creative people seem to me to have a pretty rough time,' he wrote. Fred wondered whether there might be a great deal of truth in those words.

Fred began to despair of his novel ever being published, but then he received an encouraging telegram from George, his brother, who, as a student in Cambridge, had not yet been called up to fight, and had the time to function as Fred's literary agent.

'GOOD NEWS SECKERS ARE NIBBLING SHOULD HEAR FROM SENHOUSE MONDAY = GEORGE'.

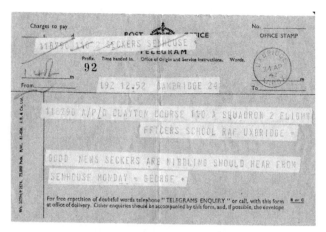

Finally, an exciting telegram from George.

Soon enough, amazingly, a letter arrived for Fred at the RAF Officer's School in Uxbridge –

Martin Secker and Warburg Ltd
Publishers: 22 Essex Street, Strand, London, WC2

29 April, 1942

Dear Mr Clayton,
    Although I have never had the pleasure of meeting you at Cambridge when I have been to stay with George Rylands, he sent me your novel – THE CLOVEN PINE – some weeks ago. We are now writing to make you an offer for its publication. ... Both my partner and I were very impressed by the CLOVEN PINE ...
    Yours sincerely
    Roger Senhouse

Fred was delighted. He couldn't keep it in – he had to talk about it. He was profoundly grateful that, at a time when the course of the war was so bad, when Hitler was sweeping all before him, when Rommel's Afrikakorps were trouncing the Allies in the North African desert and pushing them back into Egypt and were nearly at Alexandria, he was part of a nation which was still sane and civilised and tolerant enough for a young English soldier to write; for an English publisher to produce; for English critics and readers to praise a book which deliberately offended both patriotic and moral prejudices in order to state that it was possible to love deeply children brought up under the Nazi regime, as one might feel for any young creature trapped and condemned.

MARTIN SECKER & WARBURG LTD   Phone : Temple Bar 5357
Telegrams : Psophidian

PUBLISHERS : 22 ESSEX STREET · STRAND · LONDON · WC2

29th April, 1942.

118790 A/P/O Clayton F.W.,
Course 110, A Sqd. 2 Flight,
Officers' School, R.A.F.,
UXBRIDGE.

Dear Mr. Clayton,

       Although I have never had the pleasure of meeting you at Cambridge when I have been to stay with George Rylands, he sent me your novel - THE CLOVEN PINE - some weeks ago. We are now writing to make you an offer for its publication.

       We would offer what I believe are the usual terms for a first novel, based on a royalty of 10% of the published price for the first 2,000 copies sold, 12½% for the next 3,000 copies sold, and 15% thereafter; with 10% of the amount received, on copies sold for export or to the colonies; with an advance of £30 on publication, and an option on your two next non-fiction books. If these terms seem suitable to you, we would send you our usual printed contract for perusal.

       Both my partner and myself were very impressed by the CLOVEN PINE, and I then gave it to Norman Douglas, who is at the moment reading novels for us, and we have a short report from him, a copy of which, of course, I will send you if you would care to see it.

       Rylands tells me that he believes that while you were on short leave, you tried to experiment in modifying certain passages, and perhaps the most helpful offer which we could make to you is that you should meet Norman Douglas and discuss that question in the light of his report, if ever you could manage to come to London for some leave.

       Yours sincerely,

RHS:

The letter from Secker and Warburg, confirming publication of The Cloven Pine.

Fred signed his contract with Secker and Warburg in the barrack-room in Uxbridge and couldn't wait to get his hands on a copy. It was then that he was sent for by the Adjutant.

'Clayton,' the Adjutant said, sounding rather surprised, 'you seem to be a VIP. You're wanted urgently at Bletchley.' Fred's immediate feeling was one of relief – at last, the powers that be had seen sense by cutting short his square-bashing so he could truly join the war effort, using the two key skills that he had, and could wield, to try and defeat the enemy. The skills he'd developed at King's, learning and teaching classics, decoding and interpreting those ancient languages, when combined with his fluency in German, would surely make a potent combination – hadn't his short time at Cheadle proven that? He knew that some of his friends – Duncan and Kinloch and Turing – had been based at Bletchley for some time, and he looked forward to joining them. He looked forward to feeling less, well, useless. He couldn't escape the feeling that until now he had had a very soft war. The closest he'd got to enemy action was when he was seeking to master the rifle, and nearly killed himself in the process. He'd been constantly berated for his inability to acquire the soldierly arts. He brought out all the latent menace in inanimate objects. 'Spastic' was how one of his superior officers had uncharitably referred to him in a fit of frustration. But now he was needed, he had been asked for personally. A VIP. For the first time in a while, he felt important. Wanted.

When he arrived in Bletchley, he felt that this was somewhere he could feel at home. At the gate he was gruffly greeted by two guards, one younger and another more elderly. 'Clayton, to see Josh Cooper? I've been summoned here.'

'Go to the hut at the left of the gates,' replied the older guard. 'Somebody will come to see to you. Welcome to Bletchley Park…'

'The biggest lunatic asylum in Britain,' sniggered a younger guard.

'I'll fit right in, then,' remarked Fred. He went to the hut as instructed and didn't have to wait long before he was whisked into Josh Cooper's office, in Hut 10, which had been built specifically to house the Air Section when the work at Bletchley had been expanded. Cooper was head of the Air Section of the Government Code and Cypher School (GCCS) at Bletchley. He had been a classicist at Oxford with a high linguistic ability and he'd turned out to be an excellent cryptanalyst. He'd been working for GCCS since 1925 and had been head of the Air Section since 1936. Cooper's office was near that of old Professor Adcock, who had been a fellow-Kingsman and whom Fred suspected had been responsible for adding him to the list of Kingsmen involved in the codebreaking business. Fred and Cooper shook hands. Given that Cooper was a physically imposing presence, known to some as 'the bear' and that Fred was quite the opposite, Fred tried not to be too intimidated by the man who towered above him. 'Good to see you, Clayton. Do sit down.' He motioned to a chair opposite him. 'We met once before, didn't we? In Bedford, wasn't it?'

'That's right, sir.'

'I tested your German if I remember rightly. Very impressive.'

'Thank you, sir,' He himself couldn't imagine anyone less suited to the military life than he was; unlike his younger brother, George, who was training to be a fighter pilot. It was gratifying that while he was a hopeless soldier, someone had finally recognised that he did have something unique to offer.

'And we have heard good accounts of your work in Cheadle.'

'Thank you, sir.'

'Now, as you know, I've always said that no one can break codes without knowing the language, and that we've always had strict linguist tests for our codebreakers.'

'Yes, sir.'

'Well, as you'll be aware, the war is really hotting up in the Far East. Those Japs are a real threat, and we need to do what we can to stop them. We're going to have to break our linguistic rules. Too few people know Japanese. We're putting clever young men, who will be able to break the codes, through a crash course of six months. But we can't wait for them to be ready. We need people out there now, urgently. People of quality who have the skills to tackle the enemy.'

It took a while for the import of Cooper's words to register with Fred, but he was beginning to realise where this was going, and as this dawned on him, a sense of rising dread threatened to overwhelm him.

'People like you, Clayton,' Cooper continued. 'You see, you have a real flair for languages, for the codebreaker's art. You've been recommended to us as a good guesser – they say you're a bit of a maverick, but that you're independent. You could be just what we need in India to defeat the Japs. You could make a start on low-level stuff while we get these people through the crash course.'

Just what they need. Fred felt flattered, he'd been recommended, his skills recognised! And yet the feeling of pride was quickly overtaken with apprehension. He knew more than most about India, having read about it in books: the poverty, the diseases one must expect to encounter; the terrifyingly alien culture with which he had never wished to become involved. India, the one place he didn't want to go, was the very place he was being sent, and Fred was afraid.

'Of course,' Cooper said, 'you can opt out. It might be a fiasco out there, which might leave you stuck out in India for no sensible purpose. We won't force you to go.'

But Fred couldn't refuse. Apart from the narrow escape in August 1940 when Mossley Hill was bombed, he had had a cushy war. He knew he had to accept this challenge. 'No sir, I will go.' And as he said these words, he was swept with a sick feeling of fatalistic acceptance. His course was set. While his friends would be in heaven in Bletchley, he was journeying to hell on the other side of the world.

'That's very good,' Cooper beamed. 'I'm very pleased. Now, we need you urgently. You're to be flown out. We haven't finalised yet how we're going to get you out there ...'

Fred could say nothing. He felt physically sick.

The next few days were a blur as the authorities sought to find a way of spiriting Fred out to India. And the plans changed on seemingly a daily basis. First, he was to be flown out high over the Mediterranean in a Wellington bomber, and he was sent to

Farnborough to be tested in a pressure-chamber, an experience he found incredibly uncomfortable since he'd damaged his Eustachian tube swimming underwater. Evidently, he was to grin and bear it. But then the plan changed. Apparently, it was too risky – a Wellington high over the Mediterranean might crash. So, Fred was summoned to the Air Ministry where he slept in the basement of that august building, and where he was informed of the revised plan. 'Clayton, we need you to travel in disguise as a civilian. You have a top-secret role, you know. You can carry your RAF uniform in your luggage. Make sure no one sees it.'

'But sir,' Fred mused, 'civilians need passports. Mine's run out.' The superior officer tutted and sent Fred to get some passport photos done.

The journey began inauspiciously when Fred, to the fury of his guide and mentor, missed his train from Victoria because of an administrative cock-up. ('I'll tear a strip off that man,' he vowed to Fred after slamming the phone down. He'd go far in the services, Fred thought, being so quick to blame the other chap – whoever he might be.) Fred felt very sanguine about the delay. He'd get to India eventually. There was no need to get angry or anxious. He took another train to Bournemouth, and he began his journey from nearby Poole – to Shannon. The goal was India, but apparently, like Columbus, they would travel west, violating the neutrality of Ireland in the process.

On board Fred noticed other so-called civilians, 'civil servants' in the passports on that flight, though the tan on their faces suggested an acquaintance with African suns. One Irish official ventured in his rich native accent to ask one of these if the ministry involved could by any chance be the war ministry. Fred enjoyed watching the man squirm a little as he replied, flustered, as if suddenly remembering, 'Yes, war ministry.'

From Shannon, Fred was flown to Lisbon, Portugal, where Germans, Britons and Italians were lodged in different quarters. It had already taken a couple of days and there was still a long way to go. As he travelled, Fred made a note of each stop – snaking across Africa: Bathurst (Gambia Colony and Protectorate), Freetown (Sierra Leone), Lagos (Nigeria), Bangui (French Equatorial Africa), Stanleyville (Belgian Congo), Juba, Khartoum and Wadi Halfa (Anglo Egyptian Sudan); the Middle East: Cairo (Egypt), Galilee (Palestine), Habbaniyah and Basra (Iraq), Bahrain, somewhere in Baluchistan, before arriving in India: Karachi and Gwalior, then, finally, by train to Delhi.

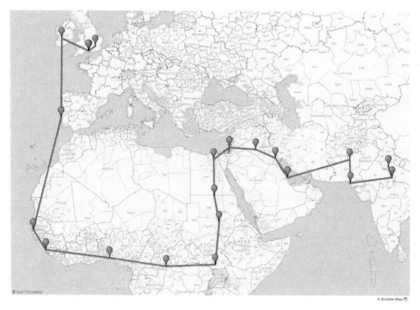

Fred's epic ten day journey from London to Delhi

The journey had taken ten days. So much for the urgency. But, it had been an adventure. He'd enjoyed the crazy journey. It was all so funny, and yet it also made him feel important. This feeling didn't last long, however, once he arrived, finally at the headquarters. 'Squadron Leader Clayton reporting for duty, sir.'

'Clayton?' the commanding officer looked surprised, 'Where have you come from?'

'From England, sir. I was told – by Josh Cooper – that I was required urgently,' Fred replied.

'And what is it you do, Clayton?'

'Codebreaking, sir.'

'No, I think there must have been a misunderstanding. We

made no such request. We certainly weren't expecting you. There's certainly not going to be much work for you for – I reckon, another six months.'

Another six months. Fred's heart sank, and he felt like a fool. A fool, to allow himself to be flattered so easily. 'I don't really know what we'll do with you, Clayton,' the CO continued. 'We have, however, just started a course for officers who will be working here.'

'I hope you don't mind me saying, sir, but I've done that course already – last year, in Bedford,'

'Oh, right,' the CO paused,' well, we'll have to find something else for you to do, then, won't we? In the meantime, you may as well get yourself settled in here. I'll arrange for you to be shown to your billets.'

'Yes, sir, thank you, sir,' Fred replied. He felt numb as he was shown his digs – a bungalow near the Jinnah Road – and unpacked his bag. He had only two books with him - the two-volume corpus of Latin poets - *Corpus Poetarum Latinorum* – and he felt so alone, so far from home – far from his family, from Karl, from those Dresden boys.

CHAPTER SEVEN
1942-1944: Delhi – A desert experience

Squadron Leader Clayton (RAF Intelligence) found himself as a breaker of Japanese Codes, based at the Wireless Experimental Centre (WEC) at Anand Parbat, on the outskirts of Delhi, India, one of two overseas outposts of Station X, Bletchley Park. Fred was part of a nerve centre of intelligence tracking military wireless sources against Japan. One of many classics scholars to be involved in codebreaking in Bletchley and India, he didn't speak the Japanese language, so needed to utilise all his skills and talents he'd learned as a classics scholar to fight the Japanese. War, he would say, made guessing his game, if you could call it guessing and not the imagination and logic of a verbal mind, pushed to the limit. The work entailed doing what he had unconsciously done at King's with Latin unseens – pushing the deciphering of messages to the furthest limits with combined logic and imagination, and practically no Japanese. He worked on the premise 'the only thing he can be saying next is …' eliminating alternatives, and he was good at it.

Situated on the site of Ramjas College, a Protestant Hindu foundation which had been evacuated elsewhere and taken over by the Allied armed forces, the centre's hilly and isolated position on the edge of the Thar desert made it ideal for its role as a wireless station, although the thousand or so people who were based there – from Intelligence Corps, RAF Signals Wing, Women's auxiliary corps, Indian airmen and many others, including civilians – lived with the perpetual fear of being caught in the *anhi* – the dust storm. Fred's digs were in a commandeered villa that he shared with other Allied officers, on the Aurangzeb Road, Delhi, India.

With little work coming his way, Fred thought he might alleviate the boredom by both learning a little of the language and, at the same time, discovering more about the people. He ignored the fact that there were officially recognised teachers and inserted an advertisement in the *Star of India* – inviting some young Indian to teach him the language.

In time, a young man appeared of somewhat haughty mien in spotless white garments, a little muddied by the monsoon rain. Azid was a Muslim – he would be happy to teach Fred. They agreed a fee.

Over the next four or five weeks, Fred found that he actually learned very little of the language but a bewildering amount about the people. Fred found the language baffling – Azid dismissed certain words that Fred heard used all around him as bad news – not classical Hindi. When Fred asked Azid about other religions, he treated him rather as a curious child seeking undesirable knowledge. Azid replied, 'The Sikhs? They are feelthy people. They do not cut or shave any arm. And one shaves, at least – excuse me – under the armpits, is it not?'

Fred didn't know quite how to respond because, actually, he didn't, and was painfully aware that his shirtsleeves were very short; Azid could easily have seen and even smelt his armpits. Perhaps, in a hot climate, Azid might have a point, Fred conceded. He knew English women sometimes did it, but he hadn't taken enough pride in his appearance to bother about unsightly hair.

One day in old Delhi in the midst of a jostling crowd, Azid turned to Fred, 'Excuse me,' (he always began like that if he thought he was about to mention an unpleasant matter), 'some of them are calling me 'the Englishman's monkey.' He clearly felt he was facing some nasty music in the interests of interracial friendship. Fred respected him for that. But then he asked him about the Hindus, and Azid said dismissively, 'They worship – excuse me – cow dung and the female organ.' That's disposed of them then, Fred thought, and he wondered if the Indians calling Azid 'Fred's monkey' were all Hindus. This was typical of Azid, who was apt to brush aside as unimportant those he viewed as inferior creatures.

Suddenly after four or five weeks, the colonel sent for Fred. He respected the man – he wasn't some stupid Colonel Blimp character – no, Fred found him sensitive and civilised.

'Now, Clayton, I've been told about the regular meetings you've been having with a young Indian man?'

'Yes, sir.' Azid. 'I've been paying him a bit to help me learn the language and culture.'

'Yes, very good, very good. The trouble is, Clayton, our work is very secret. I'm sure you're very careful, but this native – well, he's a threat to our security. We can't have him learning too much about our work, can we?'

'No sir.' Fred resisted the urge to point out that the work was non-existent. He had arrived too early. However, he conceded that the Colonel did have a point.

'So, we think it's best for you to stop these meetings.'

'Yes sir, I understand. Thank you, sir.'

On reflection, Fred and Azid were getting tired of each other. It was probably for the best. At their next meeting, he gave Azid some lame excuse about not having time for their lessons anymore. This didn't reveal in any way the top-secret nature of his work, and they parted very amicably.

Time dragged on and the work began to trickle in. Fred did all he could to stave off the boredom. He found a local bookshop in Delhi and sought to keep his mind alert. Serious study was not easy as he shared rooms and was constantly shuttled to and fro between Delhi and Barrackpore. He bought English poetry and novels and, as a prophylactic against boredom, learned Milton, Shakespeare, and Matthew Arnold off by heart. He recited these to himself during interminable delays in Indian Railway stations, 'And we are here as on a darkling plain /Swept with confused alarms of struggle and flight, /Where ignorant armies clash by night.' shutting his ears against the monotone of women begging with starving babies.

He envied his friends back home who could fall back on their academic work, enjoying the culture of Oxford or Cambridge when they weren't on duty. He did, however, meet old Cambridge friends at Anand Parbat, and they formed a mini-Bletchley colony, keeping themselves going under the adverse conditions.

Fred hoped he was justifying Josh Cooper's trust in him, though results were often disappointing. 'I do my best,' he said one day to Hugh Lloyd Jones, a rapidly trained Japanese linguist testifying once more to trust in classics, 'by the light of an Ex-operator's Morse and a dictionary.'

He had no choice but to make the best of it. And he did – he managed to adapt to life better than one might expect – in fact, by day, he appeared curiously cheerful and untroubled, in spite of the appalling poverty around him, the unnatural life, loneliness, and a climate that was uncomfortable and unhealthy to a northern Englishman like himself. The war seemed very far off and unreal. By day he sometimes seemed scarcely to feel the impact of events at all. By night, however, it was different. …

He had a recurring dream of standing in the auditorium in the Kreuzschule. Amidst the sea of boys, he spotted Götz, Karl, Wolf and George. Wolf and Karl were smiling, Götz was leaning back in his chair, a mixture of puzzlement and defiance on his face. In the corner of his eye, he could see his father at the side, a few rows back; his expression disapproving. Fred was speaking from the podium, 'Hitler is a danger. You have to escape, before it's too late. You must get out. Your lives are in danger. Get out!' His voice rose and began to shake as he was speaking, seeing the blank expressions on their faces. They didn't comprehend what he was telling them. How could he make them understand before it was too late? He tried again, 'You must escape –' He didn't get to finish his sentence. He was interrupted by the loudest noise he had ever heard. The walls melted away and the flames engulfed them from all sides. The air roared. There was no escape. His mouth opened into a shriek of utter terror.

'Are you all right, Clayton?' An irritated voice came from the bed across the room.

Fred woke with a start, drenched in sweat. He looked around, taking a while to reorient himself. He was in Delhi, officer's sleeping quarters, miles from home.

'Clayton,' the voice was more insistent this time, 'what the bloody hell's the matter with you now?'

'Oh, sorry. Nothing.' Fred replied. 'It was a nightmare, that's all.'

'What was that?' another voice asked...

'It's only Clayton with the bloody shivers again,' and then, more loudly addressing him, 'Hold it together, won't you? You'll wake up half the mess with that bloody racket you make.'

Fred would have the same nightmare. Night after night. He'd dream of Dresden being bombed and the boys being killed. In the moment of waking he'd realise that his apparent cheerfulness was a front. He was deeply anxious.

Only letters from home, when they arrived, broke through the monotony. He continued to receive letters from Karl, now 17. Karl seemed to sense Fred's loneliness, for his letters seemed to get extra affectionate. Fred found it strange how instinctively perceptive boys can be, compared to the blindness of one's otherwise sensitive adult friends. He told a friend, a professor who had recently married, about his dreams of Dresden, and his friend, perhaps concerned for him, wrote back, recommending marriage as the remedy against such maladies. Marriage? In India? India was an emotional desert, and there were very few women about. Marriage would have to wait – if it would come at all.

In the late summer Fred received out of the blue a Red Cross card which simply said. *Thank you for all you did for my boys – H.S.'* Fred was amazed. The card had come from Helene Schneider, Karl's mother. She had used her monthly Red Cross word ration on him, not the boys. Somehow the card had got through, been forwarded from home and found him in those huts, a world, a war away. Fred had heard no new horror about the intensified persecution of the Jews.

In their correspondence Karl had made no mention at all of his mother, and his silence had suggested to Fred that she must have a job – war work perhaps – but he had never expressed this to Karl – after all, he knew he was probably being overly optimistic. Now, Fred basked in this restored contact, this warm sign of life. And he began to hope. He began to hope for Helene, and he began to hope for the Dresden boys. The dreams still troubled him, but perhaps they wouldn't come true.

Fred heard little of how his book went down back home in England, although he feared that it wouldn't be well-received. The first criticism he saw was in a Forces' newspaper. He noticed the title 'Three books to read and one to avoid', and knew at once. He looked around, wishing vaguely there was someone to share the joke with. Fred himself never received a copy from the publishers – apparently it had been torpedoed or something. He bought a copy in the Calcutta bookshop from an Indian who assured Fred that it was a 'well recommended work'. Later, by what seemed at first a most unfortunate as well as an unlikely coincidence, someone came out to Fred's unit who knew that Fred had written under the pseudonym 'Frank Clare' and he told others. They were intrigued and casually borrowed the book, pretending to notice it by chance among the very few Fred possessions had in his room.

　　Some frankly asked him about it, one alluding to the confused sexuality that was suggested by the novel. Fred didn't want to be labelled. He longed to be a husband and a father – nothing had diminished that; in fact, his experience with Karl had only increased that feeling. But there was no getting away from the fact that he was sometimes overwhelmed by the feelings and emotions experienced with other men. They understood him more, gave him more time – and this had left him in turmoil, although he hoped the problem simply came down to the fact that he simply hadn't had the opportunity to build relationships with women. After all, he was born into a family of all boys, was then educated in an all-boys secondary school before spending the next decade in the all-male environment of King's – time which was only interrupted significantly by a year teaching in all an all-boys school in Dresden, and now he was in the male dominated environment of India. Was this simply an excuse or was he homosexual and simply repressing this? Could he ever form a 'normal' relationship with a woman given the opportunity? Would these deep longings for a family of his own ever be fulfilled? Perhaps this time would never come, but he was not going to give up hope yet.

As for *The Cloven Pine*, someone finally 'borrowed' Fred's copy and never returned it. He heard that the publishers Secker and Warburg had been blitzed. They had no copy.

Fred in India, maintaining a cheerful exterior.

The days in India dragged on and cracks were developing in his cheerful exterior; in late 1942, famine struck Bengal, and Fred watched as the population starved to death. He couldn't escape the terrible poverty, coming face to face with the horror of it. The familiar cries of 'Sahib, Sahib' as he walked down the street would nearly drive him mad, filling him with despair and powerlessness. Always, he attempted to steel his heart and shut his pocket to the emaciated women with beseeching hands.

One day he tripped on something in the road, catching his breath as he realised with horror this bundle was the corpse of a tiny baby. It had been left in the street, like a piece of rubbish. Had anyone known its name? What desperation and despair drove someone to discard a human life like that? Where was the mother? Was she dead too? With a sob in his throat, he ran from the scene, seeking refuge in the barracks where he could pretend the suffering wasn't happening on his doorstep. It didn't work. He saw that baby when his eyes were closed.

It wasn't just the women; boys and girls too were driven to do anything for money; they would do anything simply to survive. Once Fred and his company were going up to Durghpur, near the 14th Army GHQ at Camilla, via the Brahmaputra Ferry. At Chandpur there was a long delay in landing, and no one knew why. Fred, and several others with him, stood watching thin, native boys diving. Suddenly someone plucked at Fred's sleeve. He looked down and saw it was a young Indian boy, not as starved and thin as most, dressed only in a green Dhoti. The boy grinned hopefully and said, 'Carry bags, sahib?'

'Okay kid,' said Fred and smiled.

He had wanted to be kind, to show compassion for the poverty-stricken child but later, that unbearably hot afternoon when Fred had retreated into a cabin on the boat for the three or four officers, the boy had appeared, standing in the doorway with a confident smile and, offering to undo his dhoti, lay down on one of the couches. Fred was incredulous and horrified, 'Get away,' he spluttered, and waved his hands frantically, indicating as best he could, that the boy should go away at once. The boy did.

Later, when darkness had fallen, Fred was told the boat wouldn't leave for another hour. In the compartment it seemed unbearably hot, and the wailing begging women were there again. Fred got out, tried to find a roadside chaiwala who'd sell him some tea, and walked across the railway line.

Suddenly the boy appeared again. He sprang out from behind a truck, stark naked, threw his arms around Fred and said, 'Nice sahib!' He knew what sahibs wanted from Indian boys. As well as feeling horror, in that moment Fred felt love and pity for the boy. It was an awful substitute for Karl, a sickening caricature of him. Fred thrust a ridiculous number of rupees on the boy, who said,

'Nice sahib. Sahib good man.'

Fred stumbled away, wondering whether he was the one obvious customer among the sahibs, or whether there was something about him that indicated he might offer some compassion. Absurd as it might seem, did the boy pick Fred out as the one sahib who would be kind, hold him, with some transitory trace of love, gently and tenderly, and not use him for his own sexual gratification?

Amidst the hardship and horror, Fred was bored and underworked, which meant he had no way of finding distraction or escape from all that he was experiencing. He was burdened by the pointlessness of what he did – and he was not the only one questioning the worth of their efforts. One morning he sat with a clever junior officer, who asked him, 'Do you think we are contributing anything at all to the war effort?'

'Probably not,' Fred answered, 'but, it will be a lot bloody easier if you stop going on about it.'

But the man was right. Fred's war was characterised by boredom. It wasn't just the work, endlessly listening to Japanese chatting about the weather, day in day out, it was the lack of human or humane contact that wore Fred down until he felt emotionally numb. Living in an officers' mess and doing 'top secret' work, he felt so isolated, and desperately missed proper contact with people, He was worn down by the poverty that he felt helpless to relieve.

And Fred wasn't alone: all over India thousands of ordinary British lads, not tough professional soldiers or officers or administrators, but truck drivers and teachers and clerks saw their glorious empire for the first time and never wanted to see it again. Fred knew this because as an unwilling censor, he read their disillusioned letters. What, in their vague imaginings, had they expected? He, at least, had been forewarned, had read left wing books about India. One of his lads, a teacher, made friends with a local teacher in Durghpur. On leave in Calcutta Fred suddenly thought of this teacher, bought some easy reading books for Indian kids and took them to him. The Indian teacher looked at

Fred very kindly, but a little sadly. 'Sahib,' he said, 'children must work to eat, not read. No books. Forget how to read.'

Fred found the poverty and suffering of the people unbearable. He had a sense that the locals thought it was all the occupiers' fault – on top of which, he had the insight and honesty to know they were right. He barely dared to admit this, however; the sense of guilt he felt and what he represented only made matters worse. Fred wished he could apologise to them and make it all better. But he felt powerless. He could not turn back the clock. He could not undo the years of exploitation under the guise of colonisation. He and his army colleagues had come too late: the damage had been done over hundreds of years. Fred and the other ordinary lads, whom the locals might more easily have liked, were hindered by this history, and the locals were not so easily beguiled by their belated attempts at friendliness. Fred felt frustrated that he, as an officer, had been able to make even fewer contacts than his men. The bridges he yearned to build, the human contact he sought, wherever he was, remained unbuilt.

There were glimpses of humanity, glimmers of light in the darkness. At Christmas 1944, an American liaison man, Klein, came in like some rich merchant and unloaded boxes of Camel cigarettes, by the hundred, on Fred's unit. They were not too proud to accept. Fred was flattered, if amazed, when one of the American officers, highly amused, asked him to guess what Klein had said. 'He told us – the British officers I work with are hard-working and know their stuff, not like you lazy bums.' They had been starved of both cigarettes and appreciation and the American had provided them with both. It wasn't much, but still felt like rain falling on a parched land.

CHAPTER EIGHT
1945: A mind unravelling

In February 1945, perhaps in pursuit of some sort of normality, Fred used up some leave to become a tourist for a few days, staying in Agra to visit the Taj Mahal and other attractions. He got up at dawn to avoid the crowds and because he had heard that this was the best time to visit. He stood gazing at this immense mausoleum of white marble with its towering minarets and onion dome that gleamed in the early morning sunshine, reflecting on how apt it was that this, the most famous building in the country and perhaps the world, was a monument to heartbreak (the Mughal emperor, Shah Jahan had it built in memory of his beloved wife, Mumtaz Mahal, after she died in childbirth).

Fred's reverie was interrupted by a small boy who was offering himself – or his sister – to Fred. 'No, thank you,' mumbled Fred, and then he paused. 'Actually, would you guide me around?' he said, pointing to the Taj Mahal. The boy looked puzzled, as being a tour guide wasn't the normal service he performed for tourists and it was also one for which he had no qualifications, either as an antiquarian or linguist. One or two people stared at them as the curious pair went round together. The boy tried to point out objects of interest, and Fred nodded. It was, Fred thought, all a sad joke. The boy seemed to enjoy the joke and grinned when Fred gave him money – too much, of course. An adult Indian guide glared at them.

Next Fred wanted to travel from Agra to Fatehpur-Sikri, a vast ruined city 30 miles away, but he couldn't get anyone to share a taxi with him, so he took the local Indian bus, squashed in among the locals, and they seemed quite friendly. Then the bus broke down. The Indians all peed by the roadside. Another long Indian delay seemed threatened, so Fred walked on alone under the hot sun, hoping for a tanga (a horse drawn carriage) to take him there. An elderly Indian came along on a bicycle, with greying moustache, turban, and tucked up dhoti. He smiled and pointed behind him – he was offering Fred a lift.

This had never happened to him since the age of 10, when a bigger boy in the village gave him that kind of lift, and Fred, if a little scared, put his hands happily on his shoulders. The road was rough and bumpy; they ran into a headwind, tracked, veered, wobbled. Fred feared he might fall off at any moment and look somewhat silly. In the end they both gave up. The elderly man indicated regret, Fred gratitude. They both smiled. And then Fred knew, instinctively and with incredible joy, that there was no question of payment. He was simply a nice, lonely young sahib who might have been the man's son. Fred could almost have kissed him! They shook hands, and the man pedalled on his wobbly way.

India was like that for Fred. Every now and then one was allowed by the downtrodden natives to feel common humanity… but sometimes they seemed so stubborn, apathetic, stupid. Fred had caught himself once or twice trying, in vain, to coax a smile, because he could not bear to feel such a total lack of human contact.

A tanga came, and Fred was back in the old atmosphere of sullen bargaining, with a sour, emaciated man with sore-marked, emaciated and beaten beasts.

He wandered alone among the ruins of Fatehpur-Sikri.

On his return from leave, he was given startling news. A junior officer came up and sat next to him in the mess. 'Sir, while you were away, I thought you'd like to know…' He tailed off. Fred knew from the worried expression in his voice that it had to be bad.

'What is it?' he asked.

'Dresden,' he replied.

'What about it?' Although he knew the answer already.

'It's been bombed by a joint American and British force.'

'How badly?'

'It's been…obliterated. Bomber Command is pleased. Rumour has it that there was some sort of firestorm and thousands have been caught up in it. It's like hell over there.'

'Oh God,' Fred replied, and he felt the all-too-familiar sense of panic and helplessness rising within him. He had to keep a lid on it, keep a grip on himself, somehow. If he gave in to those feelings he felt he would unravel completely.

So, his nightmares had come true. As well as suppressing the despair, Fred tried to rationalise it, to think logically, as if doing so would make him feel better. Of course, the day of reckoning had to come. It could not remain forever the one miraculously spared city. What right did that city have to remain unscathed when other great cities suffered? There were arms factories and all that…But then, over time as he'd heard news of other German cities being bombed while Dresden remained untouched, Fred had almost come to believe that the Allies were deliberately forbearing to destroy this historical jewel, and that was wise and fine and magnanimous, worthy of a man like Churchill. But now, like a chapter in some grim ancient myth, it appeared that Dresden had been saved up only for the war masters' final feast, saved up to show how ruthless in all their righteous wrath, they could be – the final touch to the whole hideous business.

Fred found, with a sort of shamed shock, that he no longer really felt anything. He wanted to. He ought to. But his heart was dead. He was no longer capable of feeling. He longed for the end, longed to be out of it all, back home. Dresden was an item in the utter, singed greyness of life.

As Fred thought about the destruction of his once beloved city and his time in Dresden, which, along with his whole pre-war world, felt unreal and remote, one thought at the back of his burned-out mind was, 'Back in Dresden, I argued for the virtue of our democracy and values. I argued that we were the nobler for it. Now, barbarism on our side as well as theirs has beaten tolerance.' Fred now felt less shame about his very non-combatant war, believing there might be some reason for his sort to survive; but that thought was scant consolation.

* * *

In April 1945 came the stroke of luck which turned out to be the final turn of the screw. Fred drew a prize in a lottery – a month's home leave. He'd qualified for the draw having been long enough in India. Repatriations, demobilisation, and the retreating Japanese were, for many of them, like running a curious kind of race. As the Japs retired out of radio reach, Fred's job began to fold up. He had to find silly jobs for his clerks, instead of telling them to go down to Delhi and enjoy themselves. The Germans surrendered before Fred left. With any luck Fred would soon be out of it all for all of these reasons.

The plane stopped off at Porno in Nigeria ('When I was in Porno' became one of Fred's little jokes) where they spent one night on the airfield. One or two chaps were part of the group and they had been prisoners of the Japs. Fred thought that one of them looked very peculiar and they had terrible tales to tell.

Thankfully, the journey home was a two days' flight, not the ten-day tour of Africa he'd experienced three years previously. They flew via Karachi, Lydda; Fred bathed at Tel Aviv, which reminded him vaguely of Vienna, and had one final stop in Tripoli. (As a senior officer, Fred had all the documents, and, very typically, left them in the toilets at Tripoli and had to run back for them.) They were finally bound for home. They landed in the green fields of Somerset, and Fred delighted in the green. It was so beautiful.

His leave was sheer delight. With his family, he went from Liverpool to some friends at Penmaenmawr, Conwy, on the North Wales coast. There, his younger brother, George, flew overhead, trying to make recognisable signals. George was an instructor by then and shortly afterwards transferred to the Fleet Air Arm.

Fred went to Bletchley of his own accord and told them that his work had dried up. He could no longer hear the communications – his job was running away with the retreating Japanese. Of course,

Fred was trying to get out, but he wasn't lying. He didn't want to –
couldn't bear the thought – of going back. Fred's aim was to
return to Germany with the occupying army. He had lived there,
knew the people, spoke the language fluently. He was encouraged
by someone saying Fred was just the type they needed out there.
Karl (who now went by the name Charles Lacey, because of anti-
German post-war sentiment) and his brother had by now joined
the British army and were getting ready for their return with the
victors via Dovercourt, the refugee camp of seven years
previously. And Fred thought he might see Götz and Wolf again –
if, if, if they had survived – and show them that he fraternised, if
no one else did. He was, in their hearts, their older brother. Of
course, he still heard nothing of them. Were they dead or alive?

And then – nothing. If Fred was pulling any strings, they'd
broken. He left it at that. He was given a second month's leave,
because they lacked planes to take the men back. Well, that surely
meant he was out of India for good. For the first (and last) time in
his life he had won a prize in a lottery. But then the month
expired. He was recalled for service and, along with some
colleagues, was suddenly herded into a transit camp in some
houses in St John's Wood, London.

While he was there, the Atom bomb fell. Fred was badly shaken
by the first news of it. For years before the war, pacifists had
painted the horrors of any future conflict, and he had felt that they
were exaggerating. But his dreams and illusions turned to dust. He
had dreamed that Dresden would be spared, had dreamed that
mankind would be spared that ultimate horror – for, had not the
wise, atom-splitting scientists themselves declared their discoveries
could never have any military use? In six short months he twice
drained the bitter cup to the dregs. It would not pass from him.

However, there was, for the men in that camp, a silver lining to
the cloud closing in on all mankind. At least the authorities could
not send them back to India now. Their jobs were gone, the
Japanese had surrendered, both repatriations and de-mob would
be sped up. They would be out, in two or three months, they
reckoned.

But they all underestimated Them. As if galvanised into action, as if that bomb had been the long-awaited signal, they were all bundled into a train, bound for a secret destination, which proved to be all too familiar. It was his hometown, Liverpool. Morosely Fred and his companions looked down from their moored liner as the citizens of Liverpool celebrated VJ day all around them in assorted ferry-boats. Fred turned his gaze towards the city itself. He could almost see Mossley Hill from there. He was being sent back to India, yet he was so near to home. It seemed impossibly cruel.

Though he would remember little of the voyage, he found himself back in Bombay, and joined the queue to find out where he would be billeted. The chap just before Fred had left some stuff in Karachi and had hoped to return by the same route and recover it. That was naive of him. His destination now was Rangoon, Burma. He vainly protested. Fred was next. Well, he knew that large unit which had grown so much over the years on the hilltop outside Delhi, could not possibly have been moved to Rangoon. There would be no point. He had quite a lot of books there, accumulated over three years. Fred gave the number of the unit.

'Rangoon,' said the transport officer.

Fred stared. 'That's impossible,' he stammered.

'No son, you gave me that number, and the number of the unit is based in Rangoon. You're going to Rangoon via Calcutta.'

Fred tried to argue, to explain his position, 'No, please, my unit was based in Delhi – that's where all my colleagues have been based for years. I need to go back there. I think there's been a mistake. Could I travel to Calcutta via Delhi first?'

'I'm afraid not, son,' he said cheerfully. 'Look, I can't bloody redraw the map of India for your benefit. You've been lucky on the swing, getting home leave, but now you're losing on the roundabout. That's life. Sorry, son. Nothing I can do.'

Speechless, Fred stared at the man and turned away. He couldn't believe it. He felt he should appeal, should fight, but all fight had left him. He walked away numbly. Looking back, he felt he should probably have insisted on getting in touch with Delhi. Moreover, he shouldn't be in India at all: he should have made sure of a job in Germany, instead of trusting in their smooth, meaningless, non-committal chat. Miserably, passively, Fred had let it all happen. Meaning was ebbing away. He was a cog in a maniacal machine, utterly out of any human control. He felt he did not exist any more. They had shoved him around so much before. It didn't matter. Soon, soon, it must end. Sanity would return.

Fred found the Grand Hotel at Calcutta full of officers milling aimlessly around, waiting for non-existent transport to Rangoon, Singapore, God knows where else. Later he would ask himself why didn't he argue more forcibly to go back to Barrackpore where there would still be chaps that knew him? His head, as well as his heart, had finally succumbed to dreary listlessness. He was a pawn, puppet, pushed around as They, high above, decreed.

It was hot, the fans weren't working properly. Everyone was irritable, but none so much as a Colonel at Fred's table, who bawled the bearer out for everything - rancid butter, insipid curry. Fred found him unbearable – his countrymen in India sometimes made him sick with shame. He remembered a major coming up to him in a mass of jostling Indians and telling him you had to yell at the buggers or they'd happily ignore you.

Once, at Howrah Station, a high-pitched Indian wrangle broke out between a porter Fred had engaged and the chap in the luggage office. Suddenly Fred's quite expensive large thermos was between their grabbing hands, smashed to smithereens. A little bit wearily, a little mechanically, he'd shrugged his shoulders and smiled. The men stared incredulously at the silent unmoved sahib. A pleasant Englishman just behind Fred said, 'You took that very well. I don't think I could have. Perhaps it pays in the end to be more tolerant and decent than they deserve. They get shouted at enough, poor bastards.'

They did indeed, Fred, thought. We all deserve to be treated with some humanity. The crestfallen cringing bearer approached Fred, pushed a napkin onto his bare knees and seemed to seek some better response than the Colonel had given him. Poor bastard, Fred thought, and smiled - his old mechanical smile, meant to cheer himself up, as well as others. There was nothing conspiratorial about it, no furtive wink at the Colonel's expense. Nothing.

Fred went to his room which he shared with an Australian major whom he had not yet met. Fred wondered where he was — and thought the man might still be at lunch. The mosquito net was up. Fred left it so. Fred always found siestas unsatisfactory. One never slept, but he was exhausted, and beyond hot. So, he lay there, just in his underwear wondering whether the fan above his head would start up again.

Suddenly, with the slightest of knocks, the bearer appeared, with some bills in his hand, muttering something about the major sahib's wine bill. Fred hadn't understood. He indicated that the major, quite obviously, was not there. The bearer grinned and called the absent major a 'strong man'. He closed the door and approached the bed. Fred couldn't believe the man's impudence — he stared, startled, stung, incredulous. What was being hinted at? That they... that he...?

'Major sahib's not here. Come back later.' The bearer leaned over, smiling, and brazenly felt the texture of Fred's pants.

He said something like, 'First class cotton, sahib.' Fred felt frozen in the most grotesque of nightmares and he wondered how to escape. What should he do? Shout? Beat him off? He was much bigger than Fred and was gently pulling Fred's pants down. Fred did the most foolish, weak, thing possible. He fainted. Next thing he knew, the major was there, telling the bearer to bugger off, as the bearer was furtively buttoning himself up, and Fred was saying he was all right really — it was just the heat.

Somehow Fred recovered his poise, claiming nothing worse had happened with that filthy, immoral beast. But, of course, the old question, with new anguish, gnawed at him. Why was he picked on? Did smiles between Raj and Ruled betoken only one thing? Or had the man seen something else, something Fred dare not admit to?

Later, Fred made his way dazedly down to the hotel restaurant. There he met two young officers from Delhi, whom he recognised. They asked what Fred was doing there. He had been officially posted absent without leave in Delhi. Everyone was asking where he had vanished to. Fred explained the conversation he'd had with the officer in Bombay, and the men solved the Rangoon riddle for him. A small detachment had been given the old number of his unit (the number he had always known), but it had been assigned to Rangoon. Fred's unit now had a new number.

It dawned on him with a sickening realisation: his experience at the Grand Hotel could so easily not have happened. He daren't allow himself to dwell on this: the waves of nausea brought on by this encounter already threatened to swamp him; if he mulled too much on the cruelty of coincidence, he would surely drown. It was too much to bear.

So, at last, he went back to Barrackpore. He could so easily have done that before. From there he got in touch with Delhi. The lost sheep had been found, and there could be appropriate rejoicing at his pointless homecoming.

One of the tasks Fred was given – he suspected that this was mainly to fill his time – was to run 'Education for the Forces in India'. The Wing Commander, for whom the war was just a part – quite an enjoyable part – of his career, for whom the whole thing was therefore real, took all this education of the forces seriously. Fred noticed that they certainly had a wealth of talent. The word 'intelligence' was not without point, except that Fred felt there was no point in having intelligence when you were not allowed to use it. The talent, unfortunately, kept disappearing. It was damned difficult to put on a good show when, every day, one of the cast was missing. He was the producer of the circus. He sat in an almost empty office, waiting for the day's casualties. 'Please, sir, what about the Russian class?' he was asked as a typical request. 'Sorry, Sergeant Rossinsky's gone – repatriations.' He'd heard academics moaning that timetabling could be a tricky business, but had they ever tried it with lecturer after lecturer resigning, and a mob of conscripted, unwilling, impatient students having to be kept hard at it – at what? For God's sake? All day?

Fred reckoned his students had legitimate grievances, like the chap who'd had lessons in elementary Italian objecting to being switched to accountancy. It was a reasonable objection; after all, the subjects were nothing like each other. He had to shrug his shoulders, make gestures of resigned impotence.

He was asked to do a talk, to provide some sort of education and entertainment, on current affairs. The problem was, he did not know, did not care, what was going on in the world. So, he put on his single, cracked dusty record – Dresden, Germany, those boys – all in the same bloody, unbelievable boat. He had talked about it for years, bored himself and everyone else about the hopeless, helpless dilemma of lads of their own age on the other side of the great divide between good and evil. It would have to do. He was so tired. He knew it by heart. He didn't need to think. It would all come out automatically. And suddenly he felt a faint, forlorn quiver of pride, the mock heroics of the tragic actor. 'If it's the last thing I do–'. It might well be the last. So out it came. God knows what they made of it. 'I'm sorry, lads, if I was bloody boring. I wasn't feeling very fit. I had maggots in my brain, and the truth you got was maggot soup, made in Germany.'

Despite everything, so far, Fred was managing to hold everything together, to suppress that nausea that ate away at him, but he could do so no longer. Suddenly something snapped and things really began to unravel in his mind. He became obsessed with the idea that he was fatally ill, gripped by some foul disease. Whatever that horrible encounter in Calcutta had done to him, it had certainly done *that*. He was dying, dying, dying – and, as always, Fred could not tell anyone or turn anywhere for help. Never, never should anyone know his shame. It ate into his brain of course. So, Fred could not tell whether he imagined, simulated, or simply had, definite physical symptoms. He was convinced his nails and hair stopped growing – surely that was an observable fact.

Yet his imagination had already played a pretty sad psychosomatic trick in Durghpur. They had been playing some ball game, the ball had gone into some undergrowth. He had tried to retrieve it, felt a sudden sting – a thorn perhaps, but he thought, naturally, that it was a snake bite, and in a few minutes, he had cramp in his arm, it was going numb. Burton, the young first aid officer, couldn't cope, of course. Fred was whisked in a jeep to Camilla. Somehow, they reassured him that nothing whatsoever had happened. Even though they doubted his sanity, everyone treated him in a friendly way – perhaps they felt that his head and heart had always been in the right place – he was intelligent, considerate, and conscientious – and perhaps there was this feeling of being in the same crazy boat where anyone might suddenly go a bit bonkers.

Fred had visited various chaps in hospital, fellow officers and clerks working under him – with various conditions – dysentery, malaria, polio, boils, DTs, nervous breakdown. Fred did what he could for his clerks. One of them, Sergeant Taylor, had come to Fred with a worry about his mate, who had been an accountant in Civvy Street. He was ill in hospital, but no one was allowed to visit him. They had brusquely brushed off Sergeant Taylor's request for information. Fred should, of course, have guessed at once, that he had VD, but he promised, to go to the hospital and sort things out. He suspected Taylor had been a little tactless and – he could be.

The Scots medical orderly was at first taciturn, almost rude. 'I'm his officer,' Fred said, beginning at last to have an inkling. 'You can trust me.' They looked at each other.

'Well, sir, he begged me not to tell –.'

'You've told me.' The orderly sighed, conceding the point. 'I'll see him,' Fred said. 'Where is the hospital?'

He would never forget that trip across the Hooghly – India at its woeful worst. Glare and gloom mingled in the monsoon air. The small boat was ragged and wretched. So were the old man and the boy. The boy stood by the mast, thin and ugly. A rag of a loincloth flapped on and off his lank buttocks. The earth on the other side was arid, red, dusty. Urchins ran out of wretched hovels and offered the sahib themselves or their sisters, according to his taste. (He had no taste, no taste at all. He felt, in fact, sick.)

Fred came at last to that specialist hospital, an old fort as far as he could judge. There was a stifling, airless, abject sort of central hall, where visitors were asked to wait. The flies buzzed. The fan revolved languidly as the patients padded up-and-down in slippers. Fred had some chocolate and a couple of books from his own slender store, reasonable reading for a man of his education.

The patient seemed half glad, half distressed to see Fred. 'Thanks for coming,' he said, 'It was good of you to come. But do you know what this place is, sir?' Fred nodded, a little surprised. 'It's all a horrible mistake,' he continued, 'you must believe that, sir. I don't belong here.'

Fred felt sicker than ever. Could they not trust each other? Was truth utterly out of the question? Was he, even he, to play the grand English game of gross hypocrisy, to connive, be an accomplice to it all? But then– he was. He had been for years.

The next morning Fred met Sergeant Taylor and had his little lie ready. 'Your mate has picked up some peculiar bug. They've isolated him, kept him under observation, but he'll be back soon.'

'Can I visit him?' Taylor asked.

'No, I'm afraid not. He's quarantined.'

Fred had visited them all. But no one would visit him. Dying, dying, dying, and no one would ever know what had happened. He'd walk out one day, disappear from Delhi once more, end up in some dry ditch in the arid, alien land.

The lack of work could have killed him. He'd been barred from Germany - had MI5 got him on their list as pro-Nazi, he now wondered? Banished for a second time to India, assaulted by an Indian bearer; it was all getting too much for him.

Fred was having pain in his bowels now. He had gone to the Medical Officer and asked him to examine him, all over, very carefully, though his symptoms did seem to sound very vague and silly. The M.O. gave him some sleeping tablets. He had already had a nervous breakdown himself. Nervous breakdowns were not uncommon in India with young, inexperienced doctors trying to cope with tropical diseases.

One day in Calcutta Fred had met Eddie Owen, a boy from his village who had gone into medicine. Fred found him wonderfully cheerful that day – Eddie said he was lucky really; Fred's life, his career was being interrupted, while he was carrying on with his, enlarging his experience, meeting new and interesting diseases. He was stationed at Chittagong – Cox's Bazar or somewhere like that. Three months later Fred's mother sent him a cutting from the *Liverpool Echo* about his death in Burma. Fred didn't think this was impossible, though it struck him as odd, because when they talked, Eddie didn't seem to be expecting to go into Burma. A bit later, on leave in the monsoon in Shillong, he found himself being driven up that winding mountain road by a man from Eddie's unit. Fred asked him about Eddie and was told they had never been in Burma. Perplexed, Fred asked the man about his death. The driver went strangely taciturn. Later Fred met an officer from the unit and found out that Eddie had shot himself, very suddenly. There were vague ideas that it might be some new form of malaria which attacked the brain. Had Eddie met one more new and interesting disease, he mused.

Fred was shocked by news of the circumstances surrounding Eddie's death, but it was only a brief interlude from his obsession about his own health. He knew he was sick; he knew he was dying. He went to an Indian doctor in Delhi who listened carefully, looked at Fred's nails and hair, and diagnosed his complaint, which was not unknown in India, especially among Europeans who were unused to the country and climate. The doctor gave Fred some white tablets, which he found later were a sedative that had been much in vogue at the turn of the century. The pain didn't, wouldn't, go away. His appeals for help were falling on deaf ears. Would no one treat him? Could no one see that he was dying? Would anyone take him seriously before it was too late?

CHAPTER NINE
1946: Dumfries – Hospital confinement

At last, two or three months after his arrival in Delhi, Fred was back in Bombay, bound for demobilisation. He spent Christmas 1945 there, although he was not in the mood for celebrating. On the journey home, Fred felt like he was unravelling, but he didn't think his companion, a fellow officer from Delhi, or the missionaries with whom they lunched on board their liner noticed anything amiss. However, one of the three other officers sharing Fred's room had his suspicions. He asked Fred if he had been invalided out, explaining he'd moaned and talked in his sleep, and said some rum things.

On the ship, Fred sought help from the Medical Officer who told him impatiently there was nothing the matter and to stop wasting his time. He had enough to do with 'genuine' patients.

Fred reached London. The last lap. He would be home in Liverpool, but he dreaded meeting the family. At first, he had written regularly – all three of the brothers wrote to their mother, from Scotland, America (where Fred's younger brother, George, trained as a pilot), Africa and India. She was the family clearing house of news. Then silence had descended. Fred had ceased to write, and his mother had rightly seen something sinister in this. The family had tried to find out from the Air Ministry where he was. He was, apparently, back with his old unit, but all they got from there was silence.

A transport officer found Fred a night's lodging in London. The last lap. Obsessing about his 'disease', Fred went, without an appointment, to an eminent doctor in Harley Street. Surely, *he* would see it. It was frustrating – they didn't seem to understand each other. Fred returned to his digs.

He woke in the night with a sharp stabbing belly pain and insisted on phoning the eminent doctor. The landlady, very alarmed, called an ambulance. The response was swift. An army ambulance, doctor and medical orderly arrived. Fred refused to speak to anyone but the doctor. The orderly withdrew. Fred tried, at long last, to talk about the Grand Hotel in Calcutta. He was heavily doped with the sedative paraldehyde and taken for what seemed like an interminable ride, ending – though he did not know it – in a psychiatric ward in St Albans.

There were three of them in that room, all acting a little oddly in each other's eyes. One, a bomber pilot, crouched like a beast on his bed. Fred watched the medical staff make various attempts to calm him down; in the end (after a couple of days, may be longer, he wasn't sure) they sent the pilot to sleep, just waking him up at feeding time. Fred's brother, George, had at last – after weeks of fruitless enquiries – tracked him down and came over from Cambridge to see him but, to George's distress, Fred covered his head in his blanket and refused to talk to him or anyone.

A naval officer in the next bed reproached Fred after that futile visit. 'A damned bad show,' he said, 'after your brother had come all that bloody way.'

'Shut up,' Fred said listlessly.

They gave Fred an enema when he said his bowels had ceased to function, convinced his whole abdomen was paralysed. He kept demanding a thorough physical examination before it was too late. They sedated him. Looking back on this, he wondered whether a really good bit of acting from them might have reassured him, a convincing pretence of a physical examination. In all probability, he was beyond reassurance.

Fred lost count of how long he had been in the hospital ward in St Albans, but he eventually found himself on a train with an escort, like a prisoner. The sergeant was thoroughly unpleasant to him, and he wondered in his panic, in his confusion, if the sergeant knew what he had tried to tell the doctor? Was he annoyed at having to make that long journey? Did soft, silly, moaning officers bring out the sadist in him? Fred didn't know, but he had to suffer.

The journey ended at a forbidding institution in Dumfries, which, Fred in his dazed state, still recalled was the hometown of Burns. Ah, Burns, he thought, Burns, who after his wandering, wayward sex life, decided that 'the true pathos and sublime of human life' was 'weans and wife'. How right you were, Rabbie, how right! Weans and wife, that would save him.

Fred was still convinced he was mortally ill and 'They', in unfathomable cruelty, had deferred and deferred treatment – and now denied it. Fred was dying – he was sure; unless they did something quickly, he would die.

What they did was sedate him again and again. No physical examination was offered. Then, one day, a burly Lancashire medical orderly said, with lovely cheering kindliness, 'Well, sir, now we are going to have that physical examination. You'll feel better after that, won't you?' But it was only an X Ray for TB, a routine matter.

Worse, however, was yet to come. More radical treatment was in store for him. He was led to a chair with curious gadgets attached. He thought it was that long-deferred physical examination and sat there docilely enough. But then – a blinding flash – and he woke hours later, utterly terrified, wondering what the hell happened. Thereafter they had to drag him, struggling, to the 'electric chair' as they all called it, though that nice, kind Lancashire orderly tried to reassure him. Then came insulin, which Fred found a bit humiliating, because he always wet the bed – an embarrassment mitigated by kind, cheerful, matter-of-fact nurses. One patient had been a POW in Singapore: 'Humiliation and torture,' he murmured. 'These chaps could teach the Japs something.'

Then, one morning, Fred found he had shaved half his face with a Gillette razor. This wasn't odd in itself, of course, but he had clearly already done a whole lot of things, like getting dressed, without being able to recall doing them – he'd done all this before the recording tape of his memory was set in motion. He was perplexed. Did he have concussion? How was that even possible? He began to fear that his memory was going entirely, that, somehow, they had blasted great holes in it, and the whole edifice was crumbling.

When Fred saw his doctor some days later (he was a busy man) Fred thought him a bit offhand when he said, 'That must've been the day we gave you your electroconvulsive therapy on the insulin.' It was, at least, an explanation.

Fred was locked in with the other patients in their dormitory. There was a young Etonian from Ireland, with a hole in the head from a tank battle, who had been taught by a friend of Fred's at King's. He seemed sane enough. There was a serious young Scotsman whose movements had slowed down practically to a full stop; he would stand for an hour, apparently doing nothing but carefully folding his tie and putting it in a drawer. There was an air pilot who, by curious coincidence, knew George. He seemed quite sane, except that he believed the police were after him for some unspecified offence and that one of the medical orderlies was a homosexual and was attempting to seduce him. He had been on more missions than the safe average, which Fred suspected was the source of his trouble. Fred and the pilot tried to talk each other into sanity, though they were not supposed to discuss their complaints. There was a chap who had been a POW with the Japs who seemed to be writing furtive notes all the time, as if secretly informing on everyone. Later, during a hockey game, he suddenly stripped and ran stark naked all over the place. And suddenly Fred had the odd thought that it was a relief to be mad; one could do absolutely anything, one had a valid excuse. There was a weird Pole, who accused Fred of having lain on his bed and dirtied it with his boots. There was a middle-aged carpet maker who had a paralysed wife and had kept a mistress for years. He refused the Doctor's encouragement to simply admit he was ashamed of himself. There was a tall black-haired Scotsman who asserted, with a sort of self-assured impudence, that the doctors were all crazy and that they might as well have the snake as their emblem, for they were all devious devils. He said to Fred one day, 'The norm? What the hell is the norm? I bet in Russia they'd make you conform to another norm, and say you were mad if you didn't.' How right he was, Fred thought in a flash of clarity. How wise are those who have opted for madness!

Most of this awareness of the others came late. Fred moaned a lot at the beginning, attention-seeking, wanting that thorough physical check-up, till the matron said he really must stop, he was upsetting the others.

He had regular sessions with a psychiatrist who, one day revealed that based on testimony provided by Fred himself, it was clear he was attracted to his own sex and needed to live with the fact of his homosexuality. Fred had been stunned. 'But I always meant to marry,' he murmured. He explained how a woman had rejected him before the war, and six years in the forces, with three in India, hadn't allowed him to meet any women. He'd had little contact with women in his life. In India, he had come to idealise family and fatherhood, but without the possibility of nearing this goal. Karl's letters had only reinforced this paternal feeling. The psychiatrist looked sceptical. 'You might find marriage a strain.'

Fred looked at him, slightly bewildered. Had the man forgotten for a moment that his experience in India had been such an awful strain on him, and that the near rape had played such a key part in his mind unravelling? The psychiatrist had looked on sceptically. Had he forgotten the bewilderment, fear, and shame? Would marriage match the strain of his life experiences? Fred demanded. No, he refused and denied the psychiatrist's conclusion. Even if he no longer harboured realistic expectations that marital bliss would come his way, he would not accept a diagnosis of homosexuality.

Nevertheless, he improved as time went by. The matron who had remonstrated with him was kind and he believed it was her gender which helped most. The young Irish nurse said that tiresome lad in the corner was really a nice-looking boy, though there seemed to be something badly amiss with him. Then – much later – there was a lady doctor, Hussey. Their conversation was short but very, very helpful to him.

Fred had put it to her, 'As a woman, you must loathe and despise me, and men like me.'

She answered briskly, matter-of-fact but kindly, 'Why should I?' Fred felt a relief he could not understand and tried to explain a bit more. She had no time really, she just patted him on the shoulder reassuringly. That these women could be kind and understanding with the repulsive young male animal he saw himself to be, was deeply healing. They seemed to take him as they found him and the floodgates of his soul were opened when he realised that these women – doctors, nurses, saw him simply as a young man.

After a time, Fred began to gravitate to the view expressed by another patient, 'Act sane. Act sane like mad, and they'll let you out.' Fred 'decided' to give up being physically ill. After all, he reasoned, he ought to be dead by now if all that was true. But it was very bewildering. He could argue to himself that the sanitorium finally had cured him, or perhaps just drove all that firmly lodged nonsense out of his head - somewhat drastically, it must be said. He knew he'd been pretty unmanageable at first, with all his moaning. But in April 1946, after nearly three months in hospital, he was promoted to the upper floor, the convalescents, with a room of his own – how he welcomed that peace, that privacy and with it visits from George and his mother.

As part of his rehabilitation, Fred had to organise talks about patients' jobs in Civvy Street or any other topic. Fred did a talk, unsurprisingly, about German education under the Nazis. At the end a young man came up to him and said he'd found Fred's talk very interesting, since he'd been brought up in Germany. Fred feared criticism of his rash generalisations, but no, he agreed with Fred on the whole. They had quizzes, debates on national character, occupational therapy where Fred made rugs and a cloth rabbit. Fred, with his clumsy fingers, found no comfort in all this reminder of his inadequacy.

Then they let Fred have his typewriter. Fred wrote poems for some sort of magazine they produced. One was about a German boy – Götz, in fact, a memory of him standing one day a little sulkily as his mother fussed about his health. Fred's point was that so many mothers, all over the world, had fussed over their sons in vain. For reasons he still did not understand, they did not print it, though he thought it much the best.

The return of Fred's typewriter also enabled him to fix his gaze beyond his incarceration. He wrote to King's friends, to old friends from Dresden, including his former colleague from the Kreuzschule, Friedrich Jehn, who was still one of the staff there. Although the school building was now in ruins, along with much of Dresden, Jehn had survived the war and, typically open-hearted, was able to give Fred insight into life in post-war Germany:

> We are very worried about the negotiations in Moscow. I would be so glad to talk in person with you about all these <u>burning</u> problems, since I know you too always look at things from an elevated perspective. By letter that is unfortunately not possible.   Anyway, we are all in extreme concern about a <u>division</u> of Germany. You can well imagine what that would mean for <u>us</u> here. So we have not only our everyday worries but also those around what fate has in store.

Fred had been aware of these negotiations. Until now he hadn't had the capacity to care much for the plight of his friends, but now he felt keenly the anxiety and helplessness that Jehn and others must be experiencing.

Fred also wrote to Karl, who with his brother was now in the British Army of the Rhine, in the British Zone of Occupied Germany, interrogating Nazis. Since that note she had sent in 1942, Helene had never been far from Fred's thoughts, so he suggested now Karl was in Germany, couldn't he try to trace his mother? Karl's response came a couple of weeks later:

> Dear Fred,
>   I'm sorry to hear you're ill. …
>   But, about my mother, Fred, it's no good. My brother caught our uncle dying in Zurich just in time to be told that our mother and her

sister were deported to Poland in September 1942 …

Fred wept. Poor, poor Helene, poor Karl and Robert. He began to make sense of the note he'd received so suddenly in 1942. The date determined it – it was a note of farewell and final thanks as the end neared. During the war Fred had heard rumours of the mass-murder of the Jewish people that had been carried out by the Nazis; and he'd been sickened to see the newsreels at the end of the war showing the death camps and the extent of the Genocide that had been wrought on Helene's people. Helene too must have seen that the writing was on the wall and wanted to let Fred know while she still could how much she appreciated all he did to ensure that her sons were spared the same fate. In the midst of his grief Fred marvelled that she in her moment of deepest crisis had taken time to think of him.

Fred also wrote a letter to the Büttner-Wobst family. Ever since the war had broken out seven years beforehand, he had wondered, what had happened to them? Were they still alive? How was Götz? How was Wolf? That dear, dear family. He dreaded and longed for their response. And then, finally, a letter came. It was postmarked 'Dresden'. At last, he would find out the answer to his question. Fred sat down in his room and, with trembling fingers, opened the envelope and began to read.

PART THREE

Rike: The Reality of Death
1939-1946

CHAPTER TEN
The early years

Friederike Luise Büttner-Wobst was twenty in 1946, the youngest of five children. She had been the surprise addition to the family, being the fifth child in what hitherto, with two boys (Götz and Wolf) and two girls (Mädi and Traudi), had been a perfectly balanced family. Rike, then, was, as she was sometimes uncharitably called, the runt of the litter. The family rumour was that Dora, their mother, had had her head turned by a younger colleague of Werner, their doctor father. A fresh passion had ensued between the doctor and his wife, made hotter by jealousy, and Rike was the result. Werner doted on her; far from finding her a burden, he welcomed the new life she brought. New life was incredibly welcome; by now Werner knew he was dying of tuberculosis, the disease in which he was a medical specialist.

Rike as a baby with Dora

Far from being the runt, Rike was a miracle, especially as she nearly didn't survive the first few days of life. She was born with the umbilical cord wrapped around her neck and as a result the uvula, the visible nodule at the back of the throat, was unable to form. A couple of days after she was born doctors realised she couldn't drink – her throat was enlarged and her tongue was narrow and underdeveloped. On sucking, her tongue fell back into her throat and blocked her oesophagus. She would have suffocated if it hadn't been for the quick-thinking doctor who held baby Rike up by her feet and patted her on the back to make her tongue fall back.

Worried that she would starve to death since she'd lost so much weight and warned by the doctor that there was only a slight chance of survival, her parents arranged an emergency baptism for her on 27 February 1926 in the family home when she was less than three weeks old. The short service took place with the priest in the middle and her weeping parents dressed in black.

Desperate, they employed a wet-nurse to spoon expelled milk into her, but she was sacked on the spot when Dora saw her pouring the milk away. Feeding was still only moderately successful, so Werner found a recipe for baby food from the hospital he'd worked in, and that seemed to work. Feeding was still an effort, but Rike had the will to survive. She lived, and thrived.

Rike's parents employed a house-help, who took care of the other children and the household, whilst their mother dedicated herself entirely to little Rike's care. Following two operations during her infancy an artificial uvula was implanted, but her voice remained problematic for quite a while and she spoke as though she had a cleft palate.

Rike was her father's declared favourite. Whenever her brothers and sisters were annoyed with her, they were immediately chastised. 'Leave the child in peace – she's ill!' She was also the only child who was allowed to kiss the back of her father's bald head – a special privilege, since Werner avoided any kind of physical contact with his children; he would do all he could to ensure that they didn't contract his tuberculosis. Rike, meanwhile, embraced life, and was determined to make the most of every moment she was given, no matter what came her way.

Happy family – Top: the five Büttner-Wobst children in the late 1920s (from L to R: Wolf, Mädi, Götz, Rike and Traudi) with their mother, Dora. Bottom: Werner Büttner-Wobst

Superficially, at least, Rike's childhood had been idyllic. She lived a life of privilege, in a substantial house outside the city, served by a cook and a housekeeper, with the only car in the village driven by the chauffeur. Unlike many of her contemporaries whose families had been badly hit by the Great Depression that had wiped out many people's life savings, her father was determined that her future would be as financially secure as possible: while she was still an infant her father took out a life policy for her at the Deutsche Bank, and he built a house in the village for her to move into when she was an adult.

She would never forget the day she was told about her house. She remembered being invited to go for a walk with her father. It had felt particularly special, because being one of five, it was rare for Rike to have Werner all to herself, especially as he worked such long hours during the week – often not getting home until eight or nine in the evening – and was only really free on Sundays, when he was quite frequently out hunting in the afternoon. He would skin and gut what he'd caught, and Dora would gamely cook it. As well as being out working or hunting, Werner also spent quite long periods of time in bed, which Rike had not really understood – she'd wanted to be with her dear Papa, but had been shooed away by her mother, saying that he needed to rest. Sunday mornings, then, were precious – the one time he was there just for the children. Over breakfast he'd test their memory and observation, and talk to them about God and the world. In good weather he'd point out things in the garden.

So, on a cloudless Spring day, one of the first of the season, they went through Langebrück holding hands, Rike skipping and chatting away about everything and nothing. Occasionally they had to stop so that Werner could catch his breath or cough – he often had coughing fits that frightened her. When they arrived at a large pink house, Werner murmured, 'Darling Rike, you see this house?'

'Yes, Papa,' she replied.

'Do you like it?'

'Yes, Papa. Why?'

'Well, it's yours – or it will be when you're older.'

Rike didn't know quite what to say. 'But Papa, I don't want to live there when I'm older. I want to live with you – and mama.' At this, Werner looked sad, old, somehow. Rike would never forget the look on his face that Sunday morning. He knelt down in front of her and took both of her hands, looking into her eyes.

'Mein Liebling,' he said, 'I would love that too. I really would. But, you know, I'm not going to always be around.' He paused. 'I'm poorly.'

'Yes, I know, but you're going to get better?'

'No. I'm very poorly. I have an illness called tuberculosis. That is the reason I cough so much and find it so hard to walk with you. This illness will not go away. There is no cure.'

'But Papa, you treat people with that illness every day. Surely you can – ' she started.

Werner shook his head. 'I'm dying, darling. But not tomorrow. I hope I have a few years ahead of me. I hope I'll be able to see you grow up, but I simply don't know.' He tenderly wiped the tears from her cheek and embraced her. 'You are my little miracle,' he said. 'You've made me feel young again, dear Rike.' Rike had nuzzled herself into his chest and swore she'd heard his quiet sobs.

The house built for Rike.

That day was the day she had to grow up a little. Until then she had never really understood the life-threatening nature of his illness, whereas it had been a daily reality for the rest of the family for many years. Dora, her mother, had been fully occupied looking after Werner, who had a severe bleed soon after Rike's birth. Defying medical advice to rest, Werner had worked so hard trying to provide for the family in these difficult times. When he collapsed in 1927 the family feared the worst but, by some miracle, he recovered. However, word spread around the village that he was suffering from tuberculosis, a feared disease. A local in the train once said to the children, 'This carriage is infected with TB – we're not staying here!' But the hard times did bring the family together. His hard work had meant that he could employ an assistant doctor, afford a car, and have time to rest at home. But the cloud of illness was always there.

Yes, to the outsider, Rike had the ideal life, but she would have swapped all that privilege for having a healthy father. She would never forget the day during Easter 1938, when she was 12, that he came down to breakfast and said, 'I had an X-ray taken yesterday – I've probably got another two years to live.' He was both angry and sad – the news was a shock, no-one had really believed it.

Left - Rike as a young girl with her siblings; Right – in Venice with some family friends in 1939.

Life outside the Büttner-Wobst home was also overshadowing family life. Her parents had done all they could to shield Rike from the maelstrom of politics that was sweeping the entire country, but they didn't, couldn't, entirely succeed. She overheard the arguments in the house on 30 May 1934 when her elder sister Traudi had insisted on joining the crowd when the Führer was in Dresden to open the Reich Theatre Festival Week. Her father had tried to stop her from attending. 'The Bohemian Corporal is a dangerous moron!' he had shouted, 'I don't want you to listen to his rubbish.' Traudi had then silenced him by saying that her teachers wouldn't be impressed to hear him speaking that way about their great leader. Rike remembered how Wolf and Götz had said how exciting the city had looked that day bedecked with the swastika flags and banners.

The next morning over breakfast Traudi, flushed with excitement, commented on how especially beautiful the city's buildings looked that night as they had been lit up for the first time. Hitler had, she told the family, declared that, "Dresden is a pearl, and National Socialism will give it a new setting." 'He will make our city great again,' Traudi had insisted. Her father had made as if to speak, but got up from the table and went into his study, asking not to be disturbed. Dora, their mother, looked helplessly on, and quickly changed the subject.

Rike herself remembered being quite excited in those early days. She remembered reciting every day the same special prayer in class before starting school, 'And bless the deed that has liberated our homeland. For our glorious Führer we thank You. Bless him and the Fatherland forever and ever. Amen.' She joined in enthusiastically enough, but over time became increasingly aware of the cloud that hovered over their house.

She heard stories of violence. She remembered once sitting on the stairs overhearing a family friend from Munich expressing his concerns about what was going on at Dachau, and those awful times when they were made to listen to *his* ranting and shouting over the wireless, watching her father pacing up and down, shaking his head. He would have liked to switch it off, of course, but he didn't dare anymore, not since that time, in the early days of the Third Reich, when her mother had incurred the wrath of their maid, when she had swept into the kitchen and bid her switch that rubbish off – that rubbish being their Führer, no less! The maid, a fanatical Nazi, had denounced her and shortly afterwards they received a visit from a man in uniform who had encouraged her as a responsible citizen to show more loyalty to their great leader. Since that visit, Dora, at least, had been much more careful about what she said.

Then there had been that time when her parents had been really afraid – the only time they'd ever displayed true fear. Two men carrying guns, in black with SS badges on their uniforms, had appeared at the door, asking for Götz, then only thirteen or fourteen. Despite Dora's frantic protestations and pleading, Götz was taken away. He still hadn't returned when Rike was ushered to bed. She remembered being very relieved to see him the next morning, although he was very quiet and pale and after that moment seemed very reluctant to join in with the family's criticism of the regime. In fact, he did his best to fall in line and be a good little Nazi. Although she never found out the exact details, Rike later learned that Götz had been taken away that evening because of his association with another boy whose unorthodoxy had landed him in a concentration camp for a time. Götz had been taken to the Gestapo headquarters in Dresden and shown a thing or two which might make rebellious boys think twice. The lesson did its job; afterwards Götz wasn't quite the same boy she remembered.

Despite the shadow cast over her and the family by Werner's illness and the Nazi regime, Rike was almost determinedly happy. At school her teachers often commented on how cheerful and eager to learn she was, although she was chastised for being too chatty and occasionally absentminded – a trait that she shared with Wolf and Götz. Despite – or perhaps because of – the precariousness of her first few weeks of life and also the death sentence that hung over her father, she didn't take herself or life itself too seriously. She loved to laugh. She loved to run and play. The Dresdner Heide was her playground, and she felt so liberated when she was deemed old enough to go out on her own to explore the forest. It was even better when she could persuade her older siblings to play with her and she was grateful that Wolf, who shared her sense of humour and appetite for mischief, would join her in playing games of chase or hide and seek.

Of course, she missed Götz when he went away to join the Labour Service in April 1938. He wrote many letters home and Rike enjoyed gathering round with the rest of the family as Dora read out his updates. Clearly Götz was adapting well to life away and enjoying the challenge of the new routine. Then, he was called up into the infantry in November that year, although he expressed his hope to re-apply for training as a medical officer, following in their father and grandfather's footsteps. Rike was slightly jealous of Götz's life – it seemed so exciting – he was able to see the world – and he was posted to Prague, after Czechoslovakia was incorporated into the Greater German Reich in March 1939. From there he wrote letters and cards telling of tourist explorations, theatre visits and contacts with the Czech population. It was such an adventure! What fun her big brother was having!

*   *   *

Of course, war had changed all that. War had changed almost everything. Now it was 1946, she was an adult and those pre-war days seemed far, far away. She was sitting alone in her room at home, where she now spent much of her time. She was trying to read, but found herself re-reading the same sentence time and again without taking any of it in. She had read this same book – and all the others – countless times, anyway. Oh, how she longed to be able to read something new.

   Her reverie was broken by the clatter of the letterbox. Grateful for the excuse to leave her room, she skipped down the stairs, went to the front door and saw one solitary letter on the mat. When she picked it up, she was surprised to see it was postmarked Scotland. She racked her brains, tried to work out who could possibly be writing. Surely, she didn't know anyone from Scotland? The letter was addressed to Götz Büttner-Wobst. They rarely received mail anymore, let alone mail from somewhere as exotic as Scotland. Intrigued, she walked through to the living room where

Mädi was playing with her daughter Christina. 'Mädi, we've received a letter from Scotland for Götz. What shall we do?'

'Scotland? We don't know anyone from there, do we? Who's it from?' Mädi asked.

'I don't know. Shall I open it?'

'Yes, go on, read it to me.' So Rike sat down, opened the envelope, and began to read.

She saw that the letter came from Fred Clayton. The name sounded familiar, but she couldn't place it at first. Then she remembered. He was the English teacher who had stayed in Dresden for a year in 1936. (This, she remembered with a start, was nearly a decade ago. It seemed like those days were part of a different lifetime.) Fred had taught her older brothers and become friendly with Wolf in particular. He had visited the family home a number of times and she recalled him sitting on the sofa next to Papa with a massive scarf round his neck. She'd been overawed by the presence of 'Mr Teacher', even though he was young and friendly and even made an effort to talk to her, asking her once about the storybook she was reading. A foreigner – an Englishman – in the house was at once something exciting and possibly dangerous. Should she mention it at school, or had she better hold her tongue?

She was surprised when his social visits to their home suddenly ceased, although she heard her mother mutter something about it being inappropriate to make these kinds of uninvited visits to the boys' home. Apparently Rike's Aunt and Uncle had tried to warn them away from Mr Clayton, saying he was dangerous, and Dora had acted in the best interests of her family.

Rike's Papa hadn't seen any menace in Mr Clayton; in fact, he liked him – he encouraged the young teacher's frequent visits to Blumenstraße, and he never discouraged the correspondence that sprang up between Wolf and Mr Clayton after the Englishman's return to England. This continued regularly and was only stopped by the outbreak of war between their nations. That friends were forced to be enemies had, she knew, been a great source of pain to Wolf and their father in particular. Wolf had spoken so warmly, and with some pride, of his holiday with Mr Clayton's family on the Isle of Man the year before the war broke out – how he'd been described by Mr Clayton's mother as a wonderful ambassador for the German people. Her father had said in response that Mr Clayton was a good ambassador for the English, and he looked forward to welcoming him back to Dresden for a summer holiday in 1939 to return the favour for the hospitality he and his family had shown Wolf. She remembered Wolf's disappointment when Mr Clayton had written to say that he wouldn't be able to visit them after all. Fred had expressed his hope that they would remain friends even if their countries were at war and now, seven years on, he was clearly hoping to rekindle that friendship.

> Dear Götz,
>
> I know it has been a long time since I last wrote to you. Over the past seven years since war broke out, I have thought of you and your family often. I deeply regret the enmity that sprang up between our nations. I have never thought of you all without a deep sense of love and friendship. I was always very grateful for the kindness you all showed me during my time in Dresden, which seems such a long time ago now.
>
> I am writing simply to ask how you have fared in these difficult times? I spent most of the war years in India as part of the Allied forces fighting against the Japanese. These were difficult times, but I'm sure that is no different from many other people.
>
> I was horrified when I heard about the bombing of Dresden and thought about you all and your wellbeing. Please write whenever you can; I am anxious to know how you all are.
>
> With kindest greetings
> Fred Clayton

'That's a very kind letter, isn't it? It's good of him to be so concerned about us after all this time,' Rike said, 'I think we should write back to him.'

'Yes, you're right,' Mädi agreed, 'Of course you should write, tell him everything.'

Rike began to write her response that evening. Where to begin? So much had happened since those pre-war days of peace; there was so much to tell...

Dear Mr Clayton

Thank you so much for your letter. It was such a lovely surprise to hear from you; you were always such a valued friend to our family. Wolf in particular saw you as the greatest of friends.

So much has happened in the time since you last heard from us. It has been a very difficult and sad time for our family. I will do my best to fill you in as much as I can.

Firstly, I need to tell you about Götz. As you know he was part of the German army, serving as a Flag Officer in the 3rd battalion of the 102nd Infantry Regiment. He had been promoted to the rank of 2nd Lieutenant. He marched with the German army into Poland in the first days of the war. ...

* * *

Götz had received a hero's welcome when he visited for a short home leave in the days before the war began. It'd been so lovely to see her brother, even for such a short time. He'd looked splendid in his uniform and had been in good spirits, making jokes. He'd been so proud of his promotion in the army. She'd felt proud of him too when she learned he was marching off to war, part of the Führer's army of conquering heroes who would liberate Poland from oppression.

Götz in his Labour Service uniform, 1938.

It was very exciting to receive post from him from the front.
On 21 September he had written:

> Dear parents, The war now seems to be over. We're marching
> towards Warsaw, there'll be a final parade there. Really quickly I must
> thank you for the many lovely parcels that have arrived here.
> Stohberg and Uncle Schade have written to me. Many thanks too for
> the pipe. Afraid I don't have time to smoke it now. Excuse my
> writing, I'm writing in the dark in the barn by the light of a torch.
> But it's lovely to be able to sleep in a barn. Send me dried bananas,
> figs or fruit or trail mix, something like that. But enough now, more
> tomorrow, if possible. Warm wishes, filius.

She'd felt a swell of pride that her big brother would be part of a
victory parade in Warsaw. She wished she could be part of the
crowd to cheer him on. A few days later the family received
another letter, one addressed to her father. Rike had been the one
who picked up the envelope. The children often raced to the front
of the house as soon as they heard the sound of the post arriving.
Rike got there first and flicked through the letters as she walked
back to the drawing room. 'They're all for you, Papa,' she said.
'They're always for you. I never get any letters.'

'You should write some more then!' chided Wolf.

'Anyway, who'd want to write to you?' chipped in Mädi.

Ignoring his children, Werner asked, 'Anything interesting?'

'No, apart from there's one from Warsaw,' she replied.

'Another letter from Warsaw? That's strange. We only got one
from Götz yesterday.'

'Well,' said Mama, 'Maybe he had time to write another letter.
His postcard was very short after all.'

'But Mama, it doesn't look like Götz's handwriting,' said Rike,
'Look – '

Mama and Papa both went very pale. Papa said very quietly,
'Could I have a look, please, darling?' He took the envelope and
opened it. Rike noticed that his hand was shaking. It seemed to
take him hours to read the letter. When he finished, he wordlessly
folded up the paper and handed it to Mama, got up and went into
the garden. She unfolded it and put her hand to her mouth.

'Oh no,' she moaned. 'No, no, no!'

'What's wrong, Mama?' asked Wolf.

'It's Götz, he – he – '

'Is he hurt?' asked Rike.

'Can I have a look, Mama?' asked Mädi.

'What's happening?' asked Rike, 'what's wrong? Could you read the letter, please Mädi?'

Mädi did so, her voice trembling as she read.

Dear Mr Doctor!

Your dear son Götz fell yesterday, 21 September 1939, in the field of honour in an offensive near Warsaw. We buried him today on the battlefield together with eighteen other comrades under military honours and with the prayers and blessings of the division priest.

Dear Mr Doctor, I probably needn't assure you how painful to me the death of your brave, noble son is. His loss has greatly affected me. In genuine, sincere grief I want to express my deeply heartfelt condolences to you and your dear wife.

Your dear son Götz had blossomed so splendidly in the months of his period of service, and I took great pleasure in his development; he was becoming such a fine officer. In his time in service, he always gave of his best and his attitude was always positive. He was a brave and useful soldier and a true man. In the last assault he fought bravely against the enemy. It was whilst attempting this assault he was killed instantly with a shot to the head. He did not suffer for a moment, showing himself truly worthy of his calling as a soldier.

May you, in this time of trial, take comfort from these words. You can be proud of your son, who in the noble performance of his duty, gave his life for Germany.

With deepest sympathy,
Your constantly devoted
Hans Hammer
Lieutenant Colonel

The following days seemed to blur into each other. The family received condolence letters from many people as well as visits from well-meaning neighbours who expressed their sympathy by giving gifts like fish, chicken, duck, and butter. Rike remembered little of the memorial service in Langebrück church, except that many candles burned for him. They couldn't believe it; it was a horrible mistake, they'd surely wake up soon from this nightmare. It didn't seem possible that the good, fresh, blossoming, Götz, so full of life, had to die.

The announcement of Götz's death in Dresdner Nachrichten *on 1 October 1939*

They tried to get on with normal life, but life would never feel normal again, and there was barely a day that they could escape their grief. Daily reports from the war came over the wireless and in the newspapers; Werner, whose habit was to read the *Dresdner Anzeiger* newspaper in his favourite chair while smoking his pipe, normally skipped over any articles that mentioned the war, but on 18 October, he found himself drawn to a headline that crowed "Saxons annihilate Polish snipers" and he spotted the date, 21 September – the day that would forever be etched into his memory; the day his son died.

He knew that reading it wouldn't do any good, but he couldn't help himself, he had to know more about this fateful day. It seemed that everything began smoothly, all according to the plan of the efficient German military machine. 'It already looked as though it was all over and won. The terrain before us was wide and open. It was speedily crossed,' he read, and he pictured his firstborn son full of the excitement of battle and exhilaration of certain impending victory, rushing on with his comrades imagining all being swept before them. They must have felt invincible. Not for long. He read on ...

> But hardly had the battalions entered the forest – some of them had already reached the road from Modlin to Warsaw – when at the town of Młociny the 1st Battalion came under murderous gunfire from houses, manholes and trees. They seemed to be snipers, Polish elite troops, who defended the terrain doggedly. Their camouflage was excellent and they showered the advancing infantry with dum-dum-bullets and shells.
>
> The attack faltered. The riflemen dug in. Immediately, the Polish started a counter offensive. But the Saxons didn't give ground. They kept the terrain they won, even though many a comrade dropped out.

He couldn't read any more. He felt sick. Tears blinded his eyes, so he wouldn't have been able to read on, even if he'd wanted to. He imagined his poor Götz being caught in the hail of bullets. Had he known what was coming? Was he the first to fall? Or were his final moments filled with confusion, the horror of watching his comrades falling, maimed and stricken all around him, and terror, that the bullets would get him too? Werner fervently hoped that Götz knew nothing about it: that one moment he was full of confidence, excitement, and the certainty of victory and that these thoughts and feelings were the last he knew. It was all too much. Wordlessly, Werner closed the newspaper, got up and left the house.

Rike and the other children did what they could to look after their parents. Added to their parents' overwhelming grief was a feeling of guilt. They had pushed him and harried him too hard, made him feel that he had been a disappointment, especially compared to clever Mädi. They would never forget his vow to them, '*Ihr werdet euch noch über mich wundern*' – 'I'll surprise you one day.' Was it their fault that he landed up so early in the front-line? Did they drive him away? Did they drive him to his too early death? Should they have left him in his short life to be happier, less under pressure? Werner was a broken man, liable to lapse into fits of weeping at any moment. He wasn't alone. The tears flowed readily in that awful season – and there were more to come.

CHAPTER ELEVEN
Sorrow upon sorrow

On 4 November 1939, a month after Götz's funeral, the family was back in Langebrück church, this time for a wedding. Traudi married Heinz Sandmann, from the chocolate firm in Aachen. It should have been a happy occasion and they did their best under the circumstances, but no one was really in the mood for celebration. After their marriage in the registry office, the family gathered for a church blessing in the afternoon. The wedding party was dressed in black, still in mourning for their lost son and brother. To make matters worse, three days beforehand Werner had suffered a dreadful haemorrhage, which terrified the family. He had been too ill to attend the wedding and had to give the couple his blessing from his sickbed.

Mingled with the children's grief for their brother was a growing concern for the health of both of their parents. Their papa's health never really recovered from the blow of losing his son and he lost interest in life. Rike watched him fade away. She tried to tell him stories, make him laugh as she always used to be able to do, but he was listless, disinterested. Then, Mama fell sick with an apparent lung infection and got increasingly ill. In January 1940 Papa called Mädi to his sickbed, looking again and again at Mama's X-ray, he couldn't tell what the changes meant. Mädi knew all too well. There was a mass on her lungs. It was probably a tumour. She told Traudi but swore her to secrecy. She needed to protect the younger siblings from yet more grief. As for their father, he was already ailing too much. It seemed like only a matter of time.

Papa died of a stroke in the arms of Mama at about 6pm on 28 March 1940. Rike would never forget seeing her father, so still, so pale. She sought to console herself that at least he was at peace now – wasn't that what people said on these occasions? He had been robbed of peace when the Nazis came to power, and had talked a great deal, almost obsessively about their warmongering. Even she, although still so young, had been palpably aware of her father's anxiety when Götz had joined the armed forces, an anxiety which had grown when the army invaded with Götz on the frontline, right in the heat of the battle. He'd muttered that nothing good could come of it. And now he was dead.

As they walked into the church behind their father's coffin, Mama needed to lean on Mädi and Wolf for support. Rike didn't hear a word of the service; she was constantly looking at her mother, deeply worried, thinking she had never seen her look so awful. She looked so pale, so thin, so old. 'Are you ok, Mama?', Rike asked.

'Yes, dear. I'll be just fine. Please don't worry about me.'
And then, on the way to the graveside, Mama collapsed completely. Her legs seemed to give way. Despite her protestations she was brought home before her husband's body had been committed.

Rike stood with the rest of her family in front of the family grave in the graveyard of Langebrück church, reading the inscription on Götz's tombstone – those words from John's Gospel that she'd known so well. 'Greater love hath no man than this, that a man lay down his life for his friends,' and then, under his name, those words, *'Gefallen fürs Vaterland'* – 'Fallen for the Fatherland'. She wondered whether he had really needed to lay down his life for the Fatherland. She certainly hadn't asked him for that sacrifice. And now the war had claimed another victim.

And the war would soon claim another. Mama's health had deteriorated over the first few months of 1940, and the children became terribly worried and felt utterly helpless. Her grief as well as the constant care she had given to Papa clearly had worn her down. Only Mädi and Traudi knew the truth. They silently prayed for some sort of miracle.

Days after the funeral she was taken to Munich, her parents' home, and she was examined by a Dr Bähr. He diagnosed lung cancer. It was a bitter irony that she was the only one of the family who never smoked. She was taken back to Dresden to have radiotherapy treatment, which enabled her to go home where she would spend hours lying on the veranda. Rike watched her mother simply wasting away.

By the summer, Rike's schoolmates were full of excitement as news came from the West of the incredible success of the German army's Blitzkrieg campaign. They had swept all before them and conquered most of Western Europe. The German Reich was bigger than it had ever been in history. Hitler was the nation's hero, the greatest statesman since Bismarck, acclaimed as the 'greatest military commander of all time'. On 9 August, many of her schoolmates joined the throngs of Dresdeners who gathered in the Altmarkt in the blazing sunshine to welcome home their all-conquering heroes, the returning Fourth Saxony-Dresden Infantry Regiment which marched through the streets and formed ranks in that great cobbled square. The newspapers reported that hundreds of thousands of all ages had stood cheering on the pavements. All hoped and believed that the war had been won. Rike stayed away.

As summer moved into autumn, the children watched their mother slowly die. In November she demanded to go back into hospital for further treatment, but on 19 November 1940, the children were called to her bedside. She'd died by the time they got there. The doctor told them she could have suffered for another two years but, in the end, it was heart failure that caused her death. A kind nurse told them that she hadn't suffered any pain at the end, and that in the moments before her death, she had murmured, 'I'm glad I'll be with my boy and my husband.' Both parents had died within just over a year of Götz's untimely death. Sorrow upon sorrow had fallen upon the family.

Family grave in Langebrück churchyard. Photo taken in 2011.

Rike was aged just fourteen and was an orphan. War had robbed her of her brother and both parents in the space of just fourteen devastating months. Rike was now left in Nr. 4 Blumenstraße with Wolf and Mädi. Traudi and Heinz, now parents, had moved into their new house down the road on Jakob-Weinheimer Straße after their wedding the previous year. Wolf was now eighteen. He had always taken life more lightly than his elder brother, but he had to grow up very quickly in that one fateful year for the family. He finished his school career in the early summer of 1940, soon after his father's death and was preparing to leave home to study medicine. Once it became clear that his mother was so ill, he decided to defer his studies for a year. Mädi, meanwhile, as a lecturer in Chemistry in Dresden was the family's main breadwinner and became responsible for this orphaned household.

Rike was restive under her elder sister's rule, and the situation was made worse when she lost an ally; Wolf left home all too soon to study medicine in far-away Marburg. Although he made sure he returned to Langebrück whenever he could, Rike and Mädi were left with each other. In time Wolf had to interrupt his studies to go to war; he was sent to join the German occupying forces in Holland. From there, he wrote as often as possible, and his letters were a source of comfort and reassurance that at least one of her brothers was still alive.

Rike and Mädi were relieved that their brother had been sent West where his role was as an occupier rather than East, where millions of personnel were sent to join in with the invasion of Russia. The small family listened to Goebbels' announcement of the invasion on the radio on 22 June 1941 as he declared, 'At this moment a march is taking place that, for its extent, compares with the greatest the world has ever seen. I have decided today to place the fate and future of the Reich and our people in the hands of our soldiers. May God aid us, especially in this fight!'. Rike felt sick. The invasion, two years previously, had been so costly for her own family, and she thought of the many others who would receive terrible news that summer as their sons were sacrificed for the Fatherland.

The tensions in that desolate household increased further when, shortly after Rike's sixteenth birthday, Mädi married Fritz Scheibitz on Valentine's Day 1942. Scheibitz was a clever chemist from a humble home in the Erzgebirge. He was a fanatical Nazi and tried to make young Rike – and Wolf, when he was at home, more Nazi themselves, though he discovered that they weren't apt pupils. Rike resented Fritz hanging his hat up in the family home, and the newly married couple begrudged the presence of Mädi's little sister who was cramping their style; for Rike the house became less and less of a home. With the arrival of Mädi's children, Wolfgang and Christina, she felt even more of an intruder, although she was grateful for the companionship of Marianne, whom Mädi hired as home help.

To get by, Rike retreated into books, becoming more introverted and only conversed with Fritz on a superficial level. Ultimately, she struggled most from having to watch two people who were so absorbed with each other and their family that they failed to realise that she too was in need of love and understanding. Young men didn't interest her, and there wasn't a single person she could confide in. She knew that their response to her confidences would be pity and she believed any sympathy would have to be rejected if she were to stay strong.

Rike's great desire had been to follow in her father's footsteps and become a doctor; although, like her eldest brother Götz, she wasn't academic. She applied herself as much as she could but simply couldn't get the grades, so she chose agriculture as a second choice. School did, however, give her a life outside the oppression of Nr 4. Blumenstraße, although she looked forward to the day when she could leave home and become more independent.

She left school at Easter 1944 and made her contribution to the war effort, working on a farm in Hochweitzschen as part of the compulsory Labour Service devised by the Nazis to support the war effort. She relished the freedom that this life away from home gave her.

The setting for her labour service was beautiful; Rike fell in love with the hills that surrounded her and found peace and satisfaction in her work; the war felt a long way away. She discovered independence and community. She was making a life for herself and found people who valued her and who didn't tell her she was just a spoilt girl who wouldn't achieve anything. With so much privilege growing up, it may have been tempting for Rike to be snooty, to see herself as above other people, but she had no airs and graces. She hated barriers of class. She had discovered that ordinary people were very often of much more worth than the so-called educated ones, who were perhaps outwardly friendly and polite but the next moment produced a torrent of abuse towards their fellow humans. She preferred honest and simple folk.

Being put in a shared home for young women enabled her to make good friends there. In her room were three other school leavers from Dresden with whom she got on so well that she felt they would be friends for life. They were so cheerful and completely unconstrained with each other, and that provided real relief from the hard daily grind. With these friends Rike formed an 'antifascist' club. The leaders soon looked on them as reactionary, but they felt really good.

In the evening after work, they'd sit down and make plans for the future. They discussed how they could alleviate some of the problems in their community and they managed to raise morale a little in their camp. The other school leavers envied them their friendship. They organised cosy at-home evenings, chatting about anything but politics. When everyone else was asleep, they got up quietly and held banquets under an old knotty oak not far from the camp. Once someone got hold of a bottle of advocaat and another the obligatory cake. They celebrated long into the night. These activities eventually led them to being split up, probably because the camp leaders thought they were too subversive.

She also struck up a particular friendship with the house mother, known as Aunt Dörte, whose appearance had something calming and attractive about it. She chose Rike to be in charge of the house and, having easier access to her than the other girls, Rike gradually became her confidante.

Rike with her friends on her Labour Service

Advent was approaching, which Rike had always felt was the most beautiful time of the year in Germany. She found it mysterious and exciting, bringing strong associations of the wonderful smells of gingerbread. And the Christmas market in Dresden had been magical. She had such wonderful memories of paradise. But those times were gone – there were only cardboard replicas of gingerbread in the shop windows.

One day as she was working in the field, she recalled the last journey with her mother and siblings – when there had still been the five of them – to the Chiemsee in 1938. They'd decided to visit her mother's home in the mountains and rented a cottage with a view over both lake and mountains. They were the most carefree days of her life; each day better than the last. She loved the drama of the boat trips when their mother was terrified that the boat would capsize or that a storm would blow up. Once the family drove to Reichenhall, where Rike's grandfather had once been a senior district judge, and Dora showed them the prison garden where she had often smuggled in beer for the 'poor prisoners'. Highlights of the holiday were the evenings on the terrace when they played music on a wind-up gramophone they'd got hold of in the village. When she recalled playing the record of a really shrill voice bawling out into the evening air: 'The police have the nicest men!' it made her smile. It was better than any variety show!

These recollections provided an escape from what was becoming an increasingly painful present. Her house mother Dörte had suddenly become very ill. Though she was worried about her new friend, Rike was consoled by the fact that Dörte's suffering allowed her to look after her and demonstrate that she cared. When the Christmas holiday approached it was a profound wrench, because it meant she would have to be parted from Aunt Dörte for whom she would have gladly sacrificed her holidays. Dörte was still ill, and the house Christmas celebrations took place without her. Rike knew that she would have to leave her in the house. She stayed for another night with her after all the girls had gone, then she too had to travel, or she wouldn't have been home for Christmas Eve.

Rike usually treasured holidays, but this time she was so worried and couldn't wait for the holiday to be over. She returned a day early to spend a day alone with the person whom she truly loved and with whom she'd really have liked to celebrate Christmas. Seeing Dörte again was a real joy and all the concerns Rike had brought from home were dispelled by Dörte's idealism and her trust in fate – she was serene about her future, whether she would recover or not. Rike relished that day, which belonged to just the two of them. She basked in mutual love and understanding, of which she had been starved at home for so long. Over the following six weeks their friendship deepened, although Rike began to feel that she was perhaps becoming too emotionally involved in this relationship, so she asked to leave the house and lived in another part of the farm. This meant they only saw each other for short periods.

And then war broke in, destroying the bliss that she had enjoyed.

As the war progressed, news came of one after another German cities being devastated by the British bombing campaigns, but Dresden remained untouched and Rike, like many other Dresdeners, had begun to hope, to believe that 'Florence on the Elbe', their beloved city, would be spared. The Americans and British after all, loved the city so much, attracted by the fine buildings, baroque palaces and pleasant landscapes; it was harmless, a city of culture that played no significant part in the war effort. The Allies were planning to use Dresden as their administrative base after the war. And didn't Churchill have a favourite aunt who lived in Dresden? He had spared the city for her sake.

Rike would never forget hearing the sound of the planes that February night. It was like a humming that got louder and louder and went on for two days. By 16 February 1945, the news arrived that Dresden, her home city, had been annihilated. 35,000 citizens had been killed, most burnt to death in a strategy that, it was believed, had deliberately targeted the citizens, mostly women, children, and the elderly. All their illusions were shattered that day. A press release from the German News Bureau said that 'cultural and residential areas were deliberately attacked and destroyed,' although there was no clear indication about the full extent of the damage. Rike worried for Mädi and her young family and hoped that their home being outside the city limits would protect them.

Nine days later, on 25 February everyone was sent home. Not only had Dresden been bombed, but the situation in the East had worsened so much that the farm would be an easy target for the invading Russian armies, and it was argued that the workforce would be safer and better provided for in their own homes. Rike suspected, however, that they were being abandoned to whatever fate awaited them; it was every man and woman for themselves.

Saying farewell to Dörte was unspeakably hard. Rike was comforted only by the hope that they would see each other again soon. But she had to wrench herself away from the sanctuary of the farm and confront whatever was left of her beloved Dresden. On the train home she didn't know where she was; it looked like she had entered a scene of apocalyptic hell. It was a dull day, and the clouds were still hanging over the city.

When she stepped out of the bomb-ravaged station, she looked around and gasped. The city was gone. The shock was tremendous: the sights – of the city's skeletal, still smoking ruins, and the smell – the stench of corpses, of burning flesh, threatened to overwhelm her as she clambered over the rubble. The smoke made her throat constrict, and her eyes burned hotly. She didn't see anybody – there was no life at all. The city that she'd loved was gone. It was a dead town, just rubble, rats, and charred corpses. She felt overwhelmed by a great fury. How could people do such a terrible thing?

Dresden devastated by the bombing on 13/14 February 1945. Here, we're looking from Lüttichaustraße, where Fred lived, towards the station.

She was still in shock when she got home. Chaos and devastation were all around her. Difficult weeks followed. Rike learned that amongst many friends, an aunt and a cousin had been killed in the bombing. Another aunt, who had lived near the Hauptbahnhof, had lost everything. They had tried to dig in the rubble where their home once stood to recover something, anything, but found nothing – it had all been destroyed.

Anger flared up as Rike heard stories of the atrocities that had been committed by the British and Americans. On the second day of bombing, the animals broke out of the zoo and ran towards the river, and so did the people running away from the fire. According to these stories, the aeroplanes had machine guns and they shot the animals and the people. Rumours spread of tens of thousands, possibly hundreds of thousands, dead in a strategy known as 'terror bombing'. Heaven had become hell. It was an outrage.

Only letters from Dörte pierced the darkness, bringing some comfort. But then the letters stopped. Alarmed, Rike wrote to Dörte's home to find out what had happened. She received a small card from Dörte's mother, 'the fate of Dörte is in God's hands.' She had died of diphtheria. An idealist and a good German would no longer have to see the misery in the East – and that was good. For Rike it was like a thunderclap, another shock in these terrible times. 'Rest in peace, dear Aunt Dörte,' she murmured through her tears, 'I will never forget you.'

Despite all this, Rike found comfort in a faith in God whom she believed still guided her steps and loved her. The friendship with Dörte, though cut short, she saw as a gift from above that had come just when she'd needed it.

As winter turned to Spring, news from the East worsened. The Russians were coming closer. The hysteria grew. Anxious neighbours advised Rike to remove the Stahlhelm symbol of the steel helmet above their front door as it would antagonise the soldiers of the Red Army. She and Maria set to work and soon only the motto was visible. Rike shivered as, one day, walking through the ruined city she saw graffiti proclaiming, 'Enjoy the war, for the peace will be terrible'. She tried not to allow herself to be engulfed by fear. Rike decided to keep a diary to record her experiences of these troubled times; after all, her future was uncertain.

Langebrück, 17 April 1945
Ill will makes you unspeakably sad. Even though I know this, I can't help feeling bitter. My lovely peace has gone.

Hunger is my constant companion. For the foreseeable future my motto will be that of the great Socrates: 'I do not live to eat, I eat to live.'

I wish I were still in Hochweitzschen with Dörte, but those happy days have passed. Will I ever be as happy again?

On 1 May Rike listened in disbelief to Admiral Dönitz's announcement that Hitler was dead. He called upon the German people to mourn their Führer who died the death of a hero in the capital of the Reich. In response Mutschmann, Gauleiter of Dresden, one of the few cities where the Nazis still clung to power, called upon the people to fight to the end and to observe a period of mourning for their fallen leader. Rike, though she dared not express this, did not mourn the passing of the man who had brought so much suffering upon her country.

However, she had no time to reflect on this, because the clamour grew: the Russians were coming. Tales of the great vengeance they meted out on the German people were legion: widespread and brutal rape and murder. Women, girls, even children violated at will. And now, these Russians were near Dresden. There would be no escape. Hearing of this, Mädi fled with her two small children, Wolfgang and Christina to her husband's family home in the beautiful village of Kipsdorf, in the Erzgebirge, near the Czech border twenty miles south of Dresden, leaving Rike and their home help, Marianne, in Langebrück.

Mädi tried to persuade Rike to leave with her, but she insisted on remaining. The pastor met her on the village street and said, 'Fräulein, you realise the Russians are coming. You can't stay.'

'But there's the house,' she replied. 'There's Marianne. I can't leave them. I must go back.'

So, Rike went back, despite the warnings, and steeled herself for the confrontation with the feared Russian troops. She held onto life lightly. If she died, so be it.

Langebrück, 17 May 1945.

In the last few days, I've decided to describe my most significant experiences so that later other people can know the truth about these terrible times.

On 5 May, a Saturday, I had set out to surprise my sister, who had fled to Kipsdorf with Wolfgang and Christina, with apples and other little things. But the pleasure was short-lived, for they'd announced on the radio the expected massed Russian attack on Saxony.

Mädi would have preferred to keep me with her, but the thought that, unless I left Kipsdorf immediately I might never be able to return to Langebrück, was so dreadful that I took my leave a few minutes later and set off on the road.

The only way to get to Dresden unharmed was to stop a car if you were lucky enough to find one. So about 6pm I stood expectantly on the road from Altenberg – Dippoldiswalde. Unfortunately, the weather was very inclement and rainy, so that I began to lose hope. But, against the odds, and sooner than expected, a van stopped and promised to get me safe and sound to Dresden. The driver was going there, because the car needed a new spring and as it was going to the Benz factory, I could stay sitting on the wood gas stove at the back. It would, of course, have been far more pleasant to sit up front with the driver, but this wasn't possible because there were other passengers. Although it was a bit cool and windy, I was glad to be so safe. My new acquaintance graciously took me with him as far as Heidehof, where his unit lay.

I'll never forget that journey and the generosity of the driver. I was even given lots of sweets and was offered a jar of honey that I could lick out, like the bear in the stories. You can imagine what that meant to a wartime stomach.

After a warm farewell, I walked to Blumenstraße where it was clear that even here at home, we were now in the immediate war zone. The sky glowed from the huge fires over Meissen and Kamenz. The roar of battle shattered the silence of our village. By now it was nearly midnight, and I was glad to be home with a roof over my head. Our Mariannchen, the faithful soul of our house, had packed everything up so that we'd be prepared in the event of a military evacuation.

A calm Sunday followed, though the radio carried news of Germany's capitulation, which I was still unable to believe. On Monday morning we were ordered to evacuate by 10am. We got ourselves ready, but a rumour made us stay behind: Dönitz was going to speak to the German people. The day passed in an unending to and fro, and I decided to travel to Kipsdorf the next morning since everyone advised me to. At 5am I was looking about the village and - lo and behold! - two Russians on a motorbike came towards me. Too late! Now I had to prove myself, keep my nerve and show myself in control of the situation.

At about 9am the first carts drove down the stone road and then followed column after column – all Russians. I felt numb. Our worst fears had been realised and we dreaded what was to come; nevertheless, we had to carry on.

Marianne and I went into the village to fetch bread, and there we heard of the first atrocities and scare stories. We forgot all about bread and ran home, locked the door behind us and waited in terror for what might happen. When the morning stayed quiet, we decided we would plant a few potatoes in the afternoon. At least we'd have them safe in the ground.

Lunch was interrupted by loud foreign voices. Our hearts were in our mouths, and we rushed to the window. The Russians were entering the neighbours' house. All you could hear on Blumenstraße were shouts in Russian and doors banging. We raced from one window to another. We put on Bolshevik headscarves that almost covered our eyes so that we really did look like Russian girls. I think I've never felt more relieved when the first group of Allies avoided our house. I have to say I thought it was a blessing from our parents that we were spared. Since the coast seemed clear we went out in the afternoon with buckets of potatoes into the garden. We had almost finished when the bell rang, and three Russians stood at the door. They seemed to have their eye on the car. They were very disappointed that we didn't speak Russian, but all in all they were pretty decent. They left without having once looked inside the house.

We were just about to continue our work when a Russian called to us from the neighbours' garden and asked us to sit next to him on the edge of the wall. To refuse would have been an insult. He quickly explained that he was a Russian major and wanted to get to Weißig: could we show him the way on the map and point him in the right direction? Why not do him this favour? Still one sentence from the capitulation announcement rang in my ears: the German people are now at the mercy of the enemy, for good or ill. And as a result, our actions had to take account of that. But I must say that the Russian officer's behaviour was exemplary; he was a real gentleman. He even gave me a watch to say thank you for helping him.

This encounter strengthened me enormously, which was a good

thing because what followed was awful. Another four Russians came to the house and examined the car; we watched from the veranda as they hadn't rung the bell. Very soon they demanded to come in. They hammered on the door, and we opened up. Of course, they asked again about the car. I noticed straight away that they were drunk, making them coarse and aggressive. Violently they tried to separate Marianne and me, but we held each other tightly. One of these barbarians tore the watch from me that, shortly before, the major had given me. Perhaps that was the only means of preventing them from emptying the house.

Incredibly they left soon after. We said a prayer of thanks to God when finally, these four shut the door behind them. But not long afterwards two of them returned and wanted to be let in. They made their demands in Polish. We called over to Frau David, who is from Upper Silesia and speaks their language, and the novelty of being able to make ourselves understood caused the two to forget what they had come for. They came into the house and made themselves at home, telling stories of Siberia and reminiscing about life in the army. As they left, we gave them to understand that next time they should ring the bell, which with much gesticulating they promised to do. That was the last of that first day's visits. We were more than exhausted. Now we had to turn our thoughts to the night.

As we were still talking over the day's events with the neighbour, I saw a man with his daughter and lots of luggage approach Reuthers Hotel. Mindful of our security, I invited him, since he needed lodgings, to stay with us. He gladly agreed, and we felt all the safer for his presence that night. The next morning, we put his bike together again for him and he promised to return very soon with much needed food in exchange for two bottles of wine we'd buried.

The Russians returned the next day and, once again, Rike found herself needing all her guile to dissuade them from raping her. Somehow, they listened, not all the soldiers were the same, and she was left unhurt. Rike didn't know why she had survived when so many other women, not so different from her, hadn't the same fortune. Why had God answered her prayers and not theirs? Had her parents been looking after her? Had God simply decided that she and her poor family had suffered enough? Whatever the reason, she was grateful for the small mercy she experienced.

The military war was over, but the battle for survival continued.

Dresden was at the mercy of the Russians, on whom Germany had brought unimaginable suffering and now would learn to fear. One thing Russians did, was release emergency provisions and initiate a rationing scheme, which meant that at least Rike and Mädi's family wouldn't starve. There was no political freedom, but as the Nazis came to power when she was not yet seven, Rike knew no different; the extreme right had been swapped for the extreme left, one sort of dictatorship swapped for another. Rather than fretting about politics and other things over which she had no control, Rike focused on looking for work.

At the end of May, after going round a number of farms, she found work as a labourer in Kleinwolmsdorf, where she travelled daily from home, some seven miles. She had to work hard and was on her feet from 4.30 in the morning till 9 at night, but she gained solace from the fact it was healthy work and she knew that the farmers valued what she was doing.

Like many families in Germany, they waited for news of the men in their family; as far as they knew, Wolf, Traudi's husband Heinz and Mädi's husband Fritz, were all still alive. With the menfolk absent, Rike became the provider for the family, bringing provisions from the farm and making sure Mädi and her children would have food on the table. At least now she was able to prove her worth.

In time, Fritz and Heinz did return to their families, but they still heard no news of Wolf. He had been good at writing to them recounting his experiences during the war, but the letters had dried up in January 1945. They feared the worst, but no dreaded letter arrived. They heard a rumour that he was part of the German army that had surrendered to the Americans and had been taken as a prisoner of war. They believed he was alive, but they had no idea how well he was faring. They hoped that no news was good news. They hoped they would see their brother again.

* * *

Rike looked up from the letter she was writing. She found it hard to express her thoughts and feelings as she reflected on the past seven years. How can one put the experience of such deep sorrows into words to a man who was almost a stranger and yet had been a significant part of her family's life for a time?   How could she explain the optimism, the love of life that still coursed through her? She refused to allow herself to be defined by misery, to become known above all as the orphan girl. And, as she wrote, she began to think of Fred and how difficult he would find it to read this letter that had such bad news for him too; she knew how much he'd cared for them all, particularly her brothers. She looked at the clock. It was getting late – time to stop writing. She could send off the letter in the morning before her day's work on the farm.

As you can imagine, the war years have been very difficult, but we are alive and can still count our blessings despite our many sorrows. Food is scarce, and hunger is a daily reality, but I am in good health, for which I am grateful. I try to stay cheerful as much as possible and not to take this precious life for granted.

We are still deeply concerned about Wolf's welfare – we believe he's a prisoner of war – and we wonder if it would be possible for you to find out where and how he is? He treasures your friendship so much and I'm sure he would be very pleased to hear from you.

I was very sorry to hear of your own suffering. And I'm also sorry for the pain and sorrow that this letter will bring you. It seems that we were all victims of this war.

With heartfelt greetings

Friederike Büttner-Wobst

PART FOUR

Fred and Rike:
Joy from Ashes
1946-1948

CHAPTER TWELVE
1946: A correspondence begins

Fred was reeling. He sat on his bed with Friederike's letter in his hand. Again, as a year previously when in India he learned of the fate of Dresden, he felt shock and then nothing. It was all too much; Götz, Werner, and Dora all dead. Wolf missing.

He thought back to the family whose lives had been the inspiration for his novel. *The Cloven Pine* had ended with the suicide of Götz's father and Götz still trapped in the net of Nazism, facing an uncertain future but determined to find what freedom he could. But the truth was stranger and more tragic: Götz died, aged just 18, within three weeks of the war's beginning, before Fred had written a word of the book. The conclusion of the half-fiction he wrote five long years previously was lame and artificial; the reality brought a more poignant, definite end – war; Götz killed in Poland, his parents dying perhaps in part of grief within the year. He would have done anything to rewrite *that* horrific ending.

When the cloud of numbing shock began to lift a little, Fred was able to reflect on the young woman who'd written the letter. She had experienced extraordinary tragedy at such a young age. He couldn't imagine how it must have been for her to have lived through that awful period of time when she lost three members of her family, left orphaned at only fourteen. And, to see her city burned down and to face the wrath of the Russians – she had said nothing of her experience at the end of the war, but everyone had heard stories of the treatment meted out to thousands of German women and girls. It didn't bear thinking about. This sort of experience would have destroyed Fred. He had been through so much less and look where he had ended up. She, however, remained warm, strong, human, sensible, in spite it all. He remembered her as just a girl, aged 11 with those solemn eyes and pigtails. Nothing more than Wolf's sister. But there was something more about her now. He allowed himself to feel, to feel for her, experience sadness and admiration for her.

After years of feeling powerless, an impotent pawn in a War Machine which had gradually worn him down and led him to the hospital, Friederike's letter gave him a stirring and unfamiliar sensation. Perhaps he was needed. Suddenly he saw some purpose. She had asked him for his help. It wasn't much, but Fred was grateful for this. She had also given him reason to write back to her – he would need to tell her what he had found out about Wolf. This was as good a justification to start correspondence as any. While Fred felt helpless, stuck in the mental hospital, he knew that Karl was active on the continent. Perhaps he could locate Wolf and enable him to re-establish contact? So, Fred wrote once more to Karl, asking for his help.

Days later, Karl wrote back, telling Fred that Wolf was indeed in a prisoner of war camp in Göppingen, Baden-Württemberg, where he had been interned for over a year. He was alive and in reasonable health. Fred would be able to write to Wolf there. Fred was so relieved. There was a definite sign of life, at last! And then came the much longed-for confirmation. On one of her frequent visits, Fred's mother brought with her a card from Wolf, in which he wrote that Götz had fallen, his parents dead and he a POW. For the first time, although he had known the truth for some weeks, he felt the pain of grief, and through his tears he felt palpable relief … he was beginning to feel again.

As soon as Fred received news from Wolf, he wrote back to Friederike, hoping that this might be the beginning of correspondence, even a friendship between them. He didn't have any particular expectation or plan, he simply hoped that he might be able to build a bridge to Friederike. Of course, he couldn't help feeling anxious. How much would she want to get to know this wreck of a man branded a freak by the psychiatrist in Dumfries, burnt out, on the scrap heap of life?

After six long months in the hospital, in June 1946, Fred was told he could be released along with other patients. They ended their sojourn with a party, dancing reels. Fred didn't dance but was asked to give a speech in honour of the matron who was retiring; he felt the satisfaction of feeling useful once again.

When Fred returned home to Liverpool, he asked himself, what next? He faced the wreck of three careers at 32; he had forgotten all his Classics; he had been studying for Bar examinations which he never finished, because war had intervened; and his novel writing had brought in the princely sum of £120 and anyway, he felt utterly exhausted and completely uncreative. He had little money and his mental health had compromised his prospects. He tried to get a job in Germany but was twice rejected. All he wanted was to settle down and get married. Of course, he needed some sort of career, some sort of livelihood if that dream were to have any chance of being realised, and this seemed far off.

Suddenly, the fates half yielded. He was offered a position in Edinburgh, where a fellow Kingsman, the professor of Latin at Edinburgh University, with sympathy for a fellow of King's, offered Fred a junior lectureship. Then, a short time later, he received a letter from one of his former tutors at King's, D W Lucas, University Director of Studies in Classics, conveying the offer of a well-paid job in Berlin.

Until now he had been frustrated by feeling that he had no options, but now he faced having to make a decision, which was almost as vexing. Should he return to academic life which had only satisfied one half of him, or make a probable step further away from that life, which would complete a process that the war had begun? The doctor advised Fred not to go to Berlin, reasoning that it would destroy Fred's already frayed nerves quicker; coming into contact with hardship, encountering wretched conditions that he couldn't ameliorate and being confronted with the almost hopelessly complicated core problems of the times. He hesitated, but while he was still awaiting more details from Berlin, Edinburgh demanded an answer, so Fred accepted. His pay was a mere pittance compared to what he had received as a Squadron Leader during the war, but Fred didn't care; life could begin again, and he felt hope rise once more in his soul.

* * *

Wolf was alive and well! Rike was so relieved. Not knowing his fate had cast a shadow over the family in the long year that had passed. She was so grateful to Mr Clayton for putting them out of their misery and found herself intrigued by this man who, despite having only previously known her as a girl, was taking her seriously as a young woman. Rike loved the opportunity to make new friends, especially someone who seemed so open, warm, had shown himself to be genuinely interested in her and the family, and was also willing to help them as much as he could. Fred's friendliness made a stark change from the hatred she had been told about that others had encountered from the Allied powers who were now governing her country.

Having heard the terrible stories of all that the Russians had done to civilians in their military occupation of the Baltic states and the news that they were coming West, Rike's sister Traudi had fled with her young son to the relative safety of her husband Heinz's hometown of Aachen in early 1945 before the bombing of Dresden. She had gone in the expectation of better treatment and compassion at the hands of the Western Allies than she could have hoped to receive from the Russians. However, in her letters back home she wrote that while there certainly weren't the stories of rape and pillage as were rumoured in the East, she discovered that the British occupying forces seemed cruel and indifferent to the plight of the local population. Property was pilfered, women were considered 'fair game', and hunger was a daily reality. It appeared that the Allied forces were happy to let the Germans starve; after all, they were only getting what they deserved, and their attitudes, it was rumoured, mirrored those of the non-German civilian populations across Europe. German people were now figures of hate – they were all Nazis, corporately responsible, each one had blood on their hands. Mr Clayton, however, clearly had a different attitude. He understood, at least, that her family, for one, was as much a victim of Hitler as many others. To be understood, to receive someone's heartfelt sympathy, was so welcome.

In June 1946, to Rike's great relief, her brother was released from the prisoner of war camp. Although he wouldn't say much, he had been maltreated at the hands of his American captors. Now he was released, he was unable to return home to Langebrück. Post-war Germany had been carved up into four occupation zones by the victorious Allies: American, French, British and Russian. Langebrück, in the East of the country was now part of the Russian zone. Travel between the different zones proved incredibly difficult, exacerbated by the enmity between Russia and the other Allies. Wolf was forced to recover from the effects of imprisonment near Kleve, North-West Germany, in the British zone, but unfortunately, all his possessions were stuck in the Russian zone, and they had been confiscated. Rike learned that his English friend, Fred, had done what he could to help him and was continuing to do so – sending parcels of clothing, food, and such like. Rike was grateful for his continued care and, when a correspondence began between the two of them, she would leave her day's work on the farm with a spring in her step, hopeful that another letter from England would be awaiting her.

Meanwhile, Fred was now in Edinburgh and settled in his room in Howard Place, a Victorian terrace built from local sandstone. He was amused to learn that Robert Louis Stevenson was born in the very house where he was living. Would some of the inspiration rub off, he wondered? Though the room itself was small, it was well situated – the Royal Botanic Gardens were just across the road, giving him green space in which he could wander, lost in thought. The half hour walk to the university campus was pleasant as it took him through the main city centre, full of architectural gems, such as the neoclassical National Gallery whose pillars aped ancient Greece and the medieval castle that dominated the skyline.

When not teaching, preparing for lessons or marking, Fred spent most of his spare time in the evenings writing letters mainly to Germany, having got back in touch with surviving Dresden boys and teachers. Through Friedrich Jehn, Fred learnt that many pupils and teachers had died in the war, including in the firestorm that had obliterated the city; he thought of his prophetic dreams that still haunted him. Jehn described the current situation facing the Dresdeners. It made grim reading:

> Winter came early here; now, at the end of October, it's already -5⁰C, and snow is already lying. We're very afraid of the winter!   Our standard of living, which before the war was 100%, has now sunk to just about 20%! That means privations! Memories and hopes are our only sources of joy, patience and restraint are our watchwords. We hope that the German question will be solved as soon as possible and are particularly worried about the Eastern border! Unfortunately, we can't mention politics in letters. I would so gladly discuss all these problems in person with you.

Fred wished that too. He had enjoyed his discussions with Jehn in Dresden. He recalled his drunken declaration that he and Jehn would outlast Hitler, Mussolini, Stalin, and company. He hadn't been far wrong; Hitler and Mussolini were gone. Stalin, however, was very much alive and he was casting an enormous shadow over the whole of Eastern Europe. They'd been thrown out of the frying pan into the fire. Many people were trapped, and those who had managed to escape to other parts of Germany were deeply fortunate. One of these was Wolf, to whom Fred was now writing regularly. In one of his letters, Wolf remarked, 'I'm so happy that all the unpleasant things between our peoples haven't destroyed friendly relations that have existed between us.' Yes, Fred thought, hatred hadn't completely won out, although it came pretty close. He, at least, was able still to feel affection, and he felt that there was more, somehow, to come.

Fred had followed the trial of the Nazi war criminals in Nuremberg with some interest. At the end of the trial in October 1946 when the sentences were delivered with twelve of the accused condemned to death, Fred imagined what he might write to Wolf. No one was truly innocent, he felt.

> During the war, bomb after bomb rained down upon us. Europe was

blacked out, but we stubbornly survived and defiantly bid more bombs test us to the uttermost. Surely, surely, we argued, if we bomb Dresden to atoms, surely, surely, they argued, if we shatter London with v1 or v2, that stubborn foe will yield. They cannot stand it much longer. And more bombs justified bombing, more blood gave meaning to the blood already spilled. All this evidenced 'the unconquerable will, and study of revenge, immortal hate.'§

Dare I say, Götz died in vain, Wolf? You have to admit it in the end, and I have to admit that your people brought us morally down into that same dust. Fatal, we say, to yield to force. Did not Hitler teach us that?

But I'm with Chesterton: 'From all that terror teaches … deliver us, good Lord.'

Terror teaches us hate, only hate.

Wolf Büttner-Wobst as a young adult.

Fred had had enough of hatred. It was time that love won out. Through their letters, the friendship between himself and Wolf continued to grow. Among the usual conversations about falling in love, the present reality of the fight to keep fed, their

---

§ John Milton, *Paradise Lost*

correspondence was invariably littered, as it had been before the war, with political discussion and debate, about the causes of the war, about the future of Germany and of Central Europe. They also told stories of their different war experiences. Like Fred, Wolf had been (much to his disappointment) described in the Wehrmacht as completely unsoldierly. He had volunteered for military service not to take revenge for his brother, but just to fit in. As for Götz, Wolf denied he died for nothing. 'No, he did his duty to an enforced oath – the subordination of self to the general good – perhaps incomprehensible, but definitely German.' Fred disagreed. It was all futile.

Wolf expressed his desire to come to England to study, maybe through the student exchange programme – he asked Fred to find him a place at Liverpool and said he'd like to be taught by him again. Fred did his best, tried to pull strings, contact old acquaintances, but his efforts were frustrated at every turn. Despite this, their friendship thrived, and Fred did his best to help Wolf in any way he could, including arranging to have food parcels sent to him from America.

Fred was grateful for the warmth of restored contact with Wolf and the others. He found these comforting; they made him feel that he had, after all, built a few slender bridges, which survived. And a new one was being built with Rike. They'd been writing to each other on and off for a few months and each letter caused him to wonder more about this young woman, who, though she had been through so much remained bright and hopeful.

He read and re-read each letter, trying to glean from them as much as he could about her. What did she look like now she was a young woman and no longer the solemn skinny girl with the pigtails? What made her smile and laugh (he had the impression that she laughed a lot, despite not having much to laugh about)? What did she think of his own attempts to communicate with her? What did she make of his verbose and overly formal language? Would she want to keep writing to him? He knew that he wanted to keep writing to her but feared that she might think this sudden interest from a foreigner would be strange and unwelcome.

Consumed with these questions and doubts he held off writing for a few weeks while he searched for an excuse to continue the correspondence. That excuse came after a particularly long gap between letters from Wolf; he hadn't heard from him in eight weeks and wanted to know that he was ok. He also needed to know whether it was in order to arrange for a food parcel to be sent. Perhaps Rike could assist him? He wanted to do all he could to help his old friend.

Then, as he wrote, it occurred to him, was there a way he could help her? He was, after all, well aware of the situation in the Russian zone. It was clear that the ongoing difficulties of the political situation in Germany were likely to persist, and Fred felt it probable that Germany would become divided, with Wolf in the West cut off from Rike and Mädi in the East. As a single woman Rike was more vulnerable than her sisters, and Fred felt a responsibility to her somehow. So, with this in mind he wrote to her with a suggestion that she might come to England where he might help her find work:

> There is talk here that perhaps German girls will be able to come to England for certain types of jobs, but for the moment it is all very vague. I just wanted to say that I might be able to get you a reasonably pleasant position here. I hope this very uncertain comment will seem neither a firm suggestion nor presumption on my part. I don't know what the prospects in Germany are, and nothing about your current circumstances, but you will understand what the intention behind this is.

He was fretful about how this must have sounded. Was he being too patriarchal or even controlling? He didn't even know the woman and here he was offering to help her.

No sooner had he posted his letter to Rike, than he finally received one from Wolf! While he was relieved and reassured to hear from his friend, he now worried that he would cause Rike unnecessary anxiety about her brother; what if she hadn't heard from him either? What should he do? There was only one thing for it – he dashed off another letter, explaining he'd heard from Wolf; that Wolf was fine and that he'd heard that she was well too. As he finished writing and sealed the envelope, he puffed out his cheeks. 'What must she think of me? She probably thinks I'm mad.'

Fred needn't have been concerned; Rike was grateful for his interest in her and for the way he sought to help Wolf and was clearly hoping to help her too. She replied warmly from the state farm where she had worked during the war, visiting old friends –

Hochweitzschen b. Döbeln, State Farm, 10 Nov 1946.

Dear Mr Clayton!

If only you knew how much pleasure your two letters gave me.

It's a pity that Wolf is facing so many difficulties, and he's so ambitious and wants to get on. I've got the latest news from him from Marburg, and he says he hasn't managed to get a place at the university. I'm really sorry for him, because I know from experience how horrible it is always to be thrown off course. I don't want to bore you, but if you're interested, I'd happily tell you more about myself.

I found your suggestion about coming to England to work really interesting. I'd be delighted to come, because I really believe I would be well looked after under your protection. Of course, a secure job would be the first step towards such a move.

At the moment I'm working as a trainee on a farm in order to complete my second practical year in agriculture. My plan is to study agriculture so that later I can make a career as a seed propagator or animal breeder. Of course, these are only plans which can easily be derailed, because in such uncertain times we can only live from one day to the next. You might be able to agree with that!

I'm not doing badly here, but I'm very glad to be taking my exam in spring and will be able to breathe a bit more freely – but will that really ever be possible again? I think I would forget all these future plans if only I could exchange them for a peaceful life such as I knew in my parents' house. You can probably still remember how peacefully life flowed then. Of course much has changed, but hardship makes you strong and you feel able to survive without fear and without shrinking. You learn to do without everything you used to take for granted, and that's good – perhaps later I'll value it all the more. But enough of that, I mustn't keep dwelling on the downsides of life; there's always hope.

My sisters are well, given the circumstances. They're really having to earn the money for their children, because my brothers-in-law are still not home. But I'm thankful that at least they're not ill.

How are you and your mother? She doesn't know me, but please send her my greetings: Wolf spoke so much about her.

Best greetings from

Friederike Büttner-Wobst.

As their friendship evolved, plans for Rike to come to England under Fred's protection became more concrete. At first, in the early stages of their correspondence, Fred saw himself as the strong protector of a lonely child, motivated by his regard for the Büttner-Wobst family. But he began to realise she was so much more. She wasn't lonely – she had good friends, with whom she'd built a mutual respect and love. She didn't need his pity either – by the sounds of what she had told him about her experience with the Russians, she was fearless, willing to confront whatever and whoever might come her way. In fact, she was as strong as he was weak. Each letter simply added to the impression that was forming in his mind of a powerful, resilient, fearless, down-to earth – and funny young woman. She confounded his expectations – she was like no one he had ever come across before – and he discovered that he was almost desperate to get to know her more.

Rike began to occupy his thoughts: in idle moments he wondered what she was doing and what she was laughing at. Knowing her interest in agriculture he made an effort to become more interested in the plants that were growing in the nearby botanical gardens. When he was teaching, he imagined her among his students, who were, after all the same age as her, and mused at what she'd make of him.

He prized her letters; reading them so many times that he could recite parts word-for-word. Although he had not heard her speak as an adult, he imagined the way that she might read these letters aloud to him. He began to rely on them to lift his spirits, to quieten the anxiety that still followed him like his shadow – and it worked. Something about her presence, conveyed through her words on those pieces of paper, brought him peace. If she could do this through her words – he dared to think – then how much more would this be true if she were there in person? What if she came to England as his equal, not for work, but for life... for love? It was all so unfamiliar but also frightening. Although it seemed barely credible to him, he wondered, could she be more than a penfriend, more than Wolf's sister? Could she be so much more?

Jehn, meanwhile, continued to keep Fred informed about life in Dresden. On New Year's Eve 1946 he wrote:

> For us the last year brought the bitter realisation that reconstruction will proceed only very slowly. We lack everything!   No building materials, no consumer goods of any kind! So we can see that "much water will flow down the Elbe" before we can breathe again. We had hoped that after 1½ years of peace the position would change, but we have ended up in a still deeper hole. Yes, they say the lowest point has not even been reached yet! In reconstruction we see one setback after another, which leaves us despondent. You just have to grit your teeth! And then: if only we could live in one of the other three zones!!

Jehn and Rike were in the same boat. Fred wished he could help Jehn; all he could do was offer consolation and send him flints for lighting cigarettes and saccharine for sweeteners, everyday, non-essential items that were scarce in the Russian zone. As Jehn put it, these were 'little things, but still so important'. Though he was unable to help Jehn, Fred had fresh determination to help Rike. Hers was one life he could change.

A couple of days after receiving Jehn's letter, one arrived from Wolf. Although Jehn had expressed his wish to live in one of the three zones in Germany not controlled by the Russians, Wolf's letter gave him an insight into the challenges that people across Germany were facing as they adjusted to post-war life, and Fred was disabused of any notion that life was much easier for them:

Düsseldorf-Wersten
Ohligserstr. 66
2. 1. 1947

Dear Fred,
    Yesterday I arrived here again unharmed. I was very surprised to find parcels, and only on second glance I noticed it was you who had kindly thought of me. I thank you for your dear Christmas and New Year's greetings. The three books and the magazines have also

arrived here. I'll turn to them once I've finished my correspondence.

So, I'm safely returned and must agree with you that it's not always so clever to cross forbidden boundaries. But sometimes it seems to me a privilege of youth to try such things. If I were a journalist I'm sure I could write a whole book about my journey. But I lack that gift, so must do without.

But I had really interesting experiences. For example, I think of the American border guards who get a bonus for every transit passenger that they catch. Once they've caught 80 they get a special leave permit back to the USA. So even in the present severe cold they drive their Jeeps along the border and accost those on the street with 'Pass, pass, have you got a pass?' Now, I had a passport and let myself be checked quite calmly, even if they looked at me a bit suspiciously, because I had a whole bucket of herrings in my rucksack for my sisters, and I couldn't conceal it because of the smell.

Our route (we went together, my brother-in-law from Emden and I) took us through woodland, we walked about 30 km through the German Central Mountains on woodland paths whose snow didn't yet show a single footprint. At last, towards evening, we reached the first town in the Russian-occupied zone. We had not met a single person for hours and now we could travel on by railway, difficult because here it's all single track. The people are just as dull as in the West, their manner shows how afraid they all are of what will come, and their lined faces speak of suffering and their worry how they'll find their daily bread. In all the stations you see posters for the Socialist Unity Party SED, the successor to the NSDAP.

But you can't avoid the impression that it's not present troubles that oppress the people but rather the feeling that they can't see anywhere a way out of this wretchedness. It's this hopelessness which blunts people so much. They accept even the compulsory reparations to Russia and don't try to avoid them from a general feeling of dullness and acceptance of their fate. Only here and there someone escapes this atmosphere for a while. On the return journey I met a railwayman, who had been sentenced by the Russians to 12 years hard labour for sabotage. He fled to the western zone where he'll disappear among the army of thousands who have had to leave their homeland just to save their lives.

On the way back I visited an acquaintance in one of the general staff POW camps in the US zone. It seems somehow tragic to see in the camp the 'giants' of earlier times, of whom we were all in awe and whom one saw at most twice a year on visits, here still svelte, deposed from their thrones yet in their manner still showing the glory of older times. Albert Kesselring, at one time commander in Italy (during the German withdrawal), walks up and down together with Adolf Galland, one of the most successful fighter pilots, like tamed lions or tigers behind the barbed wire.**

I must recall a short conversation I had this autumn with Martin Niemöller‡ about the inner purification and strengthening of one's thoughts for which one fought in POW camps. And I wonder if it really is wise to imprison these heads of the German Wehrmacht together. Any anger they feel can be transferred to the 'enemy' who keeps them here together. In freedom they'd be demilitarised sooner than here.

These few thoughts just occur to me. I won't bore you with them any longer. I often wish I could be with you for a whole week or a whole month to talk to you and hear your opinions. Why did you not go to Berlin? I often miss not having an older friend. Two of my older friends fell in this war and one died of tuberculosis. Now I have no-one nearby and a letter is a poor substitute.

Dear Fred, I'd like to thank you for sending me a food packet. I'll write to you as soon as it arrives here. As to your kind offer to send other things, I'll be so presumptuous as to make some suggestions. Because of my long time in uniform, I have no new suits, the old ones are too small or completely worn out. But I don't suppose you can help me there – I've now reached the considerable height of 1m 78cm. Please don't go to any trouble if it's difficult to help. You'll probably have better access to books than we do here, since because of paper shortages at German publishers no academic books are being printed. So for my studies at the moment, I don't have half the titles I need. At the moment I most need German medical textbooks.

Dear Fred, that's a lot I've written here. Don't regard me as shameless.

All my best wishes for 1947 go to you.

Thankful greetings,

Your Wolf.

** These two were among the 27 most highly decorated fighters of the war. In 1947 Kesselring would be tried and convicted of war crimes and sentenced to death for ordering the murder of 335 Italian civilians in the Ardeatine massacre, and for inciting and ordering his troops to kill civilians in reprisals against the Italian resistance movement. The sentence was subsequently commuted to life imprisonment.

‡ Founder of the Confessing Church, opponents of the Nazi German Christians. Niemöller was interned in Sachsenhausen and Dachau concentration camps for 'protective custody' from 1938 to 1945.

Wolf's letter gave Fred both an increased sense of helplessness but also a determination to do what he could to help his friend in any way he could. He didn't mind being asked; on the contrary, he felt the warmth of being needed, of being able to make a difference to someone's life, however small that difference might be. He set about with renewed energy, seeking to obtain books, food parcels – he'd even try and get that suit if he could.

* * *

It was now the summer of 1947. Fred had completed his first full year's teaching at the University of Edinburgh and was back home in Liverpool where he was based for the long vacation. He had plenty of time to think and all he could think about was Rike. The more he thought, the more he wanted her to be part of his future. He tried to reason with himself that this was foolishness; after all they had only written a few letters; they had no idea what the other looked like, let alone actually met. It was ridiculous. He knew it. And yet, the thought wouldn't leave him and it began to obsess him. It prevented him from getting to sleep at night, distracted him from the writing he had sworn he would do during the holidays. No, there was only one way to stop this from dominating his mind much longer. He needed to find out whether marriage was even a possibility or if it was just his overactive imagination playing tricks with him.

First though, he needed some advice. He couldn't imagine speaking about this to his father – he couldn't bear being laughed at, and he had a suspicion that his mother would hide any reservations she might have for fear of hurting the feelings of her oversensitive son. So, he decided to talk to his older brother Don, who was himself married with children. Having gone straight from school to begin employment he remained down-to-earth and straightforward. He would not hesitate to be honest with his brother but would do so in a way that would be kind.

So, one evening in July, Fred managed to get himself invited to Don's house. After tea, Don's wife, Olwen was upstairs with the children, getting them ready for bed. This was Fred's opportunity.

He had been searching for a natural way to bring up the idea of marriage with Rike, but none had come. There was nothing for it. Throat constricting, he blurted out,

'You know I've been writing to Friederike for the past year or so?'

'Wolf's sister?'

'Yes, that's right.'

'What about it?'

'Well, I like her…very much. I had this idea that I might be able to help her. Things are tricky for the people over there in the Russian Zone, especially for a single girl like her. I suggested that she come over to England so that I might be able to help her find her work.'

'That sounds possible,' Don nodded. 'There are jobs that she could do here if she didn't mind a bit of hard work.'

'Yes, that's what I thought…' Fred paused, before stammering, 'the thing is, though, I don't want to bring her over for work. I was wondering about something else…'

'Oh yes?' Don looked at Fred, his eyebrow raised.

'Well, umm, I was wondering if she might want to come over as my, umm, wife.'

'Wife? Really?'

'Look, I know it sounds ridiculous, we don't really know each other, but from her letters I can already tell she's open, resilient, down-to-earth and strong … she could be…'

'Exactly what you need?' Don finished.

'Yes.' There was silence for a moment. 'So, umm, what do you think?'

'Well, Fred, who knows? I won't give you advice.'

'But that's what I need.'

'Well, umm, I don't know what to say. It's a surprise, certainly.' He looked out of the window as he considered what to say next, no doubt sensitive to the feelings of his brother. 'Look, I'm not saying, don't do it. … Wolf's sister could be exactly the right kind of person for you. But you must be clear with yourself what you're asking of her and of yourself.'

'Yes, I think I am.'

'Have you discussed this with anyone else? With Rike?'

'I've spent the last few weeks trying to write a letter to raise the idea, but I tear it up every time. I can't bear the thought of what she'll think of me. I mean, normal couples talk about the prospects of marriage face-to-face, or write about it perhaps after having established a solid foundation for their relationship; well, we certainly don't have that – any foundations are fragile to say the least. If she read this idea in a letter out of the blue like that, she'd surely dismiss me, which would put an end to a potentially good relationship before it had the chance to get going. I could not bear the thought of that.'

Agonised, he turned to Don. 'So, what shall I do? How can I air the idea and find out whether this was more than a dream?'

Don looked thoughtful for a moment. 'Well, there is someone who knows and cares for you both, who'd be able to give you wise counsel.'

'Wolf, of course! He would be honest with me if he thought it was a completely awful idea. Thanks Don.'

Walking back home from Don's house, he had come to a sense of resolution and a degree of peace. He would broach the idea with his friend. Wolf himself was in a more settled place, having finally been accepted to study Medicine in Düsseldorf. He'd hopefully have the mental space to give this some serious thought. So, back in his room, Fred began to write, noticing his hand shaking a little as he did so. He was so nervous that he dispensed with the usual formalities and went straight to the point.

14 July 1947

Dear Wolf,

Do you think that your sister, Friederike, would be ready to marry me?

You're stunned, but I've thought about it a long time from my perspective. …. I don't feel like 'romantic' love necessarily has to be a prerequisite for marriage. We would have a different foundation, for instance, common views and interests.

I want to feel as if I'm giving something – but not from above as one would give to charity – I want to give something, because I know that I ask a lot, especially of a younger woman. I'm trying to briefly express a complicated web of emotions and thoughts. These thoughts I have discussed with my older, married brother, whom you don't know – and he said, 'who knows, I won't give you advice. But I'm not saying, don't do it. ... Wolf's sister could be exactly the right kind of person for you. But you must be clear with yourself what you're asking of her and of yourself.'

I'm not assuming automatically that she will say yes. And I hope she won't hold it against me that I'm only writing to you for now, as if she only had a small role to play. In a conversation, or through a string of conversations I could do better. But now it seems as if I have to say all this in one letter, so that I don't have to waste weeks and months. You may have already answered with a 'no, definitely not' to my first question, so that the rest of the letter is pointless, but I must write it nonetheless.

I've been thinking about how we could get Rike to England. There's not much point negotiating with the Russian zone, she would have to come to one of the West zones and wait 3 – 6 months and sustain herself there – with which I couldn't help very much. And in the meantime, she would have to totally rely on me to make the arrangements to get her out.

It hasn't been easy for me to articulate all of this, and I have hesitated for a long time. I hope that you will help me – and maybe also your sister – with advice, and that we will avoid any misunderstandings. This isn't charity and it isn't a business deal. I don't want to offer anyone help or a way out, because I'm looking for help and a way out, and I have considered your sister for a variety of reasons.

In all cases I will remain your friend,
Fred.

Fred wondered how his letter would go down with Wolf. It sounded crazy. He barely knew Friederike, and the fact that she was in the Russian zone, which greatly affected her ability to move, meant that the chances of actually successfully getting her out of the country were quite slim. He heard the objections of friends with whom he had mooted this idea, but he couldn't shake off the sense of new possibilities. He felt excited and hopeful about life, but he was anxious to know what his friend, Wolf, felt about the prospects of their union.

A few weeks later, Wolf and Rike were sitting together in the living room in the Blumenstraße. Wolf was in Langebrück for his summer vacation and Rike, having passed her exam in the spring was preparing to go to Halle, where she was due to study agriculture. She'd enjoyed her time working on the training farm where she'd been since spring. She was in the fields from early till late, and although at first she found it difficult to adjust to the farmers' way of life she integrated so well that they suggested she stay as their foster-daughter. Rike, however, had greater ambitions.

Living in the British zone, Wolf had crossed the border illegally. This was very risky – he knew that people were being shot daily for such transgressions. Since the dawn of 1947 he had grown increasingly pessimistic about the future of the country, writing to Fred that 'it's probably a Herculean labour to unite Germany into one political unit.' Given that Germany would likely be divided, he knew his long-term future lay in the West and that he would be able to make few visits to Langebrück hereafter. Rike and Wolf were aware that their times together in future would be rare. However, they tried to avoid talking about such things so as not to spoil the precious time they had together. At any rate, there was something else far more exciting to talk about.

'Rike, I hear you've been writing letters to Fred Clayton.'

'Yes, just a few,' she said coyly.

'He likes you, you know.'

'Really? Why, did he mention me to you?'

'Yes. He had quite a lot to say about you. Do you like him?'

'Very much. Why, what did he say?'

'Well, he asked if you'd be ready to marry him.'

'M-marry?' she was amazed. 'Well, I've not really thought about it … until now, anyway.'

'Well, he has. He writes that he has given it lots of thought.' He paused, 'Well?'

'Well what?'

'What do you think of the idea?'

'I like him. We've discovered that we have lots in common. I feel I could like him much more.'

'Do you love him?'

'Not yet, but I see no reason why I couldn't love him one day.

What do *you* think of the idea?' she asked him anxiously.

'It's completely up to you. I think you should try and meet with each other before you make a final decision. You know, he told me once that he couldn't kiss.'

'There's no question of it working, then!' She laughed.

'Seriously though,' Wolf said, 'he's a good friend. I'd be very happy for you – if you wanted to – to marry him. It'd be good if you could write to him about it.'

'Yes, I will,' she replied. She enjoyed the feeling of butterflies that fluttered about her as she thought about Fred. She had been amazed at first – she had certainly not expected that he was considering marriage to her. They'd only exchanged a few letters, after all. However, he already felt like an old friend, a feeling that was already helped by the knowledge of the deep friendship between him and her brother. She didn't mind at all that he had written to Wolf about the idea first. She trusted her brother implicitly and knew he felt very protective of his younger sister. They had always been very close, principal playmates in the Büttner-Wobst family. Their relationship grew even closer after the tragedies that had befallen them. She was reassured by the fact that Wolf held Fred in such high esteem.

Fred had to wait over a month for Wolf's response. On 20 August he received his reply. Wolf, as Fred anticipated, was astonished and wrote that he didn't quite know what to say. He wrote he ought not to give an opinion; their friendship was so close he would feel responsible for whatever happened as a result. Nevertheless, he ended the letter with an encouraging note: 'I for my part would be very glad to see my sister married to a friend of mine.'

Fred was so relieved. At least he hadn't been rebuffed. Could he dare to hope that something might come out of this blossoming friendship? But what about Friederike herself? She, after all, was the one whose opinion really mattered. What did she think of this crazy scheme? Could he dare to hope that she'd be willing to love him?

Shortly after these conversations Rike wrote to Fred.

> Dear Fred!
>
> - perhaps I can call you that after Wolf yesterday showed me your letter to him which came like a bird of happiness into my rural world.
>
> When I wrote my last letter to you a long time ago, I waited eagerly for an answer and was very disappointed to wait in vain.
>
> And then Wolf came with your letter, and if I hadn't read it myself, I wouldn't have believed it. People say I'm sensible for my 21 years, perhaps a bit too common-sensical, but I don't avoid being romantic. But I nevertheless would like to get to know the man to whom I will give my whole life, for even if we build a marriage on friendship and interests in common, there must be a harmony of thoughts and actions. You knew my parents' marriage, which still seems a shining example to me.
>
> Above all, alone as a German in a foreign country, I would need much, much warmth. I think I can find it with you and know that thanks to my adaptability, I would soon find my feet and will soon find good friends. The most important for me is that we two talk frankly to each other and approach each other honestly – for I'm sure honesty is one of the most important foundations of a shared life.
>
> But I must assure you of one thing, that I would be heartily glad if I could make a person happy and could spend myself in that aim.
>
> I await your response and your plan for our meeting again after 10 years.
>
> For today take my best wishes and believe me that a little German girl loves thinking tenderly of you!

While Rike knew it was too early to commit for sure, there was no reason why they couldn't grow to love each other. Her parents' marriage, after all, grew from a chance meeting in the waiting room of Heidelberg train station back in 1916. It had been their letters to each other that had formed the foundation of their relationship. They had only known each other for five months, having met each other twice and otherwise only having written letters to each other, before they were engaged, in September 1916. They married less than a year after that first meeting. Whirlwind romances, founded on letters, then, were not so strange for her family. Who knew where *these* letters might lead?

Wolf and Rike parted that summer each with new prospects. While they were sad to leave each other at least for a few months, they were excited to feel that their lives had direction. Wolf went back West to complete his studies in medicine and Rike travelled to Halle (Saale) in Saxony-Anhalt, to begin her studies in agriculture. She left Langebrück with mixed feelings – sad to be leaving her childhood home, but relieved to be able to be independent and free from the fetters of life with her sister and brother-in-law.

When he had learned of the correspondence that had struck up between Fred and Rike, and had heard that Fred had raised the prospect of their getting married, Mädi's husband, Fritz couldn't resist the opportunity to take a swipe at her. 'There's no way this is going to happen. It's crazy. I bet you that you won't marry Herr Clayton. I bet you that you'll never make anything of yourself.'

His cruel derision only made Rike more resolute. 'How much?' she asked, with a determined glint in her eyes.

'I bet you fifty marks,' he replied, taking a note out of his wallet, and waving it in her face.

'Ok,' she said calmly, 'you're on.'

He'd see. She certainly wasn't going to let her brother-in-law get in the way of her happiness.

CHAPTER THIRTEEN
1947: Early plans

At the end of August, after Wolf's intervention, the correspondence between Rike and Fred took on a greater significance, despite the difficulties created by the vagaries of the postal service and exacerbated by Fred's uncertainty about Rike's location.

Fred wrote with excitement from his family home at the end of the summer vacation:

26 August

16 Rangemore Road, Liverpool

Dear Friederike
  I was really happy to get your letter … we are of one belief that a real love can develop, even under these circumstances. I believe it can happen when two people want to create it, work for it, and long for it. On the other hand, I'm happy that you don't underestimate the difficulties that come through a long-distance relationship.
  Concerning my own character, I want to be honest, but it's not easy. There are shadows which for some people darken the blue sky … these can turn into small clouds. I often say to myself I can't live alone, but I don't want to be the type of person who would have to live with me. This seems fantastically overdramatic. But anyone who knows my mother would have seen how she has had a calming influence on an otherwise masculine environment which so often induces suffering, and this feminine strength, this calming but not stupid, unimaginative influence, that is what I really need.
  I do very much love children. I hope we have that in common, but I have a feeling that has a good and a bad side. I love the most

when I can protect. But I'm aware that a fatherly instinct can so easily become despotic, as if a woman, like a child, wouldn't have anything to say, and would have to be grateful for everything. Under our circumstances, the danger is perhaps bigger than usual, that I expect too much of you and not of myself. But I can at least claim that I am aware of this tendency to male egotism/dominance, and maybe it's not that bad.

But now my letter must become suddenly very practical. German girls from the Russian zone have already been able to come to England. But it is much easier to negotiate with the agencies of just one country. That's why I think you should go to the British zone and wait there for the bureaucratic process to take its course. Maybe you could find refuge with the farmers in Kleve with whom Wolf previously lived. As soon as I know that you've arrived there, I will send the relevant documents to our agency in Berlin. If they need a confirmation of your move abroad from me I will send it to them, but I believe that the move to England itself will not face any bureaucratic difficulties, but just the travelling between the zones. But you would know more about that.

Under different circumstances I would prefer a much longer mutual discussion/planning but in our unsafe, political and bureaucratically tied-up world I have a feeling that time is running out. I already experienced that when I tried to help Wolf. It takes months to achieve something only for it to suddenly disappear. A door suddenly closes.

I need to inform the agencies that I intend to marry you before I can even <u>begin</u> my efforts to have you come over. Then it will still take 3-6 months. I know that in moving here, you have to trust me entirely. But I promise you that I will not let you down. And I hope to soon find out that you are already in the British zone and are only waiting for me - and unfortunately also the agencies.

Dearest Friederike, I think there shouldn't be a lack of warmth and friendliness between us. It is not a paradise here and you will not find any angels, just the usual mix of goodwill and human weakness. What from a distance initially seems so big can be overcome with time, when one really is willing to adapt to the new environment without having to lose one's own identity.

Just like you say, I knew your parents even if it was just a few visits and I adopted a somewhat romantic picture of family from your home (probably due to my loneliness at the time), so I was crushed when you told me about the three swift blows which destroyed this already in the first year of the war. I thought maybe I could create a new picture. ...

In this hope I leave you with hearty greetings and best wishes,
Your friend, Fred Clayton

Fred read his letter through once more before putting it in the
envelope. How would Rike feel about what he'd written? Her
warmth and openness to the prospect of marriage encouraged him
to be more candid than he had been previously when she was just
a penfriend, although he now fretted that he was being too honest
about the more difficult aspects of his character. What if he
frightened her off? He considered tearing up the letter and starting
again in order to present himself in a better light, but reasoned
that, were they to marry, she would discover everything about him
anyway, good and bad. She may as well know it all now.

Rike, meanwhile had begun to settle into life in Halle. There was a
severe shortage of housing in Germany, so she was grateful that
when she'd arrived in the town and looked for a room, she quite
by chance came to a house on Sophienstraße that had a room
available to let where she could move in straight away. Her joy at
finding accommodation so easily was short-lived; she found the
room had an infestation of house mites. Undeterred, she went to
the pest controller, begged him on her knees to disinfect her room,
booked a decorator, and, thanks to her persuasiveness, in three
days her room was as new.

And, thanks to Fred's letters Rike felt more optimistic about
life. Although the Weber family with whom she was lodging was
very friendly, she had felt alone in this new city away from anyone
she knew and facing an uncertain future. Now she couldn't help
smiling at the new possibilities his letters were opening up for her.

26 August 1947

Dear Fred
    Your rich gifts of letters make me glad, believe me. Three have
arrived in the last few days, and although it's late at night I must write
now because tomorrow I'm going on a car trip into the Harz
mountains and I certainly won't get round to telling you everything
on my mind. Your letters take up a huge space in my head, so that
sometimes I can think of little else, but also my heart beats a little

faster when I tear them open and expectantly absorb what perhaps will later become my second self.

Your worries and efforts almost make me ashamed – I feel I've done very little in comparison. Please don't think that this is because I no longer want to come. On the contrary, you're already a part of my still so young life, and no day now passes without my thinking of you at some point.

Rike felt compassion for Fred and the anxiety that seeped through his letters. Instinctively she sought to reassure him:

Whether your letter is depressed or not won't change my mind. I already feel the great trust you place in me and I know we'll get to know each other well, and that love will grow from that which will let us start our life together. From the start of our correspondence, I have written you only the truth, no artificial feelings or sentimentality. Sometimes the mood is not what I wanted, but I've always tried to give you a fragment of my real self.

Now to the practical arrangements. You'll have to pay for the journey anyway, because our Mark isn't worth anything and is only good for paper. I'm happy for you to use Wolf's address for papers, so things will progress without my being in the West. I'll gain time to arrange everything here. My sister wrote today that I ought to come home again for a while to put matters in order etc. But I think things will progress just with us two!

I wish from my heart we could understand each other as well as we hope to.

Today an acquaintance said to me 'If your friend in England is anything like me,' (and I think he is like you, he's a professor of linguistics) 'you'll marry happily, and I wish that for you.' Perhaps the many good honest wishes will help us a little.

Cordially, your friend Rike.

In their time together in Langebrück Wolf had made it clear just how large the obstacles ahead of them were, but Rike was determined to meet them head on. She wasn't, however, willing to leave behind everything in Halle straight away – she had only just got there after all. It was best to get some studies under her belt. And much as she wanted to join Wolf in the British zone, she had no idea if she'd be able to study there. No, she would stay put for now and throw herself as much into her life in Halle as she could.

Fred was excited; the pieces of his life that had felt so scattered just a year previously were coming together again. He had had a successful first year lecturing: the students responded with enthusiasm even applauding twice. That gave him so much pleasure, to be appreciated. When he'd been at King's he'd been directed by Dadie Rylands in productions of Shakespeare and remembered the applause for his fool (in King Lear) and gravedigger (in Hamlet). But this was different. It was for his own ideas and his passion for his field that he was being applauded, recognised. With recognition came real satisfaction. He began to think he might enjoy an academic career.

He felt comfortable too in his digs at Howard Place. Mrs Hardy was a kind landlady. He had also been able to pick up the pieces of old friendships. Karl continued to write often, and earlier in the year Fred had re-established contact with his King's friend, Alan Turing. Turing replied on 30 May,

> I was very glad to hear from you again, and should very much enjoy teaming up with you again for another sailing holiday. The best dates for me would be either the beginning of September or the beginning of July. ... I heard rumours at B.P. from time to time that you were coming there, and was disappointed that nothing came of it. You didn't really miss anything.

Bletchley Park. Fred still felt aggrieved about the way he'd been treated by the Authorities. He was convinced that they'd deliberately kept him away. Indeed, his brother had said that someone in British Intelligence had admitted that he had been posted far from Europe, because he was regarded as too pro-German. The authorities couldn't imagine that a man could be wholly committed to war with a regime while still remaining attached to those trapped by it. Too pro-German? He, who had been so insistent and early in his warnings about Nazism. He had been shouting about it well before anyone else had seen the danger. Perhaps he had been naïve... but Fred knew that dwelling too much on this would only harm his already fragile mental state and anyway, he looked forward to seeing Alan and discussing their various wartime experiences as they went sailing together.

Setting off from Bosham in September 1947 they recalled their previous sailing holiday, eight long years before. They talked about the past, but also the future. Fred told of his plans to marry Friederike, and Alan recalled his own broken engagement six years earlier. Coincidentally, as they were out on the water, they happened to see Joan Clarke, the very woman to whom Alan had been engaged, passing in a boat.

Fred was fully aware of the risk he and Rike were taking with their engagement but, as he wrote to Rike on his return from the holiday on 14 September,

> There's a risk which exists with every engagement, specifically that one changes one's mind at the last minute. The friend with which I went sailing was engaged and changed his mind. My younger brother was engaged, and his bride then changed her mind. Some people would claim that the risk is even greater for us, but I doubt it.

Enclosed with his letter were two pictures which he agonised over sending, because he worried about the impression they would make on her. The letter gave him an opportunity to reflect on their different cultures, particularly how their nationalities impacted the way they expressed their emotions. He knew at the same time he was overthinking, getting himself in a tangle, but reasoned that Rike might as well get used to it – he frequently tended to overcomplicate things, especially as fundamental issues about himself were not clear to him. He just wanted to make sure that she really knew what she was letting herself in for, although, equally, he didn't want to put her off too much.

'Are you really interested in farming?' (he continued, glad to make himself change the subject),

> That would be of a great advantage nowadays, even if we're talking about a few chickens and a vegetable garden in the suburbs. A house in the country, but not too far from the city where I work, is what I prefer - so, a small town like Langebrück. I don't love the big city. But these days one doesn't have the luxury of choice when looking for a place to live. I would nonetheless be interested to hear your views on this.

The difficulties of language should not be overestimated. I have often realised; when one is young, one doesn't need to be a genius to learn the language of a new home quickly. In school one often learns very slowly and with great effort, but one astonishingly realises how quickly one can learn.

I think you would find my mother friendly and helpful, neutral and not jealous, but rather with a certain soft spot for you as a woman, and for you as the wife of her not exactly angelic son. I have already spoken with her about it. Her main point is, it appears to me, that I as a man underestimate a little bit what I am demanding of you. She says, 'She will give up her home, her Fatherland, her family, everything for you. That is a lot. Don't forget this. She will be alone. You cannot give in to the temptation, perhaps, even subconsciously, to use your advantage and autocratically determine everything.' She knows my weaknesses, and for that reason, I believe that you would find her to be a good friend. ...

I'm sending this letter to Langebrück, because I am somewhat unsure if you are still on the State farm. Please greet your sisters for me. Let Wolf know that I'll write to him.

With hearty greetings and best wishes, and I hope to see you soon.

I remain, your Fred

Two photos that Fred sent to Rike.

Although Fred would normally have waited for a reply before sending another letter, he was beginning to realise that this relationship was far from normal for him; his head and heart were so full of Rike that after a few days had passed with no reply, he simply couldn't bear the wait and so sat down to write again.

22 September, 18 Rangemore Road

Dear Rike

I'm writing to Langebrück, because I'm not sure where you currently are. In a certain way I'm writing to the void, since up until this point I've only received the one very nice letter from you. But that can't be changed. I'm already used to that because of Wolf. One can't wait for responses. One has to, I guess, write much useless or no longer useful things.

I have found a few more pictures of myself in a cupboard – three from India and another of uncertain date. I have attached these. But, believe me, I won't read anything into it if you do not send a picture my way! I don't yet have any doubts, firstly because these pictures are very different from one another, and second, because I know that Wolf and your sisters can tell you whether the pictures are roughly accurate or not. But if I only had one picture and I had to decide whether to send it or not, or if I had to choose between the two pictures, I'd go for the one that was more honest; if your family were complete strangers, then I would be concerned.

I don't want to give Wolf and your sisters in this regard too much of a responsibility, but I must confess that I tend to find refuge in the thought, 'the Büttner-Wobst family can already say quite a lot about me, including a few odd things as well, as it seems to me.' Wolf got to know me at Dresden and also at home, and that is already quite a lot. Since my Dresdonian self surprised me quite often - and sometimes it seemed to me as if people like your father would marvel at the person that I was. Still quite young, in a foreign country, using a foreign tongue, I was like a half-drunk who doesn't realise, like others do, the impression that his manners and words have on other people. '*In vino veritas*' they say, and even this state of affairs maybe reveals some otherwise concealed truths.

So Wolf had the opportunity to get to know me well, even if not always from my good side, from Dresden and at home. So I comfort myself with two thoughts - first, that he nonetheless doesn't have too bad an opinion of me, at least not today, and secondly, that he maybe could help you in that regard. He also knows my family. That's less important, but I don't have to explain that much there.

But I do want to tell you something. So even if education, wealth and rank, are superficial to a certain degree, and the social structure is being shaken up nowadays, their environment and way that people were raised say a lot about a person.

My two granddads were builders and watchmakers. My father started his career as a simple primary teacher and will finish it as a school superintendent - he's retiring next year. My older brother didn't go to university. I guess he could have studied in Liverpool - through a scholarship - but he chose otherwise, and is now a subdirector of a (not very large) insurance company, where he earns more money than I do. I myself studied in Cambridge with a scholarship. Now, Cambridge and Oxford are not only a cut above academically: they also have a social meaning. Since it is there that the sons of the aristocracy and the rich go to study, if they even study in the first place. One is put at the same level as they are and one learns how to converse with them. One takes part in debates with the leading politicians that like to take part in the Cambridge debate.

Of course, that strengthens one's confidence. For me Cambridge was first a secret hope, a dream, for the realisation of which I worked diligently at school. But my eight-years younger brother had always thought that he, of course, would also study in Cambridge. He took that for granted. He had more confidence than I did anyway, much more than my older brother, and my example probably helped him too. In Cambridge at first, I was happy, but also scared, foreign, lost. But he socialised straight away, giving the impression that evoked the response, 'you're a cheeky brother, aren't you?' - I don't think he even needed this encouragement. Of course, the king's nephew, who lived next door, played his gramophone at midnight, at a forbidden hour. My brother, who didn't know who his neighbour was, and I guess also didn't care very much, had just gone to bed, and apparently screamed, 'Stop that noise' or something along those lines. The next day he encountered the young Duke, who politely apologised and George politely accepted his apology - 'hopefully,' said my mother, 'not too much from too high a horse.'

I'm only telling this story, because it's typical for Cambridge, so you may roughly understand what it means - the petite bourgeois family whose sons study in Cambridge. I and my younger brother knew London, and our relatives are the likes of working people. You therefore should never be surprised if, for instance, I go into a small shop and introduce you to my uncle, or go into a parliament building and introduce you to a minister, who would be an acquaintance of mine. All of this can happen and I find it interesting and valuable to be able to move in more than one circle and simultaneously feel at home.

I don't know if these letters help you very much to get to know me directly or indirectly. At least they make an impression - I fear a slightly dry emotionless impression. But I'm certainly not unemotional. Wolf can confirm that for you. But in your one letter you do a better job of that than I do. I hope to soon receive a letter from you again. In the meantime, I very much enjoy thinking fondly of you.

With many hearty wishes and greetings,
Your Fred

Much to his relief, Rike's reply to his previous letters came just a few days later. Her words were as welcome as rain on parched ground.

18 September 1947

Dear Fred, my good friend!

I'm afraid your letter has been in my hands for a little while before I found time to answer, even though it brought me great pleasure particularly because it came on a day I was really depressed by current lack of success. It's only a pity that your letter proposing the idea of marriage came a bit too late to realise your plan straight away. My training period finished a month previously, and I had the firm intention of taking my career further until all at once your letter via Wolf turned all my future plans upside down. I was already registered in the University of Halle and wanted to take the next semester so my previous work would not have been in vain, and I need the time to get to know you, which I see as a shining goal amidst the hard practicalities. I hope that my coming to England in December would not be too late for you, but now you must write very precisely when you think I should strike all sails here. Do you really think it's so urgent? If so, then you must get me an inter-zone passport and send me a permit for immigration, otherwise I can't cross the border.

How had you pictured my move to you – would I have my own room, can I bring my own crockery and clothes? If I were in a strange place, it'd be nice to have a little bit of home with me.

You see, these are things I'd much rather talk to you about. Can we not meet at least once, even if only for a couple of hours? Not just for my own sake, it'd be useful for both of us. Just a word, and I'll be wherever you want in Germany or close by. Please, please consider if that's not possible!

You must not think I'm making demands, but one shouldn't start a new phase of life under false premises. And when you write, it's as if to Wolf's sister, and I'm quite different from him. You must see in me a very lively person, full of life, who takes life lightly, who sees that unavoidable fate cannot force us to our knees if we approach it with a cheerful heart. I love life and people, and I've learnt to value people whichever class they belong to, for simple people are often better and more honourable than the so-called educated ones who can be cold and hard as stone in their hearts. That's a recognition born of my early loneliness.

I'd be glad to have found a family and build a family life that would make some envious. Though I like children I'd only want them if I knew they had a future, if I was raising proper people who would be of use to humanity. You see I have principles that I will defend with all my might and I quite admit you might have too good a picture of me.

I write all this so that you can see what kind of person you're taking on. Mutual honesty was after all a precondition.

Of the clouds that overshadow your life I have no fear. I'll dispel them. That's a golden side to my nature, to make people cheerful and help them to bear what alone might be too heavy.

Now I must stop because I have to tidy my little cell, the radio's on and because I've just found London I want to see if I can catch a single word.

Fare well!

I wait longingly for an answer. For now, the dearest greetings and best wishes. Let's hope the next letter brings us a step nearer our goal.

Send my greetings to your mother – Wolf has told me so much about her I'd really like to find in her a second mother. F B-W.

There was so much to take in within this one letter! Fred understood and shared Rike's desire to meet to discuss these key issues that she raised, but, however hard he tried to think, he could see no way of making that happen. He also appreciated her wish for mutual honesty; he agreed that it would be an essential foundation for their relationship. Above all, his heart was warmed by her desire to share his burdens. Could she really be the one to dispel the clouds overshadowing him? He longed for this to be true. When he read Rike's words about Wolf he felt that he needed to reassure her that he wasn't simply hoping to marry her because she was Wolf's sister, as he expressed in his reply:

> You're of course right when you write, that I apparently only see 'Wolf's sister' in you. Or, let's rather say, not completely wrong. I knew your family and your family home. I saw you as a child. But also Wolf. I was really surprised by that. You write that you are very different to him, and then you describe yourself as a very lively, very vivid person. Well, has Wolf changed that much then? In this case, I wouldn't have described him as lacking in joy. I guess it is possible that these sad and dark years have made a solemn and prematurely aged young man out of a happy schoolboy. That would be quite a pity. And despite a picture of a prisoner of war, and despite his post-war letters, my mother and I continue to think back to a very happy little soul who could also make others happy. We even think of him as a child even though we know that the child is no longer here. But I can very well imagine that the one year which, in such a short amount of time, took his brother and parents from him while he was still very young, and left him with responsibility for the family, affected him deeply.

Rike's university identification card, issued by her university in Halle.

Rike, meanwhile was up late. She'd received some letters from Fred at last and couldn't stop thinking about them.

19 Halle / Salle, Sophienstr. 1 1st floor right wing, c/o Weber.

25 September 1947

Dear Fred,

I should already have been in bed a long time ago, but it's no use trying, because I'm desperate to tell you that your last two letters made me very happy.

I am a student, but not a real student. My course is more about the practical side of farming than the academic side, although I am learning skills like bookkeeping, etc. I am starting to make friends here in Halle, although it isn't always easy. However, I try and stay cheerful whatever the circumstances.

I received a lovely letter from your mother. I already tried to reply, but I was scared of making too many mistakes. I know what I want to say, but find it hard to send it into the labyrinth of English language.

I haven't received any letters from Wolf for a very long time. I don't even know why he's not writing. It's important, especially because I'm waiting for a message from the authorities about a permit to visit the British zone. My decision depends on this.

This is now my last letter. Why are you actually overthinking things so much? In the first two weeks much of the things you're worrying about will become clear. We're both too rational to start a marriage on a basis that neither of us want. ...

I have known some really difficult times, so I know how important it is to pull together in the midst of them. Life is hard, but we have to get by and we have to keep laughing. A good sense of humour can get you anywhere.

I'm sorry, I am really tired. it is already half past midnight. It's time to go to bed.

With loving greetings and wishes

I remain yours, Rike

In the letter that followed (replying to Fred's letter, dated 14 September), Rike had the courage to put down her growing romantic feelings towards Fred, in contrast to her earlier pragmatism...

Halle, 4 October 1947

Dear Fred,

I've waited every day for what seems like an eternity for a nice letter to pierce my voluntary loneliness in Halle, and it seems almost symbolic that yours are the first letters I've received in my new lodgings. Perhaps this is symbolic of our futures together, of our sharing of our loneliness.

I hope you don't mind, but I really think it's better that, since we have become friends over time, that we use the informal, 'du'. This way it is so much easier to talk and even though in Germany the man has the right to suggest this change in discourse, I thought I would risk it myself and do it.

I thank you for the two pictures you've sent me. They're much too nice to throw away. Do you know that the picture of you as a student reminds me a lot of your time in Germany? I remember you as the one with the massive scarf wrapped around his neck, who sat with my dad on the sofa. Back then you were so unattainable to me, being only a fresh young girl, I didn't have the courage to think about 'Sir', Mr Teacher' (consider who you were) a little bit more. But why am I saying this? Only to prove that you were not so unknown to me. Although I must say that you look much better in the other picture, and if it resembles you more closely, then I'm happy about that. I want to fulfil your wish to send you a picture, but you will have to wait a little while until I can get the photographers to do it, because you have to pay for use of energy, the material and development of photos, but I'll try to speed up the process with cigarettes as bribery.

I am 1.68m tall and well-built, so I could almost be an advertisement for how good our rations are. I'd love to be there when you receive my next letter with the picture. Perhaps your expression will be one of disappointment, but I guess you'll write about it.

There's one thing that I would very much like to know - if we will see each other once again before I come over. Not that we will be disappointed by one another - I'm not afraid of that, since I know that we get along very well.

By the way your mother must be a fantastic woman. Perhaps she's looking for a good daughter, because I'm looking for a good mother! Your views about emotionality and feelings are in complete agreement with my own. There are those who would think differently from us, who might try to lay stones in our newly paved way, but I have realised that I don't need to be afraid of that, since the two of us will complement each other quite well.

Yes, my heart is completely bound to the countryside, and it is a punishment for me to live in the big city. But your plan is also mine, and I do think that we could build a little bit of paradise on the edges of the big city for ourselves.

You will provide everything for us and no one will be allowed to take it away from us. But I don't want to have too many pipedreams, because I'm afraid that, something will come to destroy them.

I can really be happy in all kinds of life situations. I hope I haven't bored you with my musings.

Live well for today and please accept hearty greetings from your girlfriend, Rike

PS. Please do write to Halle, if you write to home it's a 14 day diversion. Please don't forget to say hello to your mother for me.

Halle Saale 5 October, 1947 11:15pm

cont ....

Sunday is over, and I quickly have to write before I take this to the post office. I feel so happy and my heart is overflowing. Do you want to know why? Because of you. My overflowing heart still needs to express this joy a little bit more, otherwise I cannot go to sleep. I don't know if you will understand what I mean, but here in Germany we like to say, if the heart is full, the sky overflows and that's the way it was with us today.

By the way, I still need to ask you one more thing, which might not be quite fitting, but it fits quite well with my night-time silliness. Can you dance? Not anything overly complex, but just simple nice, social dances. But I think if you are sporty, as for instance, sailing, you'll probably be able to do that as well. A joyful little dance is a little part of life for me. So, feel free to picture me – your goodtime girl in Germany.

Enough for today. Good night. I'll be able to sleep now, because I've expressed my joy a little bit.

Hearty greetings

A little cheeky one

Reading this letter, Fred was touched and reassured by Rike's tender commitment to their relationship, but he couldn't rid himself of the nagging doubts that so often plagued him. He aired these worries to his mother, so often a source of support to him. 'Rike says I overthink things and worry too much about the future. I think she underestimates the difficulties we would face. The thing is, I can't stop worrying. Would it really be so difficult to live with me as I think?'

'No, of course not, you're not impossible to live with, dear. Rike will need you to help her. You would need to make an extra effort perhaps to be tolerant and patient with your wife's friends, and you'll need to help her to find friends here. But you really don't need to imagine that it'd be impossible for you to live together … that won't help anything.'

Fred felt encouraged. He hoped she was right. He wondered about the wisdom of laying himself so bare in his letters to Rike; after all, the more she knew the more chance there was that she'd reject him. It was a risk, but he reasoned that a wife needed to know about such sensitive points and weaknesses. She'd find out all about him anyway. It'd be better to give her a chance to reject him now rather than later when it would be so much costlier.

CHAPTER FOURTEEN
1947: Negotiating obstacles

By the beginning of October, the occasional showers of correspondence between Fred and Rike became a flood. Each of them was as excited to receive a letter as the other, and they were eager to write back as soon as they could. Many of the letters were filled with the practicalities of getting Rike to England. The more Fred investigated the more he realised the complexity of Rike making such a move and that this had to be attempted in stages. The first stage was for her to move to the British zone. Although he could not get the permit she needed, he was able to send her a letter from the British Foreign Office approving the move, as long as she found accommodation with her brother, or another, who would take responsibility for her care. This letter could be shown to the British authorities in Germany if they wanted a passport/identification from her to enter the British zone. Furthermore, she could tell the authorities, if it were necessary, that they wanted to get married, that he was a university lecturer, that they already knew each other, and that he would be willing to give more information if needed.

The second stage was to demonstrate that once in England, Fred would be financially responsible for Rike's welfare so she wouldn't be a burden to the British authorities. He wrote a Declaration of Intent, which could then be presented to the authorities in the British zone in Germany. They would then authorise the move to England. He reassured her, however, that she wouldn't be bound by this document – she wouldn't be forced to go ahead with the marriage against her will. She could return to Germany after a few months in England if things didn't work out. 'I would be risking less than you though, it would seem to me,' he wrote, 'And I am ready to risk that. I wouldn't be arrested after all!'

Although these documents might help persuade the British authorities to allow Rike to come to England, Fred knew that the Russians were a law unto themselves and might well frustrate their plans. Whilst he could exert some influence in the British zone, using his old university contacts, he had no way of negotiating with the Russian authorities.

Alongside this dry and practical correspondence, more personal letters were also exchanged; sometimes, Fred wrote a number of letters without waiting for a reply.

5 October

Dear Rike,

I hope you will not think I am being selfish if I continue to talk about myself. It is true that I talk too much and that I talk too much about myself, but in this case I am forced to do so (my younger brother, if he would hear this, would surely say, 'that someone would have to force you to talk about yourself would be news to me.' But he has no respect for his elders. He also talks too much. My mother mostly listens. My father never listens. But I wanted to talk about myself and oddly digressed from the topic.) Don't feel obliged to write as much as I do. This could change on my end and it is very likely that you have too little time.

Perhaps by nature I am more of a father than a husband - or at least more father and husband than lover. Certain women don't seem to take a liking to me at all. ... I don't know if this is typical, and if it is my fault or that of the woman? I have often thought that it's only because it's a specific kind of woman. But then again, I've had to believe that it is me after all. Even with your parents, for instance, I had the feeling that your father could understand and tolerate me more than your mother. Or did I just imagine it?

Maybe I'm complicated. Maybe most people are quite complicated. Only then they don't see it as clearly that they're not used to expressing themselves, to explain themselves, to analyse themselves.

Maybe you are easier, more harmonious. I almost hope that it is the case that you can approach me with sympathy and understanding, unlike most people who have no time for this illness. ...

Now you must say something about yourself. Or say something

about your family or university. It will be about you and maybe this, 'indirect method' of revealing yourself will be preferable.

I'm tempted to cross out everything that I have written, but I won't. Living together will surely give a worse impression.

See you again

With hearty greetings and best wishes

Fred

Once again, Fred agonised over the impression he was making. Was he saying, revealing too much? Would he put her off? He was relieved to receive a letter from her, dated 8 October.

Halle, 8 October 1947

Dear Fred

I've just been for a walk in the German forest and found a little bit of home in Halle. I have sent a leaf to you. I can't help wondering, will the authorities let it through? If not, it would be quite sad!

What are your thoughts about the arrangements once I arrive in England? Should I right away identify as your wife, or will you receive me as a visitor and we will only after a while enter into the 'holy yoke' of marriage? The latter would, of course, be my preference. But I would like to hear your opinion on this. I just don't want to travel to the unknown. Otherwise, I don't believe there'll be any difficulty with me leaving Germany. They'll be happy to have one less mouth to feed.

By the way, I know people say that life in Germany must be so gloomy, but I don't see it as so difficult and unbearable. Of course, we have to live somewhat more modestly than in the past, but that is healthy. It would be a shame if you pity me; it really isn't necessary, because I'm doing much better than hundreds of people here. I see life as a gift, each day is to be savoured. I also have many friends who can rely on me - good friends, rather than superficial friends.

When people try to get to know me, they're put off by my supposed hard exterior. Actually, if they manage to get through the shell to my heart, it is often not possible for them to get out again. My sister tends to say, 'You know, Rike, often no-one likes you at first but later no one will ever let you go again.'

A colleague said to me today, how come you have so much to write - since she also posted my last letter. I guess I don't understand this myself - I've never had the urge to write that much before, but I think I could write a whole novel for you. But we're not meant to write that much, because we don't have enough paper to write on here, and I don't have the time either.

I know I ought to practise my English, but please write your letters in German, so I can know exactly what you're saying to me.

I'm off to bed.

With hearty greetings and all the best wishes,

your German girlfriend

Rike

Edinburgh, 10 October

Dear Rike,

I have contacted the authorities and explained that I will pay for you to come to England. You'll need to send a statement in order to get your ID document.

Please don't think that doing this doesn't give you a choice about whether you come to England. I wanted to have everything ready in case you do say yes. I'm not forcing you to rush your decision. You could still say no at the very last second.

I hope that your *joie de vivre* - enthusiasm for life, if it is the right kind, is exactly the kind of joy I need. I may have drawn a rather negative picture of myself, but the woman who will live with me will have to see this side of me, even if the rest of the world don't believe it. On days when the rest of the world seems happy, I often feel down and alone. But at home with my wife, I'd find it stressful to have to pretend I am happier than I am. It is odd how often comedians are melancholic - the English, Lear and Carroll, and German, Kastler and Morgenstern are some examples. In the only book that I published a critic said that I didn't show any humour within it. An acquaintance to whom I told this replied, 'How did you manage to write a book that is so different to who you are?' I said, 'Well, when I write, then I am alone. And perhaps I write like a child does, because it hurts. and writing in that case helps as a comforter.'

I don't want to darken your mood with my shadows. Much rather, I hope that your mood will blow my shadows away. I also hope that Wolf will help you to complete the picture of who I am. He's certainly helped me to form a picture of you. One can be asking for a lot in such a situation. I know that I couldn't ever describe my brother. I know his weaknesses too well and I like him too much. A stranger, especially a woman, would find all kinds of other weaknesses and strengths in him.

I know that it must be difficult for you to write letters that find the right tone, as you say. I don't want to feel as if I am making you torture yourself too much in the process. On the other hand, I would so like to know a little bit more of the content of your current life, its daily worries and joys. ...

Do you think that we will one day truly love one another?

See you soon

Fred

While Rike was walking in the woods near her accommodation in Halle, she noticed the beauty of the autumn leaves turning golden and carpeting the floor. Although the leaves were dying, she reflected that in her life, the buds of springtime were beginning to show. Death had dominated her life in the past few years, and she relished the signs of new life. She naively believed that Fred could visit her in Eastern Germany during the Christmas holidays and she was confident that by Christmas itself she would be safe in the British zone. 'If only you knew how much I long for that moment!' she wrote on 10 October. 'What's so lovely is that we know so much about each other already that we'll be able to converse as though we'd been meeting every day for weeks.'

Rike had been away on a trip to the countryside as part of her course, and she wrote on her return on 13 October, enclosing a lock of hair with her letter:

Now I'm back home again in Halle from my trip into the country. It was very, very nice, and I've brought back a supply of country air for my cell, and besides that I've once more had enough to eat, so that heart and stomach are completely satisfied.

Today I'm sending you my picture and also a lock of hair, so at least you know my real hair colour. You could almost make a picture yourself, although people assert the picture isn't good, so you'll find that I look like my eldest sister, and what remains is thanks to my mother. Perhaps you've noticed the resemblance already, because you'll probably remember all the faces at home better than I could notice resemblances in your face before I had a picture. Now you can give me your hopefully honest opinion and I will expect it.

One really ought to remain true to one's principles, don't you think?

So, this week will not pass without your receiving a loving greeting from me. I don't have much to say, and you might think what I have to say is just boring stuff, but that doesn't matter, we want to get to know each other, after all, one way or another.

Outside it's gloomy and it seems as though the warm weather

which spoilt us all this year really is going.

Another letter's just come, another reason to fulfil my intention to post this one, although I don't want you to think that I write to you only because you write to me. I write <u>only</u> when I have something to tell you, if there's a letter from you or not makes no real difference. But of course news from you gives me a bit of excitement. Earlier you said that you don't know how to behave with women. It's not a problem if you're not comfortable with nice pretty women, because, I never need to be jealous. Anyway you're right if you think my father thought more highly of you than my mother, because my mother had a liking for men with a bit of polish, and couldn't understand your casual ways. Nevertheless, it was she who urged the boys to bring you to Langebrück. I can't really remember now, but I certainly know that mother never spoke disparagingly of you, on the contrary. That's really my only worry, that we might not understand each other, because my siblings maintain that I'm very similar to my mother! But we'll find out soon enough.

But now time to tell you something about myself.

When you were in Dresden back then, I still went to a private school because my parents believed my health would be more looked after - after all, I really was a very tender child (I have to stress this). But my fragile constitution didn't correspond with my very wide awake mind; my greatest pleasure was in annoying the teachers, but I always did it only up to a limit which through experience I learnt would have no serious consequences for me. I can remember once having to do a piece of work as punishment which my mother was to sign. But I knew how much mother worried about my brothers, and I was ashamed of myself too. So, I quickly made up my mind, and got up the next morning an hour earlier, picked a huge bunch of flowers and gave it, together with the work, to my strict teacher. And just fancy, she was generous enough not to require the signature. You might call it bribery, but I think it was really not so much that as a real sense of regret for what I'd done.

By the way I'm taking English lessons to refresh my knowledge a little. I was astonished that today's lesson went quite well, so much so that my teacher promised to make me into a 'perfect English miss' by Christmas.

Now I must end. I've got a little more studying to do. Is it really true that the English never talk at home about their jobs? That's what I heard recently. I think that'd be a real shame, because I'd like to share what you teach your students.

But now really the end. I send all dear greetings and many good wishes, a real friendship awaits you.

Rike in 1947. Fred wrote that this photo 'awakened feelings in me that I had never expected. … Tender, loving feelings which I might not have had otherwise.'

All of their correspondence until now had been written in German, but Rike decided to surprise Fred by trying her hand at English. She found a card with the words 'Who does not deeply desire in their heart such a great Sunday letter?' inscribed in German on the front:

15 Oct

Dear Fred!

I will try to write to you some words in my future-language. If there are many mistakes, you must not laugh, for it is a long time ago, that I write some English letters. I've worked today till my eyes closed themselves but I had to think of you and that is the matter. This card I found in the map of my past at home and I thought she'll please you like me. It's our wishing in short words with a nice picture. Oh, I have forgotten all my school-English and I shall better write in German, for I need a long time to form a sentence. (I believe that was in 'German English').

Good night! I shall dream of England.

Your friend, Rike

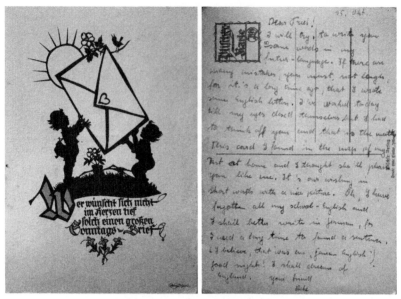

Rike's first postcard to Fred in English

Fred was so thrilled that she had taken the effort to write to him in English; he could certainly relate to her words about it taking so long to form sentences in what, for her, was a foreign and unfamiliar tongue. He remembered how long it had taken him to write letters to Karl and Helene over ten years' previously. Though he had certainly sped up and seldom needed to resort to a dictionary thanks to years of practice, writing German still didn't come naturally to him. He knew he was sounding more formal than he wanted to be and, whilst never an emotionally open person, he felt even more inhibited, restricted in the way he was communicating. Rike, in contrast, came across as lively and free, her personality leaping off the page; he doubted his letters had the same impact. He enjoyed reading her letter in English and it thrilled him to see her refer to her 'future-language' – seeing her express this in this way made their plans and dreams seem more real, possible, even plausible. And, he mused, she actually thought of him and dreamt of England. He sat down to write back to her in English – just a postcard, not one of his essay-length letters.

Dear Rike
    Your English card was quite good, though there were mistakes.

He shook his head – he couldn't resist slipping into teacher-mode; he hoped she didn't mind too much. After all, he did want to try and be encouraging to her, so he continued.

> But in any case, you know more English than I knew German at your age. I went to Vienna when I was 21, and Dresden when I was 22. At school I learned a few words – we did very little German – and then much more with a gramophone and the radio. But I learned very quickly in Vienna. Every year makes it harder, I think, but you are still young enough to find it easy – I mean, to learn a new language.

He still sounded school-masterly, and wanted to move away from that, to convey how much she meant to her.

> It's strange. I see many doubts and difficulties, and yet I find myself suddenly wishing you here as strongly as if I had long had strong feelings about you. It seems a strange, unorthodox form of romanticism. And it makes me want to say to you, 'Come quickly!'
> Yours ever,
> Fred

He was relieved to have written, albeit briefly in English. Though he was fluent in German and had written many letters, he still felt that there was a kind of barrier between him and what he was saying. It wasn't that he couldn't say it 'right' but he was using phrases he'd read or heard elsewhere, not necessarily his own words. Sometimes the letters came out a bit formal or distanced, sometimes they were somehow unnatural. Speaking two languages was like living twice over, you did have many more words to describe things, but they weren't all quite as authentic as writing in your own language. It all made the process of getting to know Rike and enabling her to get to know him that much more difficult.

* * *

As well as worrying about whether their relationship would work after having only known each other through their letters, Fred continued to turn his attention to the practicalities of how Rike could travel to England. He contacted the German section of the Foreign Office who suggested that it wouldn't be too difficult for

Rike to visit Wolf in Düsseldorf, where he was continuing his studies. The declarations Fred had signed vouching to look after her welfare should then mean that she'd be able to stay in Düsseldorf until she was able to travel on to Hamburg where she would fly to England. She would need a passport for the visit, and Fred was confident that his letters and documents would help her obtain it. It all depended on Wolf finding her somewhere to stay for three months. That would give enough time for Fred to get the necessary travel permits for Rike to travel on to England. He found out from a travel agent that he would be allowed to pay for Rike's journey across the channel if she declared in writing that she was unable to pay for the journey. This, at least, was not insurmountable.

Fred contacted Wolf with this plan, asking him to find a way of looking after Rike and finding somewhere to stay. Wolf, however, who had spoken with Rike, wasn't as encouraging as Fred had hoped and on 16 October 1947 wrote from the Orthopaedic Children's Clinic, Süchteln:

> … As you know, Rike has now settled into student digs in Halle and is happy she can study there. As far as I know, she wants to lay the foundations for eventual independent work somewhere. She doesn't want to jeopardise this by coming here; not only is the move difficult but also she wouldn't be able to return to the other zone afterwards. Here, there are strict limits on living space. Every parish has taken in so many refugees that there's hardly room left for new arrivals.
>
> In these circumstances it's practically impossible to get an immigration permit for Rike. And without a permit you can't get a ration card. Furthermore, it's questionable if she'd have the chance to continue her studies here. So you'll understand she doesn't want to move from her present location before ensuring she has secured a viable alternative. Instead, she thinks it would be better if you were able to come here so that you could get to know each other before making a commitment to leave her homeland. I know that's very difficult but I'll make enquiries if we can't invite you via the Academy to give a few lectures to the students. I assume this is not impossible as we've had several lecturers and professors from England. I just don't know how long it would take before the authorities would pass on such an invitation.
>
> The reason that this is so complicated is that the East zone is as

good as cut off from the three west zones. The four times I've been home I've had to cross the border illegally. I can't expect my sister to do likewise because the police and border guards are very hostile to illegal crossings. However, I think that even if East and West separate completely there might still be a possibility for her to move here if sufficient urgency can be conveyed to the authorities.

So, I must agree with my sister when she says it's better for you to come here, even if only in three or four months' time. I know this doesn't match your plans. But I'd like to ask you to fall in with this idea.

If you don't get any letters from the East for a month that's mostly because of the unreliability of the post. I'm often left for weeks without news from over there.

Please greet your mother from me and accept my best greetings.

Your friend,

Wolf

Fred was devastated and confused. Wolf's letter left him in no doubt about the immense challenge ahead of them. Rike had seemed much more positive and confident about moving to join Wolf. Was she having second thoughts or had she not conveyed their deepening commitment to one another? Or was Wolf merely being overprotective? It also seemed that both Fred and Rike had underestimated the implications of a move to Düsseldorf. But he was determined to rise to this challenge, as he had been nearly a decade earlier when faced with the task of extracting Karl and Robert from Vienna. He would do what he could, pull whatever strings, speak to whomever he could, to get Rike to England. And her latest letter, which he received on 28 October, contained her picture, which gave him even greater motivation. As he expressed in his next letter to her, written the same day, this photograph had quite an impact on him.

I liked your picture very much. It awakened feelings in me that I had never expected. You won't be cross with me – because they're tender, loving feelings which I might not have had otherwise.

You have a round little face that reminds me of a sweet little kitten or a teddy bear, although admittedly I only half like cats – but I've always passionately liked teddy bears. Perhaps as other men look for a wife who reminds them of their mother, I look for someone who reminds me of a teddy bear...

I have many female students in my seminars, and I amuse myself often by giving them not only public marks for their Latin but private marks for beauty. I notice that the blondes are unreliable. If they're tired, or have a cold, or have slept badly or are too pale for some reason they look nothing like as pretty. They get alternately ones and fours, like Wolf in English. The brunettes are more consistent and that pleases me more over time. I've also discovered that the moderate ones in Latin are the prettiest (with one or two exceptions).

You needn't fear. I won't fall in love either with their Latin or with their beauty. I compare them with your picture and am satisfied.

Rike laughed when she read Fred's letter. All that fuss over a picture! Although she was a sensible woman and knew that there was far more to a marriage than physical attraction, it felt good to be desired. After all, she found Fred attractive too, physically and emotionally. Crazy as it sounded, she loved the man. Yes, the more she thought about it, the more she was convinced that this match might just work. Though Wolf was still urging caution, she was determined now to move West, to embrace the possibility of a new life in England, and a new life with this man who was beginning to capture her heart.

3 November

Dear Fred,

Your letter came a couple of hours ago and encouraged me to write straight back.

My dear teddy bear, I'm so glad that my picture hasn't upset your equanimity and led to disappointment.

In six weeks I'll be in the West and am just awaiting your ticket.

I was invited to a little party but I said no because I thought of you and knew it would turn into a drinking-match, which I never like, so I'm sitting with you, glad that I've controlled myself. I've started to ask myself, before I do anything, what you might think of it.

Now do believe me that you occupy a large place in my heart. It's so nice to trust in each other completely, and when you give me courage to start each day with cheerfulness, I know I'm no longer really me without you. That's not flattery, but the truth! If you only knew how much I'm looking forward to seeing my dear teddy man, and it won't be long now!

At the weekend I'm going to my sister's and we'll talk everything through again. They laugh at us two. We're both romantics at heart though in the midst of real life. We're daring to do something, but there's an old saying: who dares wins. We'll prove that we can build an island, with its own sun, warmth and strength, we'll treasure each other and be there for each other. This is the first time I can write you this because I know you're imagining a real person and my eyes tell you this isn't just empty words but the truth.

Don't be cross that I'm finishing, it's late and bed is calling. I'll dream a little about our future. This letter might be incredible to you, but it's true.

The delay with receiving letters meant an emotional rollercoaster for Fred. Relief swept over him as he realised their tender letters and growing fondness for each other had convinced her to take the risk of moving to England, seeing as though arranging a face-to-face visit in Germany seemed almost impossible. Although Rike wrote she would be in the West by Christmas he knew nothing was set in stone and tried to guard himself against further disappointment.

Again, she wrote to him, this time whilst on a brief visit to Langebrück.

Langebrück, 9 November.
A short visit home should not pass without a sign of my thoughts of you. My sister and the children have already gone to bed and I can follow my thoughts undistracted. I've had a very nice break in Langebrück, and I was troubled to see how much my heart still thinks of home. But I'm coming to you, because once I'm decided on something I carry it out. Perhaps I'll also find a home in England. It's now only six weeks till I move West, and by the time you get this it'll only be four.

I must thank you for your last letter. I don't have brown eyes – the colour is hard to describe; I think dark blue comes nearest. I can hardly wait for the end of the semester.

In bad dreams I see myself at the airport in London with billowing coat and none too light suitcase, you're not there and I don't know where to go in a foreign country with no money or acquaintance. I think I'd hang myself on the nearest washing line post if that turned out to be true!

Just to say that your letters always produce joy, even if they seem not very successful to you. And at those times I want to be with you to help dispel the clouds. My friend in Halle says I'm the only one who can dispel her bad moods. The moods of others impel me to be cheerful, and I can usually manage to coax them out of the shadows...

This evening we looked at old family photographs and after that, they read cards for me. I don't believe all that stuff, but I had to laugh when the cards predicted a long journey to a 'dark man'. Time for bed – I'm very tired. Take my dearest greetings and best wishes.

*   *   *

Fred continued to worry and fret over everything; Rike was the source of his worry and the calm in his storm. He became increasingly convinced that far from being the rescuer, she was the one who would rescue him. He knew she was sensible, that she wasn't someone to take undue risks. She took and listened to advice; above all, from Wolf, whose emotional and practical support Rike and Fred both valued. Fred conceded to Wolf that it might be rash for Rike to give up her university place. Fred hadn't required Wolf to take any responsibility for Fred's plan and he assumed that Wolf would have been honest and said, 'I simply cannot imagine a marriage between you two. Rike would not understand your nature and your views' – but he never voiced this despite Fred's fears and so, notwithstanding the reservations Wolf expressed, Fred took this as encouragement. Rike was so perceptive; she sensed his anxiety and believed that she could help bring him the peace he so desperately needed:

> I don't wish anything for myself other than that my present calm and happiness might still be with me when I'm with you, because it's a source of the strength I need to help others. This calmness in me has actually managed more than once to make people happy and content, why should it not also work for you?

Fred read these words over and over, gaining strength and solace. He was beginning to believe she was right.

Wolf wrote to Fred on 19 November -

> I have got no further in my efforts to get an invitation for you to lecture here. I assume Rike has let you know that she'll visit me at Christmas. I hope she'll manage it.

You're right to say that Rike shouldn't give up her place at the university just like that; indeed, she's expressed a vague anxiety about leaving to me. I'm not sure why exactly; there are probably lots of reasons why she's hesitating. Maybe she enjoys being able to spread her wings among young people. Perhaps she lacks the courage to leave the area she was brought up in. I hope she'll write all this to you herself, because we siblings don't often know what really troubles the other, and often we don't dare talk about it.

The decision must be Rike's alone, although I've said I'll advise her.

Wolf was absolutely right; it needed to be Rike's decision. But, what would that decision be? He knew he could drive himself mad worrying about this, so he threw his energy into trying to get Rike to England. If only they could be together, then they would know for certain whether this would work. Her anxieties might be real, but on the other hand Wolf, as the protective older brother, may have been overemphasising her reservations. After all, her letters were full of optimism and determination to give her all to this relationship, which he found both healing and refreshing.

It may have been profound insecurity, but Fred had become obsessed that his diminutive size would push her away once she saw him. Rike's calm, candid response – to this, as well as his other worries – assuaged his fears…

Halle, 23 November

I've just found a letter that you sent me that was posted to my old landlady. Full of curiosity I opened it on the street, on the way to the student canteen. It made me both laugh and cry.

First of all your preoccupation with the 2½ cm height difference, about which I had to laugh so much because I knew already you were shorter than me and it didn't put me off. For me it's an outward thing that has no meaning. Wearing a top hat is the answer.

Seriously, why shouldn't I feel just as much respect, admiration, love and self-sacrifice for a person who is 2 cm shorter? Why would I feel superior to him just because of that?

I don't agree that marriage is a renunciation of an ideal life for both, but rather I'd like to prove that together we could create the ideal life (even with 2 ½ cm difference!)

It seems that you have the same success with women as I have with men. I've never had a problem relating to women or girls, but I've never captivated, or rather could never captivate, a man, because I, like you, react oppositely to men. My female friend once said to me, 'I don't understand you, why are you so prickly towards men you really like?' I don't understand that myself. And yet I know now that with you it'll be different because we'll approach each other differently from other mortals. I'm certain I will find the way to your heart, if reality doesn't put too many stones in the way. Up to now I've either been able to clear such stones away or climb over them.

Why do you still think that honesty frightens me? Haven't I told you that truth is the fundamental element in my life! Whoever can't bear the truth should stay out of my way. That's what seems to me so ugly, when people pretend to each other in marriage. You need have no fear that I'll keep quiet about things I don't like. I'll tell you every time!

I know I can tell you in fourteen days whether I can bind myself to you for a lifetime. I can't do that yet – we have to get to know each other properly first.

Unlike you, I don't have the time to read at the moment, I just have music which I enjoy very much. Music can often give me more than a poem or a book. I also enjoy walking, swimming, cycling. Wolf told me you didn't dance. That's disappointing; you might remember that dancing is taught as part of the general curriculum in Germany.

Now to the last thing. When we live together then we must build only on the basis of independent mutual understanding, and I think I can understand you. I will try to bring about what you dream of, and perhaps we'll see a miracle and we'll mean more to each other than we imagine at present.

I wanted to say that Wolf and I in the past ten years have become very close to each other. The letters we write are not very deep, but we're there for each other if needed. I don't know if Wolf likes me as much as I him. He's my favourite sibling, but that only developed in the last seven years. Götz was the classic big brother – chivalrous, good and helpful. As proof: when he got his first pipe at Christmas, his treasure, he once let me smoke it, so we were intimately connected even though we never said a word. I never felt so close to Wolf at first – only after our parents died, did we find a connection to each other.

Rike's letters were a lifeline to Fred. She was so reasonable, so rational. She was, he realised, more and more, the woman he yearned for…

28 November

All this week I've wanted to write to you, come quickly, come now! More than ever this week I've felt that I need you more than vice versa, that I have less to offer you than I require of you, that I'm proud and egotistical.

Academic life still leaves me unsatisfied, and this week I actually wanted to run away – from lecture rooms, from elderly colleagues with their pointed comments and emotionless lives. I have to admit that I do find myself attracted to female students – I'm not old, not made of stone – but you need not fear. Two letters arrived from you: both make me feel you're ready to give up for me your home and a pleasant life with young friends. I felt obliged to offer you a different, new, better life, and thought, Can I actually do that?

My mother said to me, 'Rike will gradually become more mature, will understand more of the world. You're too impatient, you want to explain all your character from A to Z , with all its downsides, in one go. But that takes a whole life.'

I have spoken with George, my younger brother about my plans. I told him, 'I've just written R a long letter in which I tried to be honest'. 'Ah,' he said, 'you with your honesty! You'll spoil everything with your navel-gazing and your psychologising, and your academic's love of "truth". You'll only confuse her'.

I've just read your last letter again and I think I'm making it all too complicated. Your letter is so simple and shows you are willing to overcome any problems that we might face.

Dear Rike,

I'm going to finish this letter in English. You will have to learn to be loved in English as well as in German. To hear 'darling' as well as 'Liebling', 'love' as well as 'Liebe'. When I look at your picture it seems already possible to use these words. At first, I feared your picture might not please me, and that would be a cause of uncertainty and embarrassment, but now I fear that I may fall in love with your picture more and more while I am waiting and then, if I have to wait too long, risk idealising you too much.

Don't let me wait too long – darling
Fred

Fred writes to Rike, 'You will have to learn to be loved in English as well as in German.'

At the end of November, Fred was able to say he had made some definite progress on getting Rike to England; he managed to obtain Rike's plane ticket from Hamburg to London. He intended to send this to Wolf. It was a start. There was still the matter of getting her to Hamburg, which greatly perplexed him and dominated his thoughts as well as the correspondence between the two friends.

On 9 December Wolf lamented the change in tone in their recent letters, 'I find it really unpleasant that our correspondence has now taken on an almost official character, but it's probably unavoidable,' and continued to tell Fred that while he'd made progress, he was finding it difficult to make headway on Rike's journey to Düsseldorf. He didn't want her to cross the zone border illegally because the checks were becoming more stringent and almost daily people crossing the border were shot. He didn't want that risk for Rike. The only safe option was for Rike to travel on a military train from Berlin into the British zone. It was far less risky, but permission to use this train could only be given by an official of the Control Commission for Germany (CCG) of the rank of Colonel. Wolf didn't have any connections but urged Fred to take the necessary steps to get Rike permission to use this train. Once she arrived in Düsseldorf Wolf was confident that Rike would be allowed to leave Germany and travel to England.

Wolf intended to travel to Langebrück in the Christmas vacation where he could talk over what was needed with her then. 'I'll probably be back here by the beginning of January,' he wrote. 'I hope you can take the necessary steps so Rike can be here soon.'

Wolf was also anxious to be reassured by Fred of his honourable intentions towards his little sister:

> I sometimes get the impression that Rike doesn't fully realise the significance of her decision to go to Liverpool. But perhaps I don't see it entirely objectively. She's still the little sister for me even though she's an adult now and during the first days of the occupation fully stood her ground by courageously preventing our house being plundered – that means a lot. So, I ask you today – and you will certainly understand my request – that if Rike comes to England at first she stay with your mother. I'm convinced that's the best way. Your mother will certainly advise her well. And at first Rike will need an older person to give her necessary advice and selfless help and I'm certain your mother can do that. I know they'll get on well since I know both of them. And besides your mother will teach her about customs, habits and manners that are different from ours. For that she needs a woman – a man could never do it. Also, you will understand my caution and my wishes for the sake of the good reputation your wife must bring into the marriage.

In the meantime, Rike was keen to make the best possible impression on her prospective future mother-in-law, having received a letter from her. She wrote to her in the best English she could.

Halle, 28 November 1947

Dear Mrs Clayton!

At first I was quite astonished, when I got your dear letter. But I was very glad to hear anything of you, for Wolf had told so much of you. My English is not very good, but I hope you shall understand it. I have read your letter quite alone and I'm proud to have done so – you have told me about Fred and your description was quite near the picture, what I have had.

I don't know, if I'm the right woman to marry with Fred, for we have only seen another ten years before and I think Fred means Wolf, if he speaks with me.

So I thought, I had to come to England and we shall prove our character, for a marriage is no business. The real world sometimes is quite another than all the letters and conversations. Fred is of course my best friend and his letters are so nice, so I must be fond of him. But sometimes I thought, he must not mean, that I'm the only wife to make him happy and I wish that he shall have all his future dreams, but I'll try to come soon, that we all can meet another.

I know there were many mistakes but the chief is that you shall understand my words. Those years before I have had my last English lesson and since this time I have forgotten all my English speech.

I wish you a Merry Christmas.

  With kind regards
  Yours sincerely
  Rike Büttner-Wobst

At the beginning of December, she wanted to send Fred a Christmas present. She searched everywhere for something suitable, but could only come up with a model elephant – it was the only thing that she could find that she guessed would make it, intact, through the post. 'I'm sending this elephant as a Christmas present,' she wrote. 'There is nothing else I can send you in this post-war time, but I send my love with the elephant.'

A couple of days later she sought to reassure Fred, whom she knew fretted over so much. She wasn't so worried about the future. He did enough worrying for the both of them.

When I leaf through your letters one thing stands out. You torment yourself with worries which don't seem like worries at all to me. Every time I feel I want to smooth your brow and tell you that everything is much easier than you think. My worries are of a quite different kind, because they arise from much more practical things. I hope we'll jointly overcome your problems and mine and find the way out that you seek. The master on the training farm used to say: 'A pity you're not here all the time, Friederike. Every day with you I get a day younger. That's the nice thing about you, you're always cheerful, whether loading dung, or cleaning out the horses, or spreading manure. You'll always find something to laugh or be cheerful about.' My father was a wise man and always used to regale us with wise sayings. One of his favourites was, 'Worrying in advance is like giving wings to a distant hardship.' I think we'll know in at most four weeks if we can master life better together than alone. And if it's not to be I'll continue studying and I'm sure there'll be better, nicer and prettier girls for you. So, don't worry!

Time to end, because it's my landlord's birthday with coffee and cake, and I'm solemnly invited. These days you don't say no. Tell me, what do you like to eat best? I can remember Wolf enthusing about your mother's fantastic roast mutton that really impressed him.

All the best for today. Take all my dear Christmas greetings and all the best for the New Year.

Your Rike.

CHAPTER FIFTEEN
1947-1948: New horizons

1947 drew to a close, and as their relationship flourished Fred realised that he would need to establish long term prospects for himself and Rike. He didn't know how long his post at the University of Edinburgh would last; he also wasn't sure that his current income would be sufficient to support the two of them. He applied for a job at the BBC, but was unsuccessful. Despite his success with students, he was pessimistic about his prospects of advancing his academic career; he felt he would never catch up, even if he were more intelligent than his older colleagues who, unlike him, had been able to continue their academic work during the war. He would have liked a better post than the one he had currently, but he doubted if he'd be offered one with his lack of experience. Moreover, the war had brought changes; while he didn't doubt he still possessed the talents that had won him so many awards at King's all those years ago, he'd lost confidence in his ability to apply them.

He was also finding it hard to adapt to civilian life. During the war, others had organised his time for him and, in his free time, the uncertainty of surviving the war brought an urgency and focus to his work on his novel. Now, however, he was unable to use, profitably, the freedom he had and couldn't even organise his own work.

Furthermore, for him, the academic life wasn't enough; as he expressed to Rike, 'I want another, more solid justification for my existence. So, you see, I need you. All paths lead to this conclusion. I'm trying to solve a problem in my life, or perhaps many problems, with your help. At first, I thought I was more the giver – now, I'm more the recipient. More and more I feel I need you more than vice versa.'

He wondered if he were being too honest to her in his letters – his mother and brothers certainly thought so. But Fred knew no other way. He sent the letter, hoping it didn't have too negative an effect on Rike. At least she would know what she was letting herself in for!

In mid-November Fred's colleague, W K Smith told him of a vacancy for the Chair of Classics at the University College of the South-West in Exeter, Devon. 'Have you seen this?' he asked, handing Fred the job advert in the newspaper. 'I'm putting in for it. I think you should too.'

'Really?' spluttered Fred. 'I haven't got a snowball's chance of getting that.'

'I wouldn't say that,' Smith argued. 'Look, you might have certain advantages – over me, at least. I've done only Latin for several years, whereas your Latin and Greek are more or less equal.'

'I'm not sure that's quite true,' Fred said. 'I have only a little Latin and even less Greek – at least that's how it feels.' That was the problem – the war had made him so rusty.

'Well, I think you should give it a go as well as me – and may the best man win.'

'That will probably be neither of us then!' Fred joked.

When the vacancy was talked about in the department staff room, some said they thought Exeter's advertisement was a mere token; they'd lined up renowned Latin scholar Jackson Knight, who'd been Reader of Classical Literature there since 1942. This appointment would seem fair enough, Fred thought; he'd read Knight's book on Virgil and been impressed. What did Fred have to set against that? A book which nobody read? He didn't feel his novel exactly qualified him for teaching Classics in Exeter or anywhere, really.

So, Fred, being in a hurry, and not feeling very hopeful, posted the curriculum vitae he'd composed for the BBC job. He was surprised to be shortlisted.

On 5 December, Fred went to the interview with no great hopes. There, one of the panel asked him, 'How is your health now, Fred?' Obviously someone, in a reference, had mentioned his illness. Fred remembered that George had told Donald Lucas (a lecturer at King's), one of the referees, about it; it must have been him.

'I feel fully recovered now, thank you.' Fred replied. At least, I hope to God I am, he thought. But, of course, he wasn't so certain – being bitten once, in such a horrible way, had shaken his self-assurance. But did they believe him? Would they take the risk? He was convinced that once the issue of his health had been raised in the interview, that was it. Oh well, he could put it down to experience.

When they called Fred back, he thought the candidates were all to be told, in turn, it was 'nice to have met, but they regretted…'

He didn't believe his luck. Old Gilbert Murray (retired Regius Professor of Greek at Oxford) who'd chaired the interview panel, said, 'Mr Clayton, we are going to take a gamble.'

'I think you are, sir,' Fred replied. 'Thank you. I hope I won't let you or the department down.' He was absolutely amazed, although he wasn't unfamiliar with gambles himself. He was, himself, about to take one – his marriage. They asked him about his marital state, and he had indicated his hopes.

It almost seemed as if God had relented. He was grateful to that committee – for they were the Grace of God in person to him. Where, but for that Grace, would he have gone exactly? He was also thankful for his referees, John Sheppard (Provost of King's) and Donald Lucas who had obviously been kind enough about him. Sheppard might possibly have gushed too much, his enthusiasm might have been suspect. Donald was a different matter. He did not easily enthuse.

'So, when would you want me to start?' he asked, expecting them to say February or March.

'We'd like you to start immediately – the seventh of January, start the year in the best possible way,' Murray replied.

'Yes sir, thank you, sir,' Fred replied. He was delighted. What a surprise! He felt bad about leaving his colleagues in the lurch. The head of department, however, wasn't at all perturbed. He sincerely congratulated Fred and casually handed over Fred's classes to two colleagues. Now, Fred had to make preparations for a move, which would take place sooner than he'd expected. Nevertheless, he wouldn't complain. Against all the odds he had an opportunity to establish a future for himself and, hopefully, if all went well between the two of them, Rike as well.

He couldn't wait to tell her the news that he was a real professor with twice the salary and ten times the responsibility. He wrote to tell her the news while he was on the train back to Edinburgh, having stopped en route from the interview in Liverpool. Exeter, he felt would be the perfect place for them to begin a new life as it was surrounded by countryside. He was concerned, however, by the timing of his appointment – it could be that, at the very time Rike would be arriving in England, he would be preoccupied with this new position, especially when they had an important decision to make about their long-term future. 'I'll have so little time for her,' he told his mother. 'Rike might arrive in London on a day when I can't collect her. And, just at the time we should be getting to know each other.'

'Don't worry, I'll make sure I'm around to welcome her,' she replied. 'However, she needs to get to know you – it's your job to introduce her to life in England.'

He relayed all this in his letter to Rike. It would be the first of three letters he'd write in three days – the first, to tell her his good news; the second, after he had read her response to the letter he had worried would put her off him. At the end, she signed off, 'Still yours,' and Fred breathed a sigh of relief. Unable to think of anything or anyone else, he couldn't resist putting pen to paper the very next day, beginning this time in English.

Edinburgh, 9 December, 47

Rike darling,
    For after all I must begin – I hope I must begin – some day to love you in English, not only in German. I practise it to see what it sounds like. I practise it in front of your little postage-stamp picture, that I am always afraid of losing, it is so small. I practise it, and it is

strange how convincing it sounds, how true. That does not prove it is true or will be true, but it proves how much I want it to be true. And surely that is something, if at the same time we know and see clearly, that this love is not there already, that no one is giving it to us as a present, but that it is for us – and only us – to make it true, in spite of everything, because we wish it so.

He continued in German, pouring out his thoughts to her as he was now so accustomed to doing. He found it a cathartic process to express his thoughts, worries and doubts, and found that in doing so, the doubts were dissipated. He did worry if he was oversharing, that he might scare her off, but, he reasoned, the more he poured out, the more honest he was, the better she would know him.

Overall, Fred was hopeful. It looked as though the future was opening up for him. This new post brought a new start and a sense he could rise above difficulties; together he was certain, they could overcome all problems. He was delighted when he discovered that Exeter University had an agriculture department with its own farm that might enable Rike to continue her own studies, and there were very pretty country houses in the area, one of which they could make their home. He looked again at her picture, much looked at, much loved, much spoken to. 'I need you, dear Rike,' he said. 'I will need your love of life, if it's an understanding, respectful love of life with a bit of patience with my up and down moods. But will you need me?' That was the question that mattered above everything else. Would she come? Would she love him?

Just before Christmas he received Rike's Christmas greetings and the gift of the elephant. Together, they gave him some reassurance, though they didn't dispel his doubts completely; only her presence with him in England could do that. He hoped they would not have to write to each other for much longer, delaying the time when they could really get to know each other. 'Try, please, to visit me as soon as possible – and stay,' he urged.

Meanwhile Rike was now determined to travel to England. She had finished her semester in Halle and was preparing to bid farewell to her homeland. She chose not to spend Christmas at Langebrück, because of the shortage of food and her strained relationship with her brother-in-law, Fritz. Instead, she went to the farm where she'd previously worked. The people there were very friendly and warm, and she was able to help with the Christmas celebrations for the workers.

Her visit to the church service proved disappointing; there were no decorations in church and, strangely, the sermon wasn't really about the meaning of Christmas; it hadn't given her the festive feeling she'd been looking for. This was the first time Rike had been in church since her confirmation in May 1941 although, at previous Christmases, she and her siblings went together to the graves of their parents and read the Christmas story and sang carols by candlelight. The shared experience had brought them together as a family during this difficult time and, somehow, encapsulated the true meaning of Christmas for her.

After Christmas she arrived in Langebrück for New Year, where she frequently discussed her plans with Wolf. He reiterated his belief in the necessity of a meeting between Fred and Rike before any final decision were made about their future. It was his nature to be entirely rational, thinking about it from all sides, seeing it from all perspectives, but she knew nonetheless he wasn't the kind of man who'd simply let her get emotionally involved with Fred without meeting him first.

New Year's Eve was spent celebrating their traditional festival of 'Silvester'. As usual, it was a low-key, family affair, and Rike preferred it this way. She knew this might be the last Christmas holiday she would spend in Germany, which gave these particular celebrations added poignancy. After Mädi's family went to bed, Wolf and Rike were alone. 'Well, it's nearly midnight,' he said, 'nearly the dawn of a New Year. Shall I open our last bottle of red wine?'

'Good idea,' she replied. Wolf got up, opened the wine bottle and poured out two generous glasses. They sat in companionable silence for a while. Their relationship had changed so much over the past year or so. Wolf looked fondly at her. 'You're not my little sister anymore,' he said wistfully, 'you're so grown up.'

'I am nearly twenty-two, you know,' she chided.

'I know, I know, but you've always been my little sister, it's always been my job to look after you – especially since Mutti and Papa died.'

'Yes, I know, and I really appreciate it. You know that, don't you?'

He nodded.

'And,' she continued, 'I really appreciate how much you've done for me over the last few months, helping me to get to England.'

'Well, of course, that's what big brothers are for. And anyway, we're not quite there yet, there's more to sort out.'

'I know,' she said, 'it seems to go on forever. Do you think I'll ever get there?'

'Of course. You're determined enough. You have such courage. I really admire that in you.'

'And it'll be ok?' she asked, showing a rare sign of doubt.

'Time will tell,' Wolf replied. 'Fred's a good man. He's very honourable. He's a good and loyal friend. He'd treat you well. And, of course, if it doesn't work out, he wouldn't force you to stay; he's not like that at all.'

'I know. He keeps telling me that in his letters. He worries so much – he makes me wonder whether I should be worrying more. I know he's anxious about potential misunderstandings that may spring up between us. I'm not; in fact, I'm excited about our disputes and misunderstandings, because I'm confident that we will be able to find a compromise. I have a good feeling about this. I feel, somehow, as if it's meant to be; but meeting, really meeting, could change everything.'

'Well you will know little sister… it'd be wonderful, from my perspective, if you were married to one of my best friends, but I just want what's best for you. You deserve it, after all we've been through.'

'Well,' she said, 'There's only one way to find out –'

'Oh yes, what's that?' he asked.

'*Bleigießen*,' she smiled.

It was an annual tradition in the Büttner-Wobst home, as it was for many households in Germany. Rike lit a candle. Handing Wolf the *Bleigießen* poem, she asked, 'Would you do the honours and read this?'

'It'd be a pleasure –

"In New Year's Eve

The lead is melted.

It is tilted in water, cold and clear;

What do the figures represent?

Look at them as they are;

Do not guess the figure quickly.

Hold it back,

The shadow image promises you more.

If it does not occur to you,

Look at this little book.

It tells you frankly and freely,

So all sorts of ...!"'

Rike melted small chunks of lead in a spoon held over the candle. She quickly poured the molten lead into a bowl of cold water, where it hardened almost immediately. They peered at the hardened lead, trying to work out what shape it had formed and what this told them about the year to come. Rike didn't take this sort of thing seriously; it was a bit of fun more than anything else, but nevertheless she wondered what the lead would augur for her in this most significant of years.

Watching her, Wolf asked, 'Well, what does it look like?'

She reached into the water and got it out. 'I don't know. Actually, it looks like a ship – a boat.'

'You know what that means, don't you?' Wolf said.

She nodded. 'A voyage is on the horizon.'

'And,' he said, picking up the list of meanings, 'it can also mean you'll have good luck in your plans.'

'Well, if the lead tells us that, it must be true!'. They laughed.

In their Christmas letters Rike and Fred exchanged stories about their different traditions. Rike wrote to Fred about her time in Langebrück and about that peculiarly Germanic New Year tradition. In return she had enjoyed reading Fred's accounts of the English Christmas customs, of Christmas pudding, carols, turkey, and she wondered how they would spend next Christmas. She hoped they'd be together. She hoped they'd be able to make their own traditions, perhaps a fusion of the best of both of their cultures. She hoped for many things. In just a few weeks she would discover if those hopes would become reality.

CHAPTER SIXTEEN
1948: Red tape in the Russian zone

How could Rike get to England? This was the puzzle that faced Fred as the New Year dawned. He felt that he was going round in circles. It was so complicated! She needed to get to the British Zone, but where, and how? It seemed that the best option had been connecting Rike to Wolf in Düsseldorf, but even that was beset with difficulty. Fred was, at least, well-connected. He knew, either directly, or through his brother, George, a couple of people – T R Creighton and John Hemmings, who both worked at York House in Berlin, the headquarters of the Control Commission for Germany (British Element) – CCG, part of the British military occupying forces. They might be able to help Rike obtain the necessary documentation or at least they might know someone who could. Fred would try anything and anyone – he'd write a hundred letters if he needed to, if it meant that Rike would come to him; for this is what he desired above all.

On 5 January Fred moved down to Exeter to take up his post. He knew he needed patience – this was, his mother told him, the quality he most lacked. He was relieved to be busy with his new job and with the not-too-small matter of finding a new home for them. His parents offered to help him find a house, which would mean Rike would at least be able to come straight to Exeter. Fred wondered how he'd be able to afford this, and even briefly considered whether a solution would be to find a house in which they could live together with his parents, although he doubted that he could really bear to live with his father.

Then, Fred found a home, on the outskirts of the city – a white pebble-dashed bungalow, which was smaller than he'd hoped, but it was beautifully situated, perched on the top of a hill, overlooking fields and woodland. The living room looked out over the hills. Though the house was small, it had large gardens that, being almost all on a steep slope, would give him a headache were he responsible for their management, but that he imagined Rike seeing as a challenge, and an opportunity to work at creating something beautiful out of the potential chaos. Its name was 'Halwill', which meant Holy Well. His experiences in recent years had led him to doubt the existence of God; however, he was not immune to the idea of living somewhere that was associated with healing and life. All in all, he felt it was the perfect place for them to build their future together.

Halwill. Fred writes to Rike, 'I've bought a little house ... It will be waiting for you.'

Although plans were coming together, the spectre of fear plagued him. What if, when she arrived in England and she got to know him properly, she didn't love him, didn't want to be ... near him? Though he couldn't bear the thought, the rational side of him admitted this would be a possibility. He didn't want her to feel obligated ... as he wrote to her,

> The terms of your visa are that I declare my intention to marry you. If the state prevents our getting to know each other and requires us to make a definite commitment in a relationship that hasn't had enough time to develop, then I believe we should agree to get married, even if only for form's sake. It would give you a proper existence here, English citizenship, freedom. And afterwards if you wanted to get divorced, I'd have no objection.
>
> Now, I think I know myself and understand myself well enough that I can promise to let you decide freely once you've arrived.

He paused for a moment, reflecting on how strange this all was. It was an unconventional way of speaking about marriage – it was so business-like, contractual, and felt deeply unromantic. However, he was merely trying to take care of her, and release her from being burdened or feel forced into a loveless marriage. No, that would not do. Sighing, he ran his hands through his hair and continued...

> My dear Rike, it might be hard for you to understand me. Perhaps I seem ever more strange and alien to you. Perhaps you might think I know nothing of love, marriage, women if I can write like this. It might all seem very theoretical and unreal. But it seems to me you've managed to understand and evaluate many things about me better than I'd expected.

This emotional wrangling out of the way, Fred could move onto something more positive, exciting – their home.

> Dear Rike, I've bought a little house. My mother will inspect it next week. Prices are terrible – they've trebled in Liverpool, risen five times here. A smaller and more expensive house than I expected. It will be waiting for you. Can you, do you want to, will you come soon?

Despite Fred's longing, Rike's arrival seemed no closer with a letter that arrived from John Hemmings in Berlin, written on 30 December. He was still relatively new in his post, but was more than willing to find out what could be done. He happened to be going to Düsseldorf in early January and suggested meeting with Wolf and the passport office there to ascertain what documentation they needed to allow Rike to stay there. Once he was in full possession of the facts, he would be in a better position to find out from those who worked in Entries and Exits and Inter-Zonal travel what exactly Rike needed to be allowed to cross zones. He knew that the only means of travel officially open to the Germans was the train from Berlin, which was run by the British Army of the Rhine. He continued,

> There is of course the heartbreaking trek to the frontier and a crossing which goes on regularly and which the Russians do little to prevent. If you go along the one autobahn through the Russian Zone from Helmstedt (Lower Saxony) to Berlin, which we are allowed to use for communication with Berlin, you see many pathetic little groups of Germans struggling along it. I do not know yet whether those Germans who travel on our military train are only those who live in the western sectors of Berlin or whether there are those who are in the Russian zone. However, I will try and find out.
>
> I fear that there is perhaps little of comfort to you in this letter. I don't indeed know if I shall be able to do anything, but I shall be delighted to have a shot. I may be able in a few days to give you some more certain information.

Little comfort indeed. Everything was still so uncertain. Fred certainly didn't want Rike to be forced to become part of one of those 'pathetic little groups' struggling along the autobahn in their quest for a new life away from the Russian Zone. He was, however, grateful that someone was on the case who had more influence than himself or Wolf. George had said that John Hemmings was a decent chap; Fred believed him when he said he'd try to help.

Meanwhile he waited impatiently for news from Rike. He had no idea exactly where she was. Had she made it to Wolf in Düsseldorf, or was she still marooned in the Russian zone? The trouble was that letters from Dresden took so long to get anywhere and the waiting carried on. Fred was grateful for the distraction of settling into his new role in Exeter and adjusting to a new place. He didn't have too long to think – because when he thought too much, he grew increasingly frustrated with how little he knew of Rike's situation and whereabouts, let alone his ability to influence events.

The picture became a little clearer when Fred received a letter from Wolf –

16 January 1948

Now to the matter of Rike's journey. No-one outside Germany can have any idea how complicated the issues of authority and competency are. When I came to England before the war, I needed only a visa, then I could travel. Today you need at least ten different papers. It's difficult to get each of those papers. In most cases you're lacking one or the other requirement for it to be issued. For Rike, everything's worse because she's not even registered in the British zone yet. But she doesn't want to give up her right of residence in the Soviet zone. Therefore, the requirements for her emigration can't be fulfilled. If only she could decide to come here to Düsseldorf permanently everything would be easier. But I can't demand that of her because I don't know where I'd accommodate her here. 3,000 Düsseldorfers are living in bunkers. I've sent her all the papers including the plane ticket and told her to travel to Berlin, so she can find out there if she can travel out via the British zone – after completing all necessary formalities in Berlin – directly to Hamburg and from there to you. I just don't know if she'll achieve what she wants to there.

Unfortunately, letters take a long time to travel from Dresden to Düsseldorf, which simply creates more delays. Now I'm sitting here waiting until I hear something. It's very regrettable but there's nothing I can do about it.

I'm not sure the Berlin connection will work, but it's worth trying, because I really don't want Rike to travel here illegally. I'm glad I could discuss all this with her in Langebrück over Christmas. She spoke really rationally and not without enthusiasm about her plans. But you know, too, that siblings don't always show their true feelings to one another. So I couldn't get a true picture of what she really thinks of this plan. I must ask you not to interpret the fact that we've not yet made any progress in the exit permissions as ill will on my part. It's purely down to my inability to negotiate with our officials.

Fred was perplexed. He didn't know exactly where Rike was or how she was going to get to Hamburg. It didn't look as though she'd be able to join Wolf in Düsseldorf after all, so that particular scheme had been thwarted. Hemmings' conversations with Wolf, then, looked as though they would bear little fruit. As for Rike, he continued to worry about her. He knew that the postal system was subject to interminable delays, but he hadn't heard anything from her for over a fortnight. The general uncertainty hanging over them made it so much worse. He was relieved to hear finally from Rike, and her letters over the next weeks updated him on the progress – or lack thereof – that she was making.

Hochweitzschen, 4 January 1948.

Wolf hasn't been able to get an exit permit for me to Düsseldorf. We've looked into getting an inter-zone passport, but that will take two months and to get emigration papers I have to have lived in the British zone! The present political situation makes it too dangerous to cross the border illegally. But I've got nearly all the documents I need, so I'm not giving up. I'm going to Berlin in two days' time to see if I can negotiate with the Foreign Office directly. Perhaps they can get me a proper ticket to the West, or organise all my travel from Berlin. In which case I'd not need a train to the West. That would speed things up a lot.

Now the main thing: After moving I absolutely must come back to Germany once in order to bring all my clothes, my furniture and all my possessions (if things develop between us as we wish). You must know I'm not exactly a poor girl and that my parents prided themselves on building up my dowry. You will surely understand that I'd like to have these things. Is that at all possible???

All difficulties in England seem as nothing compared to the paper war in Germany. I know you said you might be too busy with work, but I'd really appreciate if you could meet me off the plane. I'm worried that, if your mother meets me, we won't be able to make ourselves understood, and things could go wrong.

Last night I dreamt that I'd arrived with my mother, and you collected us but were two heads shorter than me. But those two heads made no difference to our happiness.

This struggle to join you feels like I'm taking on an unbeatable force so much stronger than I am, but I'm up for the challenge!

In six months, I've got to like you so much I can't imagine you out of my life even for a day.

Reading through this letter Fred tried not to think too much about the challenges and the 'unbeatable force' bearing down on them; he preferred to reflect more on this extraordinary woman who saw these substantial difficulties as challenges to be faced and overcome. Amazingly, this woman seemed to like him – with all his insecurities and idiosyncrasies – and she wanted to be part of his life. He was profoundly aware that he didn't deserve this, but equally he knew he felt the same way about her; the prospect of life without her was simply unthinkable.

Though the letter sent on 4 January was full of difficulties, the letter Fred received a week or so later gave him more cause for hope.

14 January

Dear Fred,

At last I'm back from my Berlin trip and will give you all the details.

Last Saturday I went to Berlin by car. The weather was stormy and it poured with rain all the way. I stayed with the aunt of my former teacher, who looked after me very well. She gets parcels from America, and for the first time in years I drank cocoa and ground coffee, ate rice, and smoked a really good cigarette.

I didn't look for York House, the passport control office, until the Monday, and when I explained that I needed a ticket for the military train they turned my request down flat. First, I needed an exit permit from the Russians, or an interzone passport. I tried for this in the afternoon, but without any success. So next morning I reported to the Passport Control Officer. I filled out yet another application for a visa and submitted all my papers. The officer called me, and once I'd explained my hopeless case to him, he advised me to register as a visitor to Berlin. He promised me then he'd expedite my case. So now I have hopes again. In at most eight days, I'm moving to Berlin. It's not so easy, believe me. Although negotiating with all your officialdom isn't unpleasant, I do find all these paper-pushers dreadfully unfriendly. They're people so fixated on paper you'd think they were married to laws and ordinances. *Per aspera ad astra*!

So now you have a dry and, I hope this time, a clear report. Just so that you see I'm really making efforts to reach my aim.

Semester holidays are different for us than for you. The year has only two semesters and since we have no coal to heat the university buildings the holidays are from January till 15 April. Consequently, the holidays in summer are only three weeks. So, if my plan works and I'm with you in three weeks I've got time enough to return if things don't work out.

Now, as our whole plan is becoming reality for me, because I can actively do something towards it, I'm a little afraid of all the new and unknown things. I will certainly need a very good comrade, whose strong arm I can feel and who will protect me, to restore my self-confidence in a foreign country, But I think it won't be too bad, will it?

Enough for today! I've got to send this letter. As soon as I know more in Berlin I'll telegraph my arrival time in England. See you soon!

Fred checked the date. It was 22 January. Rike could be in Berlin by now, having taken a vital step towards bringing their plans and dreams closer to reality. It was agony not knowing. Although she did express some anxiety and confessed to being 'a little afraid' of the unknown that lay before them, he admired her hugely. He wondered how she kept going, kept so determinedly positive. He knew he wouldn't be so were he in her shoes. He hoped she felt all these efforts would be worth it and that he would fulfil her desire for a strong arm to protect her. He would certainly do his best.

A week later, her next letter arrived, where she updated him on progress and also her thoughts on how they might live together.

Halle, 21 January
About the arrangements in Exeter. Ideally, we'd have a separate flat from your parents, but I'm happy to for them to share the house if that's what you want. But tensions at home can be unpleasant – I had them long enough with my brother-in-law. I'm already looking forward to meeting your mother, I don't know why – perhaps that I'll learn a lot from her.

On Saturday I'm going to Schleiz for a few days to take leave of my friend, then off to Berlin under full sail.

You must have been smoking a good cigarette when you wrote to me, because your letter smelt like the black market over here.

I'll have to stop or I'll use too much electricity. Hardly worth talking about myself anymore – you'll be able to see for yourself soon enough.

Halle, 22 January

Just a little more to add to my previous letter. I had a dream which could have lasted all night as far as I was concerned: I'd received a telegram from you: 'First experimental flight to Mecklenburg [north-east] approved! Arriving to see my little lady on Friday. Fred.' But, I thought, the plane can't land in Mecklenburg, so I'll go to Berlin Tempelhof instead – and that's where you arrived. You had to leave after a couple of hours, so I flew with you as stowaway. But half way through this lovely flight my landlady woke me up! You see, I get no peace from you, even at night.

Schleiz, 31 January.

Eight days have passed, and I haven't written to you, though I've thought a lot about you. The day after tomorrow I'm going back to Halle, and on Wednesday finally to Berlin.

Reading these letters Fred was at least clearer about Rike's situation, although he was palpably aware that he was receiving information a fortnight or so after events were taking place, so he was never on top of things – for all he knew, the situation may have changed, yet again.

*   *   *

February dawned, grey and cold. Rike was back in Halle, having spent eight days on holiday at her friend Gisela's house in Schleiz, a small town in Thüringen, south of Halle. She had gone there hoping for snow so she could go skiing, but not a flake of snow fell; instead, she was treated to unseasonably warm weather and sunshine, which made up for her disappointment. Rike also felt the warmth of hospitality from Gisela's family who treated her so kindly she immediately felt at home.

Hearing of Rike's plans, Gisela's father delighted in regaling her with stories of his visit to England in 1902 and showed her a book about life in London. Her time in Thüringen gave Rike fresh energy and resolve for the challenge ahead of her, as did the three letters from Fred that arrived while she had been away. She was particularly thrilled to read that he'd bought the house where they both longed to make their home together. She would do all in her power to make this dream come true. She wrote to Fred full of excitement at the possibilities that lay ahead of them.

Halle, 3 February 1948

Dear Fred!

Three letters from you, but I must answer the last one first because it's one of the nicest letters I ever received from you. I'd not felt before how much and how dearly you think of me. Perhaps I've not understood you as well as at this time. The letter expresses so much warmth and your resolutions are so selfless. I assume they won't be necessary because I firmly believe that I'll be able to get my way in Berlin. All complications will be removed in advance, because if I don't marry you in the next two months I'll be expelled from the country. I've found a solution for my possessions. As soon as I'm clear whether I'm going to stay in England I'll have my things transported via Berlin to the west, and then they'll be able to be brought across the channel by ship or ferry. But right now those are such unimportant matters, much more important at the moment is my leaving here, everything else will sort itself out.

So, tomorrow morning I'll travel to Berlin, then I can go to the Foreign Office the day after. Enough of that, I'm fed up of all this office nonsense and would rather tell you what I've been up to. Today I was really irresponsible and had a really fun day with my friend who accompanied me back to Halle. In the morning I had all sorts of things to sort out at the university secretariat, since for now I want to keep my right to attend lectures. It's much easier than doing everything in writing when you get that far, I find. This afternoon we went twice to the cinema. Isn't that excessive? But it was nice! You're getting a very pleasure-seeking girl to stay with you, but I will tell you honestly that I don't need any of that if I've got my 'little place in the country' and don't have to sit hemmed in by stone walls. Nice of you to look for a house a little to my taste. I hope everything will eventually be how **we** want it to be. I'm so excited! Tonight I'm tired and you won't be cross if I finish. From Berlin you'll get more letters from me. Perhaps it'll be sooner than you think! At any rate you mustn't be surprised if I telegraph you! My identifying feature will definitely be my white fur coat which I'll wear for the journey. (You know about polar bears, I assume?)

Now all the best until we meet again! A little patience and we'll manage it!

Until then I remain far away but still your own
Rike

On 4 February she arrived in Berlin to try and sort the paperwork. The city was desolate, with dirty piles of rubble seemingly on every street corner. Most surviving buildings bore battle scars, pocked by bullets or with broken windows, including the hostel where she stayed for a couple of nights. She walked past soldiers with guns, some eyed her with suspicion, others with predatory interest. She shivered, remembering her encounter with the Russian soldiers at the end of the war. It all conspired to intimidate her, to encourage her to turn back. But she wouldn't. She had reached the point of no return. It was England with Fred or nothing. Nevertheless, three days of running around the city trying to battle with bureaucracy got her nowhere. She would have to return to Halle having achieved nothing. She was worn out and dispirited…

Berlin, 6 February 1948

Dear Fred!

Three days of useless running to and fro and I'm fed up and tired. Tomorrow I'll have to leave with nothing accomplished. A pity, and I had hoped my carefully worked-out plan would leave no more cliffs to overcome. After 100 detours I found an address in the American sector where I would be accommodated until my exit permission is available. When I went to speak to the mayor, he told me the Americans don't process exit applications if you're not registered as living here. And you can't get a change of residence permit either etc. Now I'm moving on again to try to obtain an address in the English sector. Another 14 days wasted! It really makes you weep. If it doesn't work this time, I can't see a way out! Even a form stating my home 'Land' would help me very little. It's a never-ending war of paper. But only patience, I'll manage it in the end! Somewhere there must be someone with an old aunt in Charlottenburg, which is a district in the English sector, where I can bed down for a short while. Above all it's difficult because I'm not allowed to register here for food stamps because Berlin is closed, but how gladly I'd take three weeks if it would eventually succeed.

So much for my successes and/or failures. Over time, though, even the stupidest ass cottons on. You know all about that…

Now a little more about your letters. That idea of an aeroplane flight was probably just a pipe-dream, because I would so gladly have avoided all this bureaucracy. But I really don't wish you to be so short - on the contrary, you should become the main thing in my life, you mustn't be so short! If necessary I'll put a couple of bricks on my head so that I shrink a bit. As regards annual festivals I think we'll be able to agree. From all the lovely customs of your country and mine we'll choose the loveliest, and then together we'll celebrate the loveliest festivals in the world. Do you agree with that? Perhaps we could try at Easter. I'll gladly play the German Easter bunny! Perhaps I could cross the border disguised as that?

Yet again I've had no post from Wolf for a very long time. I'm almost jealous that he writes so often to you. Perhaps I'll get more post from you later. I've not heard from my sister for a long time, but I'm sure she'll show herself again, or I'll travel to Langebrück again before I come back.

But now that's all for today. I've got to go to bed. Tomorrow that pleasant crush all over again in the train.

With all my heart

Your Rike

She returned to Halle on 7 February, where two days later, she celebrated her 22nd birthday and dearly hoped it would be the last birthday in Germany. She didn't dare believe otherwise. She was, however, exhausted – all the travelling from Halle to Berlin was taking its toll – and discouraged – she was beginning to wonder if the bureaucratic mountain she had to climb would prove to be insurmountable. Yet she wouldn't give up, not yet, anyway. Surely there had to be someone she knew who had an acquaintance who lived in the British sector of Berlin? After asking around, finally, she managed to get hold of two addresses. It seemed like all the gaps in her paperwork were being filled. Only bureaucratic resistance could thwart their plans. She resolved that she would at least try everything.

Then, at last came a glimmer of light. Fred received a letter, dated

26 January, from another of his contacts in Berlin, Tom Creighton, Deputy Educational Adviser for the CCG. Tom said he would be able to help Rike if she could get from the Russian zone to visit him in his office in the British sector of Berlin. From there he could facilitate her onward travel in the British zone. He was worried, however, that Rike might be prevented from receiving this advice as any communication to her of this sort could be intercepted by Russian censors who might conceivably prevent her from leaving. One never knew what the Russians would do next.

The body of the letter was typed, but Creighton had added the following by hand:

> If she can get to Berlin and get someone to put her up in the British zone for a <u>maximum</u> period of 3 weeks, she can get travel documents and visa here, and can go direct from here by air to London. To facilitate this you must write direct to
>
> H.M. Consul-General, Political Division, HQCCG, Berlin, B.A.O.R. 2, certifying that you are
>
> a) a British subject
> b) legally free to marry
> c) intending to marry … within 2 months of her arrival in England
>
> You must pay £16 to B.E.A.C. in London and ask them to inform their Berlin office that a passage is available for her on demand.
>
> This whole process takes not more than 3 weeks. I can help her to obtain travel documents but she may have difficulty in being accommodated in the British sector and getting ration cards. I can try to arrange this, but may not succeed.
>
> Alternatively, she still can go into the British zone and do all this there, at any place which has a British Consul, if you and she prefer. It makes little difference which, except that it may be quicker in Berlin, and we have been having a little trouble with the Russians lately in getting trainloads of Germans over the border.
>
> But if she will come to me, I can give her a passage to the zone.
> Congratulations will be well in order when all this has been done!
> TRMC

At last, Fred thought, his various attempts at pulling strings were bearing fruit. He now had a plan – Rike needed to get to the British zone in Berlin, and Creighton would be able to sort the travel documents for her. Although details were still sketchy, they at least had an advocate in the form of someone of influence on the ground in Berlin who would be able to do something. Fred couldn't wait to tell her the news –

5 February

Dear Rike

I am a bit closer to getting a passport for you. I have heard from Creighton and he said that he should be able to help. And I've learned, through reading the newspapers here, that there have been serious discussions in government about employing German women here.

Opposition to employment of foreigners seems to be slackening here. With the shortages of workers and destruction of the German economy I had predicted such a step. There look to be various possibilities for me to give you a good life.

My mother has had a look at this house – she thinks it's a charming, but very expensive little box. She admits that one could fall in love with the situation and that all prices are very high. We have agreed that my parents will move in with me at the end of March and will stay as long as we all want. They will rent out the house in Liverpool, probably to my younger brother, but they won't give it up. So, you can get to know me, them, the house, and the situation, all at once.

We have a cow as a neighbour in the field, who seems quite nice, although we've not greeted each other. We ourselves have a small meadow where the present owner keeps geese. In the garden we have a few blackcurrants, hazelnut trees, gooseberries, apple trees, snowdrops and primulas and soon there will be daffodils. The house lies on a hill and looks over to the hills beyond the river. If you go a little further behind the house up the hill, you can see the valley, river, and the railway. Where we are, trees hide the valley and the railway. The house has seven tiny rooms all on the same floor – a kitchen, bathroom, five living or bedrooms – just as we wish. Does that sound nice? I was really thinking about you when I chose it, and also about me. It's well situated for the library, and the cow, for the new university buildings, and the trees, and so on and so forth.

Although the arrangements for Rike's arrival in England seemed to be falling into place, Fred was finding it difficult to keep track of Rike's progress in Germany – he hadn't received any news for over a fortnight. It was incredibly frustrating, and he felt the all too familiar sense of dread rising in him. He fought to keep it down. The day after telling her about their new home, he wrote again, 'I'm worried about you, because I haven't heard from you in 16 days. The general uncertainty is becoming unbearable.' He was grateful that during the week his mind was diverted by his work and, completely helpless to assist Rike, it gave him solace to throw his energies into the things he could control, keeping regular tabs on the progress of the house purchase.

From what Fred could piece together, the situation kept changing; although he received a letter from Berlin from Rike he couldn't read the address and work out which sector she was in. The letter had also taken nine days to reach him, which meant he felt he was always chasing after events. How he longed for the immediacy of a phone call!

* * *

Having been on the verge of giving up, when Rike received Fred's letter informing her about Creighton and the options for obtaining a visa, she had a fresh burst of energy and precious hope, although she steeled herself to face the possibility that their hopes and dreams may not work out. She wrote from Langebrück to Fred on 12 February:

> In 8 weeks my new semester starts, and if there's no way out by then I will have to plunge with new joy into my work. Of course, I almost wish that by then I'll long since have been with you, have successfully finished my studies and will have begun my role as housewife. It's actually terrible that I'm already so familiar with the thought of my new surroundings that I'd be very disappointed if it were all a dream.

Fred had painted such an idyllic picture of the home he had bought for them that it filled Rike's daydreams and gave her further resolve. So, a few days later, on 16 February, she returned to Berlin determined that *this time* would be different. She walked back to York House (Headquarters of the CCG) to meet with Tom Creighton. Though he wasn't there she sat with his secretary to complete yet more paperwork (she wondered what body parts she was going to have to give away this time!). The secretary, a middle-aged woman who had an impressive grasp of German, offered her a drink and, hearing of Rike's multiple and hitherto fruitless attempts to overcome bureaucracy, took pity on this young woman.

'Miss Büttner-Wobst,' she said kindly, 'I'm sorry you've had such difficulty so far. I can't imagine how stressful this has been for you. And I apologise that Mr Creighton can't be here for you, but he asked me to reassure you that he would give your visa priority. You should get it in three weeks, so you don't have much longer to wait.'

Three weeks. That didn't seem so far away. Rike was so relieved she felt tears welling up inside her. But she didn't want to cry all over a stranger. All she could manage was a mumbled 'thank you.' She was so excited that she wrote to Fred from Creighton's office; she couldn't wait to tell him the news. Her first concern was to seek to reassure him.

> We're a lot further forward! Your worries are completely unfounded, I'm still fine and am looking forward to things progressing. In case you don't get any post it's probably due to the postal connections, because I've been writing faithfully.
> Enough for today. Soon I'll be with you in your little house.
> I think it'll be for ever.
> Your Rike

Four days later, by 21 February she had got an address in the British sector which enabled registration. She went back to York House to get hold of the Exit Permit, but Creighton's secretary apologetically said that he was still away. Rike was flummoxed. She could envisage the three weeks becoming more like four, six, eight, and she couldn't let that happen. She talked through her dilemma with the secretary, who advised her to try the Mayor of Wilmersdorf, which was in the British sector. In the Mayor's office, a helpful lady said she would take up her case with the British authorities, and they went back together to York House. Within five minutes she was given an exit permit without the need for a Berlin identity card. That evening, exhilarated, she wrote to Fred to update him on the latest developments:

> Cheerful and in good spirits I went the next day to the Health Office, and the dear old doctor was at first sight quite sure that I was completely healthy. So that obstacle was overcome. After that I had to go to the Strangers' Police [registry office for residence permits] because they too have to confirm that I'm allowed to get out. Here I ran up against a brick wall, because the official said, 'What, you don't have a Berlin ID? Then I can't process your application. The English require your ID!'. When I explained to him that I'd already got permission from the English he answered he'd got to follow his rules. But he did take my application. Now I'll see on Monday if this fine gentleman is minded to give me that one stamp. If not I'll just have to wait until Creighton returns. Now I have another request to make of you: please send me straight away, in addition to my flight ticket from Hamburg, the ticket Berlin–Hamburg. Otherwise, the journey will cause unnecessary difficulties. My ticket number is 63 235. If this isn't possible, please send the purchase price to Creighton. But it would be better if you sent the ticket. You'd save me lots of toing and froing. Please send it to Creighton's address. At least I'll be sure that it will arrive – I'll collect it from there.
>
> I'll be so glad when I'm at last sitting in the plane. No, you can't help me with anything else, because your authorities are not as stubborn as ours, and even the best of friends cannot help when the German police have 'their regulations'. The whole thing won't take much longer. 10 days, then I'll have my exit permit and ten days later the visa. But so many things are likely to get in the way that I probably won't need my 'polar bear' coat after all. I would be really happy to have it here now, because it's got really cold again. If the newspaper reports are correct, you've also been able to enjoy the late winter.
>
> Enough for today! More on Monday!
> With all my heart, your Rike

Rike was delighted finally to be able to have something tangible to hang onto and she knew that Fred would be so pleased and relieved. After feeling they were making no progress, suddenly things were happening so quickly; so quickly, in fact, that she didn't have time to post her letter before she had further news for Fred – the news they had been wishing and hoping for so long. There were tears in her eyes as she scribbled in her haste:

23 February.
I've done it!!! In 14 days I'll have my visa. Please send me that additional ticket straight away – that'll decide when I can travel.

She was then delighted to be able to write with the greatest measure of certainty they had ever had, 'I can explain all this to you better in person. Looking forward to seeing you again soon.'

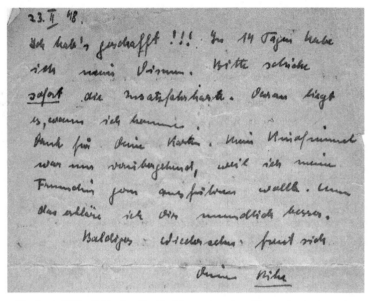

'I've done it!' Rike delights in telling Fred that, at last, they will see each other face to face.

Fred's hands shook as he read her letter. He wept with relief. Finally, she was coming. What an incredible woman she was. He admired her tenacity and strength so much, and marvelled that she was crossing an ocean for him.

CHAPTER SEVENTEEN
1948: A new life

As Rike made her preparations to leave her homeland she recorded her experiences in her journal, a large red leather notebook, that she'd been writing in since 1943. What an extraordinary five years it had been; so much had happened – and now, everything could be about to change.

7 March
I have finally received all my papers and got them together. I collected the plane ticket to Hamburg from my friend and telegraphed the siblings: Flying out Monday 15 March lunchtime.
I can't believe this is actually happening!

14 March
And they have come – the poor remnants of the family – Wolf, Mädi; they'd brought the last bottle of Arak and the farewell was cheerfully toasted at good Aunt Anna's.

15 March
This morning I was a bit apprehensive; unfortunately, neither Mädi nor Wolf could come to the plane with me, because Wolf's train to Eisenach left at 11am and Mädi had to be in Leipzig that evening. Overfull trams made the leave-taking really short. Now once again I stood quite alone, as so often in my life, but in my heart was joy that in five hours I would see the man who would make me happy for the rest of my life.
In Berlin a bus took me to Gatow [British-zone airfield]. Once I got through the tiresome passport check there I finally climbed into the aircraft.
On the plane I sat next to an English woman who was very curious. But I didn't want to talk – I couldn't. I was overwhelmed by all the new impressions which were so vivid and my expectation was so great. The route was set – Berlin – Hamburg – London.

We took off from Berlin in fog, but by Hamburg there was some visibility. In Hamburg there was a 40 minute wait. Sandwiches were provided – white bread and ham, the first cooked ham I'd had for many years. At 17.05 we took off from Hamburg, unfortunately it was almost completely foggy but still really beautiful. Above us the evening sky, below us a range of cloud-mountains. Now and then I spied a little corner of Holland and then the dark sea. The heat and the growing darkness made me tired. I leant back and tried to sleep but unfortunately my neighbour made it impossible – she couldn't keep still and wanted to know so much. Then came supper (oh how materialistic, but how nice) with pate, a white roll, cheese, and butter cream tart. Outside it became dark and the cabin was unbearably hot, a few water droplets raked across the window. I wanted nothing more than to breathe some real fresh air.

At 8 o'clock I arrived at Northolt, West London. I climbed out of the aircraft; no-one was there. After the passport checks, still no-one. Heart racing, I took the bus into the city as we'd arranged. When I arrived, I still couldn't see him. I began to wonder if I'd have to find a cheap hotel nearby, but wait – there he was at the back, half hidden by the bus shelter. Yes, it was him: bright eyes, a nice shirt and black hair.

In a short time, the ice was broken. I talked while he had to carry the terribly heavy case – he didn't have to but he wanted to. He registered me in the hotel – 'number 629', 6th floor – and we went to his room next door. There to welcome me was a host of golden daffodils and a cup of tea.

We had two wonderful hours of chatting. I don't know whether he's disappointed, but I already know that I like him a lot.

17 March

Yesterday we were together in London and we did the tour. Buckingham Palace, Queen Victoria Monument, Westminster Abbey, Downing Street, St Paul's Cathedral, Royal Courts of Justice – with case in process.

It's a completely undestroyed city, a city with smart people, smart shop windows (poor Germany, how much you've lost). Lunch à la carte. All this is a new land for me and I'm still asking myself if it's real or just a dream.

A long journey brought both of us, after many detours, to the cinema. We watched a comedy, *The Bride Goes Wild* and a French country film. Something cheerful and a bit of countryside... Then through the city 'to have a tea-time' in a nice little hotel.

Once back at the hotel, we both sat down exhausted, yet not too exhausted to start a discussion which I didn't really completely understand. He talked of the psychosis of an overstressed person. I'd like to understand but can't.

Then after supper we sat comfortably together for a while, over a cigarette and pictures of home.

At 12.30am we asked the porter, will you please wake 627 and 629 tomorrow at 8 o'clock?

Good night, sleep well.

Fred and Rike, together at last!

Exeter, 20 March

The next morning, we travelled by taxi to the station for the 10.55 train. A very talkative porter entertained me until the train arrived. I got in, and he'd already got the essentials for our journey (even a Dresden newspaper was there, for my sake). The porter must have noticed something. At any rate, he wished me a good journey in German – perhaps it was the only German word he knew.

The journey was lovely; the beginnings of spring were a joy to me. The cows and horses were already in the meadows, the catkins were blooming, and even the gardens were turning green.

11.30 we had lunch in the 1st class dining car. O life, how sweet you are!

By 3pm we were in Exeter. We took rooms directly opposite the station (Rougemont Hotel), and then a walk through the lovely old city and to the delightful little house that later might become our home. Then he had a little work to do; I tried to write, but it didn't really work. So we decided that tomorrow he would move in with his landlady while I stayed at the hotel – he had to mark the end of term essays.

So next morning I was left to my own devices. I walked into town and wrote to my sisters.

The weather was lovely, and after lunch we visited the Food Office, because without stamps I can't stay in the hotel. Amazingly, everything was arranged really quickly – how different from my experiences in Germany!

We travelled together to the coast at Exmouth and spent a lovely afternoon chatting to the deep blue sea. It was 7 o'clock before we took the bus back. We had a brief farewell, and I went to the hotel alone. Contrary to expectation dinner is great. Then I went to bed, to read and to dream.

Next day I was alone again. I went into town, bought sewing needles and thread, visited the old castle, and then I darned stockings and did the washing.

At 12.30 there was a knock: 'Please come in', but no-one entered; so I opened the door. How lovely, he was there to collect me.

He stayed until 3pm and returned at 5. Until dinner we shared stories. It's nice to have such a clever friend. Finding myself alone for the evening and hearing the cheerful dance music below I found myself weeping. I told myself not to be miserable, because I'm better off than a thousand German girls.

Sunday 21 March

At last, it was Sunday for both of us. It's Palm Sunday, and this means Fred's on holiday, at last. This morning he collected me for a walk. Although the weather wasn't particularly nice, we had a lot of fun. We came back just in time for lunch, tired and satisfied. After the meal we wanted to rest for a while. Why do I have a room with two beds? 'I don't think I can ever get away from you!'

Monday 22 March

We had beautiful weather today, which rewarded me with a walk to somewhere that looked like an enchanted castle.

In the afternoon we went to the cinema to see *Great Expectations*, which is a rather fantastic film, …

Afterwards we had supper very happily together and for the evening went to the theatre to see *The Linden Tree*. To be honest I didn't pick up much of it, but it deals with post-war problems.

Tuesday 23 March

Today we travelled to Liverpool. We encountered a disrespectful conductor who interrupted our harmonious journey, and then in Shrewsbury an enormous number of soldiers came on the train. I was a little tired, but anxious because the men kept me awake. At 11.30 am we arrived at Liverpool, Mossley Hill. Fred ran to fetch the big suitcase in the luggage compartment while I stood on the station; not far from me was a man with a dog who came up to me. I was alarmed and wondered where Fred had got to. Of course, I couldn't say a word for fright, but then I was relieved to see Fred coming towards us with our two suitcases. We ordered a taxi, had to wait half an hour, and then sit like sardines between the cases, but at least the dog grinned at me in encouragement. Then we were home, and the first thing Fred's mother said was 'lavatory, bathroom, bedroom' – I couldn't understand other words. There was fish and chips for supper. I had to force it down. All the excitement had gone to my stomach a bit.

* * *

They walked together through Sefton Park, near Fred's childhood home. The sun shone brightly on what was a warm spring day. After an intense couple of days with Fred's family, it felt good to have some space alone together. Still anxiety gnawed at Fred. Rike seemed happy, but he also knew that she was rather overwhelmed. He was desperate to know what she really thought, but was equally fearful of finding out the truth. Finally, he stumped up the courage to ask the question that had been plaguing him ever since her arrival a fortnight previously. 'Are you happy, darling?' Fred asked, anxiously.

'Yes, very,' she answered.

'Because if you're not, you don't have to go through with it – honestly. I would completely understand. So would my parents. We all know just how much we're asking of you.'

Rike stopped. She took Fred by the hands, and looked intently at him. He averted his gaze, fear in his eyes.

'Fred, look at me,' she said, 'you worry so much, don't you? You're always worrying. Do you remember that I wrote to you that many of the things that you worry about will become clear in the first couple of weeks of us being together, and that we're both too rational to start a marriage on a basis that neither of us want?'

'Yes, I remember.' His throat was dry, he dreaded what was coming next.

'The time is up, it's been a fortnight since I came to you. And I have to tell you this...'

Fred looked at her, gazing with such serious intent. He felt himself falling, as he closed his eyes, disappearing into the sum of all his fears, until her voice made him look again at her.

'I love you, I want to marry you. I don't want to go off and find anyone else, anywhere else. You're all the husband I need – even if you're smaller than me! Of course, it's not going to be easy, but things rarely are. I believe we can work on this together. We can overcome the obstacles that come our way.'

Fred was silent. Exceptionally, for him he was speechless. In truth, he daren't speak, because he was overwhelmed with the cocktail of emotion swamping him and he felt unable to string words together. He'd been steeling himself for rejection.

'Fred, look at me,' she said again, lifting his head with her hand, 'I love you.' And she took his face in both hands and drew his face to hers. They kissed for the very first time. At first it felt awkward to him and he worried that he wasn't doing it right, but his lips softened and he let himself go, feeling the pent up anxiety, questioning and doubt melt into love in that moment. His arms, that had been hanging uselessly by his side, moved up her back and he pulled her into him.

Later, as they walked hand in hand, Fred told her: 'When I first dreamed of marrying you, I admit that I thought I would be like a knight in shining armour, rescuing a poor orphan girl. Actually, I've realised that it's the other way round. You've rescued me – you'll have no idea how much. I need you. I was so afraid that you'd leave me, that you'd see who I am and turn away. Are you sure you'll stay?'

'I see who you are Fred and I'm not going anywhere. I choose to marry you. I choose you.'

* * *

On 18 April, the congregation filed into Mossley Hill Parish Church, still scarred from August 1940 when it had been the very first church to be bombed in England in the Second World War. The windows were still shattered and the front of the nave still looked like a bomb site. Fred sat at the front of the church, looking around, and reflecting on how appropriate it was to be marrying in this church; even on their wedding day there was no way of escaping the war that had left an indelible mark on both of their lives, on everyone's. Behind him family and friends filled pews on both sides of the aisle.

For Rike, no family that still survived could make the journey. Fred's uncle James had stepped in to walk Rike down the aisle. Fred hoped she wouldn't feel lonely; he hoped he could be enough for her.

His younger brother George, now a lecturer at Liverpool University, sat next to him. He was well-deserving of the honour of being best man; his care of Fred in those dark times of his breakdown in early 1946 had been instrumental in helping him to recover. They didn't say much to each other; they didn't need to. 'Ready?' asked George.

'Just about,' Fred replied. Although aware of the enormity of the words he was about to say and the promises they were about to make before the congregation, Fred felt a deep sense of serenity.

The congregation stood as his German bride walked with dignity and determination in her borrowed dress towards him. Tears formed in his eyes when he saw her. She was radiant, so beautiful. She had shrugged off the controversy of being a German bride and was for this moment, simply a bride.

As he waited, he was full of admiration for the way she had overcome every obstacle and embraced every challenge, and overwhelmed that she had done this for him. As she joined him at the front of church, they held hands. She squeezed his hand and whispered, 'I choose you.'

18 April 1948, Rike and Fred marry at Mossley Hill Parish Church. Pictured here with best man George, George's fiancée Rhian, and bridesmaid Hilary, Don's daughter.

Liverpool Echo – 18 April 1948
'German Girl Bride: A Young Liverpool Professor's Romance'

A German girl, who until recently was in the Russian zone of Germany, today married a young Liverpool man, now a professor, whom she met before the war when he was teaching in Dresden.

The bridegroom was 33-years-old Professor Frederick W. Clayton, professor of Latin and Greek at Exeter University, second son of Mr William Clayton, a retired Liverpool inspector of schools, and Mrs. Clayton, of Rangemore Road, Mossley Hill. The bride was Miss Frederika Buttna-Wobst (sic), who arrived by plane in this country about a month ago after an exciting journey from her native country.

The wedding took place at Mossley Hill Parish Church before a large congregation of friends of the bridegroom's family.

As a young lecturer with a remarkable record of academic successes, which began when he attended Liverpool Collegiate School and continued at Cambridge, Mr. F. W. Clayton had among his pupils at Dresden two German boys who, during the vacation, invited him to their home. Their father was a doctor. There were three daughters, and the romance sprang up between Fraulein Frederika and the young teacher of languages.

The war intervened, and Mr. Clayton, joining the R.A.F., served as a squadron leader on intelligence work in India and Burma. He was appointed to his present post last December.

None of the bride's family was here to see her married to-day. She was given away by Mr. James Jones of Wallasey, uncle of the bridegroom. The best man was Mr. George Clayton, younger brother of the bridegroom, himself a lecturer at Liverpool University. The bridesmaids were Miss Rhian Jones, fiancée of Mr. George Clayton, and little Miss Hilary Clayton, the child niece of the bridegroom.

'I've never been in a newspaper before,' Rike said the next morning, as she read the article.

'They didn't manage to spell your name right.'

'Well, just as well my name's now Clayton, isn't it?' she replied with a grin. 'It's much less of a mouthful for you poor English who can't cope with my grand name!'

'And they said our romance sprang up when I was in Dresden …'

'Well, how d'you know I didn't have a crush on you then, Mr Teacher … ' she said with a smile.

'And what about now?'

'Even more so, today, Mr Teacher, Mr Husband, and I meant it, you know – '

'What?'

'Those words we said at church – whether in English or German, "for better for worse, for richer for poorer, in sickness and in health, to love, cherish, and to obey, till death us do part..." I meant every word. Now, do you believe me?'

Against all odds, a bridge had been built, not to be broken. The waiting was finally over.

EPILOGUE
July 2000

It was an unseasonably cool and cloudy day in Langebrück. Rike shivered in the breeze wishing she had packed warmer clothes. She and the family walked from the station along lanes so familiar she could probably still do the route blindfolded despite the fact that this was the first time she had returned in fifty years. She envied the energy of the two young men who were striding out in front of her. They seemed in such a hurry to get to their destination. Rike remembered feeling like that. Not now. Her new hip still ached and even if she could have kept up with them, she would have chosen to walk slower to savour this precious moment, to drink in her surroundings.

Of course, there had been some development over the half century, but so much remained the same as it had been all those years ago. Langebrück had, after all, avoided the fate of Dresden, just a few miles away. Many of the same buildings still stood, as did some of the trees that she had played around, hidden behind, climbed. The wind whispering through the leaves seemed to welcome her home.

'Are we nearly there, Nanny?'

Rike was travelling with her youngest daughter, Barbara, her son-in-law, and two of her grandsons. It was their first visit to Rike's family home, a place that had meant so much to her and Fred, a place where it had all begun.

'Nearly there, boys; Blumenstraße is the next left – number four, go down the road, it's on the right half way down, a big white house.' They charged off round the corner.

'I'm sorry to be slow, darling. My hip … falling apart my love.'

'That's ok, Mum, there's no rush. The boys are excited, that's all. What about you, how do you feel?'

It was a good question. Since they had arrived in Dresden the day before, a storm of emotions had raged within. Although there had been restoration, the city was unrecognisable. When she left in 1948 it was still a wasteland of ominous spaces punctuated by the few stubborn fire-blackened buildings that had survived the bombing. The city that she knew had been wiped off the map – her brothers' school, her father's medical practice, relatives' homes annihilated.

When she had walked out from the rebuilt train station the day before, her senses had whirled in turmoil. She could hear the humming of the planes that still filled her nightmares; her eyes stung with the memory of the acrid smoke and rank stench of burning flesh. She had hurried to shut the door and lie down as soon as they reached their hotel in the Altstadt; of course, she couldn't share any of this, 'It's OK love, I'm worn out by the journey,' she'd mumbled.

Today, though, was different. Today, she was home.

When her father moved the family out of Dresden to nearby Langebrück, he thought it was the cleaner air that would save them. He could have had no idea that this decision would save their lives, spare them the utter devastation of those terrible nights that February. Had she not suffered, she might have felt some guilt at her survival, but she *had* suffered, they all had. But, Rike was ever positive, she did not allow herself to dwell on the horrors.

Instead, she focused on what she had been given in the years since she had left her hometown; on the young girl who made that journey to an enemy country to marry a man she barely knew. She focused on what they had built together. Fifty years of marriage, four children, six grandchildren, a lifetime of fidelity and love. Fred used to call their family 'The United Nations', three of their four children were married to Italian, French and Irish partners.

Two years ago they celebrated their Golden Wedding

Anniversary surrounded by their children and grandchildren, Fred's brother and sister-in-law, and their nieces and nephews. She and Fred had defied those who had said their marriage would never last. She remembered Madi's husband, Fritz, who'd derided her dreams of marriage. He still owed her those fifty marks!

Rike in 2000, visiting her hometown for the first time in over 50 years.

As she neared her childhood home, she allowed herself to feel pride. She was proud of the family she and Fred had made. As she approached the house, she saw the place where she and Marianne had obliterated the relief of the Stahlhelm helmet they feared would provoke the Russians. The words were still visible though: *Thue recht – scheue niemand* – 'Act justly – fear no one.' She remembered the defiance she had shown on the day the Russians had visited, the determination and courage she had applied to every aspect of her life. She was proud of that too.

'Mum? Are you ok?'

'Sorry, darling, I was miles away. I feel, well, all sorts of things. I feel gratitude, sadness too but also pride. In some ways I feel like I've come home. I loved it here. It was a wonderful place to grow up.'

'Like Halwill – our home,' Barbara replied.

'Yes, I did everything I could to create what I had been given.'

'You succeeded – for us, and for our children too. The boys love it there.' Barbara paused for a moment. 'I wish Dad were here.'

Rike smiled sadly. Her dear, dear husband. He had been able to flourish in his work as a Professor of Classics at Exeter with her unstinting care and the stability she gave him. Fred had delighted too in the fulfilment of his lifelong dream of being a father – two boys, Timothy and Peter were followed by twin girls, Margaret and Barbara, who filled him with a joy he had never even dared to imagine.

Of course, he was never fully free of the mental scars caused by his experience of war and his own hypersensitivity but the love and stability of life at home staved off the onslaught of depression for many years. But when his final illness came, there was little she could do; dementia robbed him bit by bit of his magnificent mind. When his death came, it was a mercy; his struggles were over.

Fred Clayton had been a good man, a man true to his word, a man blessed with rare intelligence, a man who never wavered in his love for his German wife.

'I wish he were too, my dear, I really do.' With the grandchildren's laughter carried on the summer wind, they linked arms and looked together at the place where it had all begun.

AUTHOR'S NOTE

I was 18 when my grandfather died. He'd suffered from Alzheimer's in the final years of his life, so he was a bit of a mystery to me. I remember him talking at the dinner table, accompanying him to the university library in Exeter, but otherwise, he was quite a distant figure to me as I grew up. His funeral and the weeks following his death were a revelation to me.

What I discovered through the moving and passionate eulogy delivered by his younger brother, George, was that this old, somewhat distant man I knew as Grandpa, had led an extraordinary life. From the modest beginnings of a Liverpool grammar school, his adult life had begun with astounding academic success. He won a plethora of prizes and was described by the great Alan Turing as the 'most learned man I ever met'.

In what he described as 'the redeeming act of my life' he organised the rescue of two Jewish boys from Austria and saved them from certain death. I was so proud that he was my grandfather; in fact, it was one of the first things I told my wife on the first evening we spent together.

My relationship with Rike, my grandmother (or 'Nanny', as I knew her) was different. We were always close; I loved her warmth, openness, and hospitality, I basked in her interest in my life and her pride that I was studying German for A-Level. Through her letters and journals, my admiration for her has grown. She was just as remarkable as my grandfather, but in different ways.

I didn't think much more of my grandparents and their stories until 2014, when I was a Vicar in Coventry. Both Coventry and Dresden had been destroyed by bombing in the Second World

War, and there was a strong history of reconciliation between the two cities. In February 2015, on the 70th anniversary of Dresden's bombing, The Archbishop of Canterbury, the Bishop of Coventry, the Lord Mayor of Coventry, the Dean of Coventry Cathedral, and a number of others were to make an official trip to Dresden (referred to in the Foreword). I had a deep sense that I ought to be part of this visit and to my great joy, the Bishop agreed.

I had written a blog to tell the story of my grandparents and my personal reason for going to Dresden. Much to my surprise, it attracted interest and, in a peculiarly surreal week, I ended up appearing in the Church Times, local radio, national German TV and on Radio 5 Live. With my shaky A-level German, and in the presence of the Archbishop, I shared the story in the Frauenkirche, Dresden's cathedral, rebuilt in 2005, and known as its most beloved symbol. It was a powerful experience, revealing and reliving my grandparents' experience in the place of, perhaps, the worst bombing in the European war. It made an indelible mark on my life.

A few months later I was part of a conversation about sabbaticals and I happened to mention that if I were to take a sabbatical then I'd use it to write the story of my grandparents. Much to my surprise, the Coventry Diocese said that this would be a great idea, and so the journey began.

In the months before the sabbatical, I raided my parents' attic and discovered a treasure trove of material that formed the basis of *Loving the Enemy* – my grandfather's notebooks, recalling his experiences in Dresden, Vienna and during the war; the diaries that my grandmother kept, and, of course, most importantly, the letters which established the basis of their relationship and led to their marriage.

I also managed to find one of the few surviving copies of *The Cloven Pine*, my grandfather's semi-autobiographical novel based on his experiences in Dresden and Vienna, published by Secker and Warburg in 1943, under the pseudonym Frank Clare (now out of print). I used his book as a principal source for his experience in Dresden in 1936. Though this was a fictionalised portrayal of his time there, his experiences provided the raw material for his novel, and I have, on occasions, used dialogue from it.

The letters were all in German, and I'm profoundly grateful to the generous people who helped me understand what was in their correspondence – Evan Rieder, Katy Coupe and, particularly Richard Parker, who freely, and willingly, gave his time and skills to produce the translations of the letters that you see in this book. I couldn't have done it without him.

I am also grateful to Dr. Patricia McGuire, the archivist of King's College, Cambridge who allowed me to spend a day searching for records of Fred's life at university and who sent me copies of photographs of Fred at King's, and Liam Sims, at the University of Cambridge Library, who sent me copies of his work in the *Cambridge Review*. Together, they helped form a more rounded picture of Fred as a young man, which I've shared in Chapter 1.

After the first draft was produced, I met Rainer Barczaitis from Dresden who has become a friend and advocate for this story, offering his own insights, providing valuable information about life in Dresden in the pre-war period and giving me the opportunity to speak about Fred and Rike in the Kreuzkirche, where Rike was confirmed. Rainer is also kindly working on a German translation of this book, which is no mean feat. I'm so grateful to him.

Andrew Hodges' biography of Turing was a helpful source for me and, I am also grateful for Andrew's generosity in reading and commenting on the manuscript.

My aim has been to tell Fred and Rike's story as truthfully as possible and, where dialogue is inferred in the material, I have taken the liberty of bringing it to life.

Although it has my name on the front, *Loving the Enemy* is by no means a solitary effort. I want to thank various people who have championed the cause in its different stages, particularly members of my family: my wife, Liz, my aunt, Margaret Tudeau-Clayton, my dad, Gerald, and especially my beloved mum, Barbara, with whom it's been a great joy to sit and work together on the manuscript; also, Jonathan Clayton, for his good connection and help.

My thanks also to Bishop Christopher Cocksworth for his invitation and encouragement to join the Dresden trip and, especially, for writing the beautiful foreword; to Christine Camfield, the Bishop of Coventry's PA, for her enthusiasm and encouragement and for seeing the power and potential of this story from the very beginning (if this does end up as a film then you can surely take some credit!); to Naomi Nixon for enabling me to take the sabbatical in which to research and write the first draft; and the congregation of St Christopher's Church, Allesley Park and Whoberley in Coventry, who went without their vicar for three months and for their ongoing love and support.

My thanks, too, to Simon Green for his early encouragement and to Janice Lacey, Karl's daughter, who got in touch with me and was able to give me some insight into the difference Fred made to her father's life and whose appreciation for the manuscript in its earlier stage gave me fresh motivation to get *Loving the Enemy* published. I am particularly grateful to Rowan Somerville for his detailed feedback on the manuscript, his literary expertise, and his challenge to me to bring Fred and Rike to life.

Being an unknown author writing my first book is a daunting prospect, so I'm grateful for the support of the book launch team – especially, Andy Kind, Kevin Bates, Nikolai Press, Debbie Niblett, Katy Coupe, Liz Carter, Zoe Lawton, Marc Lalonde, Jo Philpott, Michelle Giampaglia, Martin Saxby, Simon and Helen Green, Owen Entwistle, Dave Truss, Steve Legg, Jen Jenkins, Barbara Bell, Nick Bell, Yolande Davis, Susanna March, Alastair Duncan, Fiona Turner; and Stuart Hart, who proofread the book.

Ultimately, my gratitude is to Fred and Rike themselves, for their courage and example, and for their audacity in daring to build bridges when others were destroying them, allowing love to triumph against all odds. I hope many will be inspired by their story that resonates so powerfully seventy years on.

Andy March
Coventry
October 2021

SELECT BIBLIOGRAPHY AND PHOTOGRAPH CREDITS

I have relied on a number of sources to 'fill in the gaps' for me about the life of Rike and Fred and the times in which they lived.

Articles, online sources
Liverpool Collegiate Old Boys Association - The Notable - FREDERICK WILLIAM CLAYTON 1913-1999 http://www.liverpool-collegiate.org.uk/NOTABLES/F_NOTABLE_CLAYTON.htm

Wiseman, T.W. Obituary: Professor F.W. Clayton, 24 December 1999 https://www.independent.co.uk/arts-entertainment/obituary-professor-f-w-clayton-1134399.html

Neugebauer, Lt. Gen. M. Norwid 'The Defence of Poland, September 1939', http://felsztyn.tripod.com/germaninvasion/id11.html

Dresdner Anzeiger 'Saxons annihilate Polish snipers', 18 October 1939

King's College Cambridge Annual Report: Frederick William Clayton – The Man and his Work

The Cambridge Review, University of Cambridge, 1935

Books
Clare, Frank *The Cloven Pine*, London, 1942
Hodges, Andrew *Alan Turing: The Enigma*, London, 1983
Smith, Michael *The Emperor's Codes: Bletchley Park and the Breaking of*

Japan's Secret Ciphers, London, 2000

Smith, Michael *The Secrets of Station X: How the Bletchley Park codebreakers helped win the war*, London, 2011

Russell, Alan (ed.) and Clayton, Anthony (ed.) *Dresden: A City Reborn*, Oxford, 1999

Taylor, Frederick *Dresden: Tuesday, 13 February, 1945*, London, 2004

Taylor, Frederick, *Exorcising Hitler: The Occupation and Denazification of Germany*, London, 2011

Photograph Credits

All photographs come from the Clayton-Büttner-Wobst family archives, except -

Front Cover and p. 20, 'Dresden. Blick von der Neustadt', SLUB Dresden / Deutsche Fotothek / Wilhelm Stein

p. 5, 'Freshmen, 1931' King's College, Cambridge Archives by kind permission of the Provost and Scholars of King's College, Cambridge

p. 12, 'B.As 1934', King's College, Cambridge Archives by kind permission of the Provost and Scholars of King's College, Cambridge

p. 21, 'Dresden-Altstadt. Hauptbahnhof', SLUB Dresden / Deutsche Fotothek / Walter Hahn

p. 24, 'Dresden-Altstadt. Georgplatz. Kreuzschule', SLUB Dresden / Deutsche Fotothek / Reinhard Kallmer

p. 83, 'Alan Turing', Shutterstock

p.162, 'Ruinen an der Lüttichaustraße, im Hintergrund Hauptbahnhof', SLUB Dresden / Deutsche Fotothek / Günter Reichart

p. 101, Fred's epic journey, created using Scribble Maps © 2021 Scribble Maps, Open StreetMap.

Printed in Great Britain
by Amazon